Janáček's *Sinfonietta*

Frontispiece: Janáček sitting on the balcony of the Organ School in Brno on 20 May 1926, soon after completing the *Sinfonietta*. Photograph by Bohumil Vavroušek (Janáček Archive, Brno).

Janáček's *Sinfonietta*

Nigel Simeone and Jiří Zahrádka

With a foreword by Jakub Hrůša

Published with support from
The Leoš Janáček Foundation (Nadace Leoše Janáčka), Brno
and The Dvořák Society of Great Britain

THE BOYDELL PRESS

© Nigel Simeone and Jiří Zahrádka 2026

All Rights Reserved. Except as permitted under current legislation
no part of this work may be photocopied, stored in a retrieval system,
published, performed in public, adapted, broadcast,
transmitted, recorded or reproduced in any form or by any means,
without the prior permission of the copyright owner

The right of Nigel Simeone and Jiří Zahrádka to be identified as the authors of this
work has been asserted in accordance with sections 77 and 78 of the
Copyright, Designs and Patents Act 1988

First published 2026
The Boydell Press, Woodbridge

ISBN 978 1 83765 330 0 hardback
ISBN 978 1 83765 441 3 paperback

The Boydell Press is an imprint of Boydell & Brewer Ltd
and of Boydell & Brewer Inc.
website: www.boydellandbrewer.com

Our Authorised Representative for product safety in the EU is Easy Access System
Europe – Mustamäe tee 50, 10621 Tallinn, Estonia, gpsr.requests@easproject.com

A CIP catalogue record for this book is available
from the British Library

The publisher has no responsibility for the continued existence or accuracy
of URLs for external or third-party internet websites referred to in this book,
and does not guarantee that any content on such websites is,
or will remain, accurate or appropriate

Leoš Janáček Foundation

Twentieth-Century Music

Series Editors
SOPHIE REDFERN sophie.redfern@kcl.ac.uk
NIGEL SIMEONE nigel@bredon.com

This series presents incisive, single-work studies by leading authorities on major twentieth-century compositions. Focusing on works that continue to shape today's concert and opera repertoire, each volume combines scholarly clarity with interpretative insights and fresh perspectives. Encompassing orchestral, chamber and choral music, as well as song, opera and ballet, each study traces a work's historical and musical context, creative genesis, publication history and critical reception. Readers are also provided with an exploration of each composition's musical language alongside a detailed survey of its recorded legacy. Studies also seek contributions from a distinguished performer, offering a window into the work's living performance tradition and interpretative life.

Boydell & Brewer
Email: editorial@boydellandbrewer.com

Contents

List of Illustrations	viii
Foreword by Jakub Hrůša	xi
Introduction and Acknowledgements	xiii
Abbreviations and References	xv
Prologue: Janáček and the Orchestra	1
1. Inspiration – Composition – Publication	15
Supplement. Sources: Manuscripts and Editions	55
2. The *Sinfonietta* in Janáček's Lifetime: A Chronicle	70
3. The *Sinfonietta* Makes its Way into the Repertory, 1928–45	109
4. The *Sinfonietta* Recorded: 1946 Onwards	125
5. A Conductor's Perspective: Jakub Hrůša in Conversation	157
6. The *Sinfonietta*: A Musical Commentary	174
Coda: Rosa Newmarch on the *Sinfonietta*	196
Appendix: Scores Annotated by František Neumann, Otto Klemperer and Henry Wood	199
Discography	213
Select Bibliography	223
Index	228

Illustrations

Plates

Frontispiece: Janáček sitting on the balcony of the Organ School in Brno on 20 May 1926, soon after completing the *Sinfonietta*. Photograph by Bohumil Vavroušek (Janáček Archive, Brno).   ii

1   Entry in Janáček's notebook for 28 June 1924 with his jottings of fragments from the military band concert in Písek including 'Fanfáry' (Janáček Archive, Brno, Z59).   21

2   Janáček's earliest sketch for the Fanfares of the *Sinfonietta* (Janáček Archive, Brno, A 7444).   26

3a, b   The first two pages of Janáček's autograph of the Fanfares, in the manuscript submitted to *Lidové noviny*, with the first three trumpet notes on p. 2 miscopied as B flat–E flat–B flat (Leoš Janáček Foundation, Brno, Ar 3-2, A-1).   27

4   Janáček's autograph manuscript of the *Sinfonietta*, fifth movement, bars 149–56, with the cymbal clash ('Talíře', on the bottom stave) in bar 151, one bar before the entry of the fanfare trumpets (Janáček Archive, Brno, A 7444).   40

5   Václav Sedláček's authorised copy of the *Sinfonietta*, fifth movement, bars 152–6, with the cymbal clash ('Talíře') in bar 152, at the same time as the entry of the fanfare trumpets (Austrian National Library, L1. UE. 777 GFOL).   41

6   Janáček with Jan Mikota outside the Prague offices of Hudební matice Umělecké besedy in 1926 (Janáček Archive, Brno).   46

7   Janáček's contract with Universal Edition for the *Militärsymphonietta*, dated by him on 14 August 1926 (Leoš Janáček Foundation, Brno).   47

8a–d	Front covers and title pages of the two simultaneously issued pocket scores of the *Sinfonietta*, both published in January 1927 (Nigel Simeone, private collection).	59
9	The first card for the *Sinfonietta* in Universal Edition's Werke-Kartothek showing performance, hire and purchase records between January and October 1928 (UE Archive, Vienna).	60
10	Postcard reproduction of a poster by Karel Šimůnek for the Eighth Sokol Rally, Prague, 1926 (Jiří Zahrádka, private collection).	66
11	Václav Talich in the late 1920s. The photograph is signed and dated 18 May 1930 (Janáček Archive, Brno).	67
12a, b	Janáček's copy of the programme for the world premiere, 26 June 1926, with his annotations on the verso (Janáček Archive, Brno, D 165 LJ).	68
13	President Tomáš Garrigue Masaryk greeting the ceremonial procession of the Sokol Rally on 6 July 1926 in Prague's Old Town Square (Jiří Zahrádka, private collection).	69
14	Announcement of the German premiere in the *Wiesbadener Bade-blatt*, 9 December 1926.	76
15	František Neumann. Pastel portrait by Eduard Milén, c. 1924 (Nigel Simeone, private collection).	85
16	Janáček and Otto Klemperer after the Berlin premiere, 29 September 1927 (Janáček Archive, Brno).	87
17	Břetislav Bakala and the Brno Radio Symphony Orchestra in the Stadion, Brno, on 27 March 1941 at a broadcast performance of the *Sinfonietta* (Janáček Archive, Brno).	112
18	Rafael Kubelík and Břetislav Bakala in Salzburg, 1957 (Janáček Archive, Brno).	129
19	Charles Mackerras and Václav Talich in 1948 (Charles Mackerras archive).	135
20	Charles Mackerras conducting the Czech Philharmonic in 2002 (Charles Mackerras archive).	141
21	František Jílek at the Brno National Theatre (Brno National Theatre).	143

22	The end of the third movement in František Neumann's corrected score, with the added 'rit' marking over the three *Più moss*o bars, and the added upbeat Fs in the violas in the closing bars (Wienbibliothek im Rathaus).	202
23	František Neumann's corrected score, showing the *banda* trumpets playing in the last three bars, and the violin slurs deleted (Wienbibliothek im Rathaus).	204
24	Otto Klemperer's conducting score, signed and dated with his Berlin performances in September 1927 and February 1933 (Royal Academy of Music, London).	205
25	The last page of Otto Klemperer's conducting score, with additional parts for the *banda* and other retouchings written in his hand (Royal Academy of Music, London).	210

Music examples

1.1	Janáček's sketches for fanfares before the Sinfonietta (Janáček Archive, Brno, A 7444).	22–25
6.1	I. Allegretto, themes	178–80
6.2	II. Andante, themes	182
6.3	III. Moderato, themes	185–86
6.4	IV. Allegretto, themes	189–90
6.5	V. Andante con moto, themes	193–95

Tables

4.1	Timings for 26 selected recordings	155
4.2	Timings in the third movement	156

Foreword by Jakub Hrůša

In the Czech musical landscape, particularly in my native Brno, Janáček's *Sinfonietta* stands as an iconic masterpiece. Its melodies and harmonies echo throughout society, recognised and embraced by many. While its opening fanfares have become an essential part of ceremonial state events, it is the music itself that truly defines its significance. The *Sinfonietta* is, in every sense, contagious, and I believe no listener can remain untouched by its energy.

Janáček's *Sinfonietta* occupies a unique and vital place in his œuvre. It is a mature creation and a 'classic' among his works. Reflecting Janáček's fully realised, now thoroughly developed style, it marks a profound milestone in his artistic evolution. The book by Nigel Simeone and Jiří Zahrádka that you are opening is the first in any language completely devoted to the *Sinfonietta*, and the depth of the authors' understanding of this work makes it an invaluable wellspring for readers around the world. Rich with sources, correspondence and a detailed history of its performances, it offers rare insights that cannot be found elsewhere.

I was certainly not alone in finding my way to 'classical' music through the stirring tones of this piece. The *Sinfonietta* offers myriad ideals for how one might first approach classical music: it is fresh, concise, profoundly original, sonically brilliant – brimming with contrasts – yet deeply reflective of Janáček's lifetime of experience. It is youthful and invigorating, whether heard in a live performance or in recorded form. Janáček was the first of the 'old' composers to infuse his music with the pulse of life that today's audiences long for: the captivating, mobilising energy that sweeps you along, but at the same time, also the tenderness that touches the most sensitive of souls. While Janáček's critics sometimes dismissed this as primitivism, others, more attuned to the essence of its expressive power, recognised it as realism, or even a kind of democratisation of music.

This new work by Nigel Simeone and Jiří Zahrádka on Janáček's *Sinfonietta* is nothing short of exceptional. Their almost brotherly connection to the music allows them to weave together musicological scholarship with an impassioned curiosity for every note of Janáček's score and its journey through time. It was a privilege to discuss this work with Nigel, and our conversation (printed in Chapter 5) deepened my own understanding of the piece, leaving me moved by his brilliant insights.

In this book, readers will find true inspiration. It reflects the authors' profound passion for the themes they explore, and a deep love for Janáček's music. Nigel and Jiří share with the composer qualities such as originality, tenacity, a belief in the power of art, and an extraordinary sensitivity to every single phrase. This book is not merely scholarly; it captures the very heart and soul of the music.

I wish for Nigel and Jiří's work many captivated readers – those who already cherish the *Sinfonietta* (and will come to love it even more through this book) and especially those whose hearts will be won over by it.

Jakub Hrůša, Seoul, 31 May 2025
Music Director, Royal Opera, Covent Garden
Chief Conductor, Bamberg Symphony
Chief Conductor and Artistic Director designate, Czech Philharmonic

Introduction and Acknowledgements

Janáček's *Sinfonietta* had its world premiere on 26 June 1926, and this book coincides with its hundredth birthday. Given that the *Sinfonietta* is Janáček's most famous and successful orchestral work, it's perhaps surprising that this is the first book entirely devoted to it – particularly as its five movements represent such a thrilling microcosm of the composer's late musical style – but its centenary provided an ideal opportunity.

After informal discussions at the Brno Janáček Festival in November 2024, we decided to work together on a volume that would place the *Sinfonietta* in the context of Janáček's other compositions (Prologue), evaluate its inspiration, sources and first publication (Chapter 1 and its supplement listing sources), document its early performance history and reception (Chapters 2 and 3) and describe its subsequent success on records and CDs (Chapter 4). We were very fortunate that Jakub Hrůša was happy to share his insights on conducting the work, as well as considering the interpretations of some of his distinguished predecessors (Chapter 5). The structure and instrumentation of the *Sinfonietta* are both idiosyncratic and highly original, and they are examined in detail in the musical commentary (Chapter 6). An appendix discusses scores annotated by three conductors who performed the work during Janáček's lifetime (two of them in the composer's presence): František Neumann, Otto Klemperer and Henry Wood. Finally, the book includes a comprehensive discography.

The authors gratefully acknowledge the help and support of friends, colleagues and institutions.

First and foremost, our warmest thanks go to Jakub Hrůša. He has taken an enthusiastic interest in this project from the start, was extremely generous with his time for the 'conductor's perspective' (Chapter 5), and has kindly written the Foreword.

Mark Audus, a leading Janáček scholar in his own right, and a friend of many years standing, deserves special thanks for his expertise in typesetting all the musical examples in Chapter 6, as well as for his advice and wisdom.

Patrick Lambert, another distinguished Czech music scholar (and for many years a producer at BBC Radio 3) has been unstinting in his encouragement and most kindly put at our disposal his own unpublished work on the *Sinfonietta*, along with newspaper cuttings and other sources. His work is acknowledged in several footnotes, but his generosity and guidance deserve special thanks.

We are similarly grateful to Heinz Stolba of Universal Edition (UE), Vienna, for supplying scores and sharing a number of documents from the firm's archive, notably the relevant pages from the print-books of UE and the Wiener Philharmonischer Verlag, and the 'Werke–Kartothek' record cards for the *Sinfonietta*, as well as for his enthusiasm. We also give our warm personal thanks to Ludmila Loucká for her assistance and encouragement, to David Roberts for his wholehearted support, to Leo McFall and Carol Falling for supplying information about Klemperer's Wiesbaden performance in 1926, and to our friend Cathy Mackerras for the photographs of her father.

The Leoš Janáček Foundation (Nadace Leoše Janáčka) in Brno and the Dvořák Society of Great Britain have both supported this publication with generous grants and we owe them a great debt of gratitude.

Several libraries and collections have rendered valuable assistance in the preparation of this book, notably the Janáček Archive of the Moravian Museum, Brno; the Leoš Janáček Foundation, Brno; the Austrian National Library, Vienna; the Wienbibliothek im Rathaus, Vienna; and the Royal Academy of Music, London. Warm thanks are also due to Pavlína Landová, Senior Librarian at the Czech Philharmonic, for providing comprehensive details of the orchestra's performances of the *Sinfonietta* from 1926 to the present. Andrea Hoy, Archivist at the Cleveland Orchestra, provided details and press cuttings relating to the orchestra's performances. Other library collections that have been consulted are noted in the text, and our thanks go to all librarians and archivists who have helped us.

Michael Middeke has been the most encouraging and supportive of editors. Crispin Peet and Caitlin Smith at Boydell have been models of efficiency, and we thank Joyce Li for her copy-editing. Special thanks to Sophie Redfern for her very careful reading of the whole text.

For both authors, our late friend John Tyrrell was a constant inspiration. As well as cherishing his memory, we owe him an immense debt of gratitude, not only for his incomparable scholarship but also for many years of selfless encouragement and belief in our work.

On a final personal note, the authors thank their wives, Jasmine Simeone and Šárka Zahrádková, for immeasurable acts of kindness and constant support.

Nigel Simeone and Jiří Zahrádka, June 2025

Abbreviations and References

bcl	bass clarinet
BmJA	Janáček Archive of the Moravian Museum, Brno
cl	clarinet
db	double bass
edn	edition
fl	flute
HM	Hudební matice Umělecké besedy
hn	horn
HŽ	Svatava Přibáňová, ed.: *Hádanka života (dopisy Leoše Janáčka Kamile Stösslové)* (Brno: Opus musicum, 1990).
IL	John Tyrrell, ed. and trans.: *Intimate Letters: Leoš Janáček to Kamila Stösslová* (London: Faber, 1993), edited translation of HŽ (above).
JAWO	Nigel Simeone, John Tyrrell and Alena Němcová: *Janáček's Works: A Catalogue of the Music and Writings* (Oxford: Clarendon Press, 1997).
JYL2	John Tyrrell: *Janáček: Years of a Life. Vol. II (1914–1928): Tsar of the Forests* (London: Faber, 2007).
LJUE	Ernst Hilmar, ed.: *Leoš Janáček: Briefe an die Universal Edition* (Tutzing: Schneider, 1988).
mvt	movement
NZfM	*Neue Zeitschschrift für Musik*
ob	oboe
ÖNB	Austrian National Library, Vienna
PN	plate number
pubd	published
rev.	revised
SKV	*Souborné kritické vydání děl Leoše Janáčka*
TCV	Svatava Přibáňová, ed.: *Tema con variazioni: Leoš Janáček korespondence s manželkou Zdeňkou a dcerou Olgou* (Prague: Bärenreiter, 2007).
tpt	trumpet
trbn	trombone
UE	Universal Edition, Vienna
unpubd	unpublished
va	viola

vc   cello
vn   violin
WBR   Wienbibliothek im Rathaus, Vienna

Note on references to the score

Throughout this book, all references to the score of the *Sinfonietta* are to the critical-practical edition by Jiří Zahrádka, published in full score and pocket score by Universal Edition in 2017 (UE 35865 and UE 36503). As well as the most accurate representation of the text, this edition includes bar numbers that differ from those in earlier editions, and has written-out repeats. Rehearsal figures are the same as in earlier UE and Philharmonia editions.

Prologue
Janáček and the Orchestra

Janáček's early orchestral works, from the late 1870s until the early 1890s, include some charming music but little or no indication of the innovative orchestral writing that was to become such a striking feature of his mature works. The Suite for Strings was a student work, first performed in Brno's Besední dům on 2 December 1877, conducted by the composer. The *Idyll*, also scored for string orchestra, was conducted by Janáček on 15 December 1878 at a concert in Brno attended by Dvořák. Both pieces demonstrate fluent craftsmanship, but they are the products of a musical education firmly rooted in traditional Austro-German techniques. The late 1880s saw the composition of several orchestral arrangements of folk dances, many of which were recycled in 1891 for the ballet *Rákoš Rákoczy*; more than thirty years later, Janáček assembled six of his best folk arrangements as the *Lachian Dances* (*Dances from Lašsko*), first performed under that title in December 1924 and published in 1928. Janáček's nostalgic affection for them is understandable: they are delightful pieces, written under the influence of his friend Dvořák, but they have few, if any, of the features that characterise Janáček's later music.

Just as *Jenůfa* marked the emergence of Janáček's breathtaking originality as a composer for the stage, his orchestral writing started to exhibit some of its characteristic colours and gestures in *Jealousy* (*Žárlivost*). When he completed this in February 1895, Janáček conceived it as a prelude to *Jenůfa* (and still intended it to fulfil that function as late as the autumn of 1903, when it was copied into the earliest surviving orchestral parts of the opera). But having decided to cut *Jealousy* from *Jenůfa* before the opera's 1904 premiere – almost certainly because he felt that it served no useful dramatic purpose – Janáček was happy to encourage performances of it as a concert overture. František Neumann conducted the premiere with the Czech Philharmonic Orchestra in Prague on 14 November 1906, and Karel Kovařovic performed it on a visit of the Prague National Theatre Orchestra to Brno on 13 October 1917 (Janáček was present on both occasions). From the first bar, with its peremptory brass chords and arresting timpani strokes, *Jealousy* is instantly recognisable as typical Janáček. Until recently, the only available score – edited by Theodora Straková and Osvald Chlubna – included some retouchings, but a new edition by Jiří Zahrádka (Universal Edition, UE 37513) has restored Janáček's original orchestration.

Janáček's output of orchestral music from his later years is quite small: *The Fiddler's Child* was completed in April 1913 with some revisions made in March 1914; the first version of *Taras Bulba* was finished by January 1915 and a completely revised version was ready by March 1918; the *Ballad of Blaník* was composed in 1919–20; and the unfinished *Danube* was extensively sketched in 1924–5 but then put aside and subsequently abandoned. Janáček's only other purely orchestral work was the *Sinfonietta*.

Alongside these pieces, there are many examples of his very individual orchestral writing be found in the operas from *Jenůfa* onwards, and in works for chorus and orchestra, especially the *Glagolitic Mass* (1926). *Fate* (1905) is full of unusual writing (starting with the multiple time signatures of its opening bars). The opening of *Káťa Kabanová* (1921) is notable for its high timpani and muted trombones, and there are many passages elsewhere in this opera that demonstrate the range of colours that Janáček was able to create – as well as the cinematic speed with which he could change them. Near the end of Act III of *Káťa*, there's a good example of this kind of shift: clarinets, flutes and violins play delicate falling phrases over quietly insistent timpani for 14 bars as Káťa says a troubled farewell to the world; after this, she has one bar to jump into the Volga, before there's a sudden eruption into panic and turmoil, the shocking drama reflected in the orchestral writing.

Just as remarkable is Janáček's ability to conjure up completely distinctive sound worlds for each of his mature operas. This is first apparent in *Jenůfa* but became increasingly marked in *Fate*, *The Excursions of Mr Brouček*, *Káťa Kabanová*, *The Cunning Little Vixen*, *The Makropulos Affair* and *From the House of the Dead*. In each opera, the orchestral sonorities constitute an acutely sensitive reflection of their very different dramatic situations. For that reason, it is sometimes difficult to generalise about Janáček's orchestral technique since it is designed to fit the particular musical and dramatic circumstances. There are, however, features of his writing for individual instruments that demonstrate the originality of his orchestral thinking, heard at its most daring in his later music, above all in *The Makropulos Affair*, *From the House of the Dead*, the *Glagolitic Mass* and the *Sinfonietta*.

By the time he wrote these pieces, Janáček had mostly abandoned conventional manuscript paper, preferring to use plain paper with the staves he required drawn by hand. In his chapter on 'Janáček and modernism', John Tyrrell wrote,

This [innovation] is visually evident in the way he wrote his later scores: rejecting printed score paper and writing out individual staves for particular instruments only when he needed them, a practice parallel with that of Stravinsky in his sketches for *The Rite of Spring*. It means that Janáček's scores are increasingly lean, with unexpected juxtapositions of instruments in his orchestral music. They rebel against one of the principles of traditional scoring – the even spread of instruments over the entire range. Janáček liked extremes.[1]

It was, of course, the quest for 'increasingly lean' orchestral sound that led Janáček to adopt this unusual practice, not the other way around. His fondness for 'extremes' is apparent in all his later works, including many instances in the *Sinfonietta*. It is worth considering these alongside other examples of his extremely original use of instruments or instrumental groups.

Woodwind

The flute and piccolo writing in the *Sinfonietta* is characteristic of the ways Janáček used these instruments. The flute is often his instrument of choice for lyrical melodic writing, as in the start of the fifth movement of the *Sinfonietta*, or the sublime C flat major solo that accompanies Káťa's first appearance in *Káťa Kabanová*. Janáček also makes use of the flute as an atmospheric orchestral colour. Examples include the 'rushing of the wind' in the third movement of the *Sinfonietta*, numerous passages to evoke the forest in *The Cunning Little Vixen*, or adding brilliance to urgent ostinato motifs (the prelude of *Makropulos* or the 'Svet' in the *Glagolitic Mass*). His flute and piccolo writing can be heard at its most imaginative in *From the House of the Dead*, which calls for four flutes, all of which also double on piccolo. Examples include the flutes (and later piccolos) as the dominant instrumental colour that establishes the mood at the start of Act II; or the magnificently strange sound of three piccolos doubling horns and male voices (three octaves lower), as darkness falls later in the same act – a particularly striking example of Janáček's delight in 'extremes' of register.[2] Janáček also had a fondness for using flutes to play important accompaniment figures: for instance, in the luminous interlude before the final scene of *Mr Brouček's Excursion to the Moon* where the figuration alternates

---

[1] JYL2, p. 723.
[2] Act II, starting nine bars before Fig. 39.

between two flutes;³ or the oscillating quavers (also played by muted horns) in the orchestral threnody which follows the shooting the Vixen in Act III of *The Cunning Little Vixen*.⁴

Prominent oboe and cor anglais solos are a common feature in Janáček. For the oboe, the second movement of the *Sinfonietta* is one example, and others include the Prelude to *Káťa Kabanová*, the 'Gospodi pomiluj' in the *Glagolitic Mass*,⁵ or the very similar theme (presumably a deliberate self-quotation) as the curtain rises for Act I of *From the House of the Dead*. Examples of cor anglais solos include the opening of *Taras Bulba* (a theme which then moves to the oboe a few bars later), and the languorous theme in the third movement of the *Sinfonietta* (which is again handed on to the oboe – a process that is reversed in the movement's closing bars).

Janáček uses the whole clarinet section to memorable effect in the 'Věruju' of the *Glagolitic Mass* where three clarinets are placed offstage for part of the movement.⁶ That passage also demonstrates his fondness for using the clarinet's upper register – and the last movement of the *Sinfonietta* is a prime example of the same trait. So, too, is the final song (No. 19) in the expanded version of the *Nursery Rhymes*, where a pair of clarinets shriek with spiky exuberance, before Janáček demonstrates the variety of his writing for the instrument as the first clarinet takes up a lyrical phrase which leads to the instrumental coda. There are many examples of inventive but idiomatic clarinet writing elsewhere in this enchanting work, from the rapid phrases that swoop up and down the register in No. 5 to the delicate figurations in No. 16. Janáček's writing for bass clarinet is just as remarkable and it has a particularly prominent role in the *Sinfonietta*, often functioning as the bass instrument in the woodwind section.

This is largely a consequence of Janáček's wholesale neglect of the bassoons in the *Sinfonietta*; apart from a significant part in the second movement, they play only four bars in the fourth movement and nothing whatsoever in the third and fifth movements. This is not the only work where Janáček seemed to forget about these instruments: while two bassoons and a contrabassoon make an important contribution to earlier movements in the *Glagolitic Mass*, they do not play at all in the final 'Intrada'; and in *Jenůfa*, the contrabassoon plays near the end of Act I but never after that.

---

³ Piano-vocal score, p. 151.
⁴ Fig. 31.
⁵ From bar 10 onwards.
⁶ 'Věruju', bars 121–167.

Brass

Trumpets often mark some of the most spectacular moments in Janáček's scores, though he uses them expressively too. The *Glagolitic Mass* demonstrates the variety of his trumpet writing. In the orchestral Introduction ('Úvod') and the closing 'Intrada', they create splendour and jubilation in much the same way as the outer movements of the *Sinfonietta*. But the first trumpet entry in the 'Věruju' is a pair of lyrical phrases – high, exposed and muted – which add a rather haunting colour.[7] Janáček also used trumpets for moments of delicate poetry: in Act III of *The Cunning Little Vixen*, as the Forester leaves the inn musing that his dog is getting old 'just like us', there is a phrase on two trumpets, marked *dolcissimo*, which lends an unusually beautiful colour to this poignant and nostalgic scene.[8] It should be added that Janáček sometimes avoided using trumpets when we might 'expect' to hear them: the coda to *Taras Bulba* provides a clear demonstration of this. Generations of conductors, starting with Václav Talich (who conducted the premiere), have doubled the organ right-hand octaves with trumpets, but Janáček never wrote this, choosing instead to keep the trumpets in reserve until ten bars from the end of the work.

Janáček's horn writing sometimes finds him using the instruments in a relatively conventional way, such as the hunting fanfares at the start of final scene of *The Cunning Little Vixen*, but there are many instances of more unusual writing: the alarmingly high-lying solo in Act III of *Káťa Kabanová*[9] or the increasingly stratospheric ostinatos in the agitated central section of the third movement of the *Sinfonietta*.[10] This was a sound Janáček clearly relished, and while it's very demanding, it is also raw and exciting.

In a few works – notably the *Sinfonietta* – Janáček requires four trombones, but in most of the later operas, the *Glagolitic Mass* and *Taras Bulba*, he asks for the more conventional grouping of three trombones and bass tuba. In all cases, he uses the lower brass to extremely telling effect. The hushed, closely spaced chords for muted trombones and tuba accompanying the timpani in the prelude to *Káťa Kabanová* create an instrumental sonority that is not only entirely Janáček's own but also eerily evocative. The close spacing of lower-pitched instruments is a crucial component of Janáček's writing, and because they're also muted, the trombones have a slightly more brittle colour. The last three bars in Act II

[7] Bars 35–6 and 41–4.
[8] Starting four bars before Fig. 45.
[9] Starting five bars before Fig. 8.
[10] Starting at Fig. 9.

of *Káťa*, played as the curtain falls at the end of the double love duet, are again characterised by *pianissimo* chords of E major played by trombones and tuba in what conventional wisdom would consider to be unduly 'thick' harmony, but in Janáček's hands, the effect is not only unorthodox but also magical. This kind of voicing was something Janáček developed further in later works, such as the muted trombone chords in the 'Agneče božij' of the *Glagolitic Mass*.

Among Janáček's orchestral works before the *Sinfonietta*, the use of trombones in *Taras Bulba* is particularly imaginative. Whether they are playing the combative rhythms in the main *Allegro* of the first movement or at several crucial places in the third movement, what stands out is the variety of Janáček's writing for trombones and tuba, the rapid changes in their role, and how often they play completely independently from the upper brass (trumpets and horns). In the *Sinfonietta* there are parts for four trombones, with the bass tuba reserved for specific moments (like the bassoons, the tuba is omitted entirely from the final movement). With a trombone quartet, the result is a lower brass sound that has a harder edge, notably at the start of the second movement, when growling muted chords are quickly followed by a spiky repeated ostinato. By way of contrast, at the start of the third movement, it is the more rounded sonority of the tuba that underpins the whole texture.

The *Capriccio* for piano left hand and an ensemble comprising flute, two trumpets, three trombones and tenor tuba shows another aspect of Janáček's trombone writing. It was first performed in Prague by the one-armed pianist Otakar Hollmann and members of the Czech Philharmonic on 2 March 1928. Though 'three trombones' are all that Janáček specified on the score, he had already told Hollmann on 4 October 1927 that he should 'request valve trombones' (rather than slide trombones)[11] to render the fast passagework effectively. The players willingly agreed to this – and they would have been thoroughly familiar with valve instruments, sometimes known as 'Armee Posaunen' ('Army trombones'). According to Jarmila Procházková, 'these instruments were used in the opera orchestra of the Brno National Theatre until 1919.'[12] Janáček was therefore accustomed to them, and one of his favourite copyists, Jaroslav Kulhánek, was also a trombonist in the orchestra. The case of the *Capriccio* raises an intriguing broader question: were more of Janáček's complex trombone passages imagined by him as being played on valved instruments? And does this have possible implications for the performance of other works, including the *Sinfonietta*?

[11] Letter to Otakar Hollmann, 4 October 1927, BmJA G7003.
[12] Jarmila Procházková, preface to SKV E/5, p. xii.

Timpani

'That's why I never forget to write a solo for the timpani!' This is how Janáček ended his 1911 feuilleton 'Without Drums', a childhood reminiscence of an Easter Sunday Mass in Hukvaldy: 'The Mass was not triumphant – because it was without drums', he explained. Janáček was as good as his word: one of the most remarkable features of his orchestration, in works from *Jenůfa* (and its pendant *Jealousy*) onwards, is his writing for timpani. The predominant view in the nineteenth century was that the most effective use of timpani was to reinforce or emphasise the bass line, though there are moments in Berlioz, Schumann and Tchaikovsky where timpani take on a more independent role, and this expanded greatly in the music of Janáček's contemporaries such as Dvořák, Rimsky-Korsakov, Mahler, Strauss and Elgar. According to a note in Cecil Forsyth's *Orchestration* (London, 1914), 'in a current drum-maker's catalogue drums are advertised and guaranteed' for pitches up to the G below middle C. Rimsky-Korsakov's *Principles of Orchestration* (first published in 1913) suggests a range up to G sharp, a semitone higher, though he notes that 'a magnificent kettle-drum of very small size was made for my opera-ballet *Mlada*; this instrument gave the D flat [a semitone above middle C]'. Both treatises noted that mechanically tuned timpani were still a rarity at the time. According to Rimsky, 'the expensive chromatic drum permitting instant tuning is rarely met with' while Forsyth wrote that mechanical tuning can be useful for solving practical problems, but 'it should be remembered that the functions of the drums [timpani] is not to play scales, portamentos and melodies.'

In Janáček's music, however, timpani often become leading protagonists of the musical argument, and in a few cases, they are indeed required to play melodies. The boldness of Janáček's timpani writing is already apparent at the end of Act II of *Jenůfa* where the timpani become the instrumental embodiment of the Kostelnička's closing line: In the orchestral epilogue, timpani thunder out a repeated five-note rhythm derived from the Kostelnička's last word ('na-ču-ho-va-la!') to bring the act to a stunning close.

There are examples of bold timpani writing in almost every work that followed. At the start of *Káťa Kabanová*, Janáček wrote a prominent solo line for timpani that goes a tone higher than Rimsky-Korsakov's recommended upper limit: The eight-note timpani motif first heard in the Prelude – and the leading motif of the whole opera – comprises four Fs and four B flats. Janáček clearly loved the sound of high timpani: the exciting writing in *Taras Bulba* has many top A flats and also requires frequent retuning of the other drums. This indicates that Janáček had access to mechanically tuned timpani (the forerunner of modern pedal timpani), and according to Paul

Wingfield, the Brno National Theatre orchestra had a set of machine timpani.[13] Much of Janáček's later writing for the instrument would have been unplayable without them, and even with modern pedal timpani, Janáček's parts are often very demanding.

The cut 'Raspet' ('He was crucified') section of the 'Věruju' in the *Glagolitic Mass* is an example of Janáček's writing for multiple timpani requiring three players, each with sets of drums, the first part going as high as B natural (a semitone below middle C). While this is a splendidly apocalyptic (and visually striking) piece of instrumentation, this passage was deleted, largely on practical grounds. Elsewhere in the *Glagolitic Mass* there is a timpani solo in the 'Slava'[14] which, in the definitive version, is doubled by cellos and basses. But in the earlier September 1927 version these four bars were scored for timpani alone – a difficult passage requiring multiple retuning, with the timpani playing what is essentially an unaccompanied melodic line. The final 'Intrada' of the Mass is a rather different case in which the timpani hammer out a dactylic (long–short–short) rhythm. Ostensibly straightforward, there are places where quick retuning presents challenges, and unusually, the timpani part throughout this movement is entirely independent of anything else in the orchestra, with no doubling of either its rhythms or pitches.

The first and fifth movements of the *Sinfonietta* are among the most famous examples of Janáček's timpani writing (they do not play in the central movements). This music is also an example of Janáček indicating precisely the sound he wanted, adding in his own hand on Václav Sedláček's copy, 'wooden sticks' (*dřevěné paličky*). For some reason this instruction was not printed in any early editions, but it has appeared in editions since 1980. The presence of this marking perhaps hints at how Janáček may have envisaged the sound of timpani at similar points in other works. Charles Mackerras certainly thought so and often asked players to use wooden sticks for passages in *Taras Bulba*, the *Glagolitic Mass* and the late operas.

---

[13] Paul Wingfield: *Janáček: Glagolitic Mass* (Cambridge: Cambridge University Press, 1992), p. 56.
[14] Starting at bar 83.

Other percussion instruments

Xylophone
Janáček's most famous use of the xylophone is its appearance at the start of *Jenůfa* as a musical representation of the turning mill wheel, but the instrument also makes regular appearances in later operas: In *The Excursions of Mr Brouček to the Moon* it accompanies the drinking chorus at the climax of the opening scene, marks the passing of time at the end of the double love-duet in Act II of *Káťa Kabanová*, and adds edge and brilliance to the radiant close of *The Cunning Little Vixen*. Janáček's use of percussion is at its most extreme in *From the House of the Dead* and the xylophone has a particularly prominent part during the prisoners' entertainments in Act II. Janáček seems to have viewed the xylophone as an instrument that could provide dramatic colour; there is no xylophone part in either *Taras Bulba* or the *Sinfonietta*.

Bells: 'zvonky' and 'zvony'
In the fourth movement of the *Sinfonietta*, Janáček asks for 'zvonky' – 'little bells', rendered in Italian as 'campanelli'. It's perhaps surprising this has given rise to a degree of confusion, but the origin for that goes back to the instrument list in the first edition, which specifies 'campane'. Several distinguished conductors of the work have asked for the 'campanelli' to be played by tubular bells (see Chapter 4). But Jaroslav Vogel, who was present at the world premiere, was clear that Janáček meant this part to be played on a glockenspiel – and he is surely correct. In the *Glagolitic Mass*, Janáček makes a distinction between 'campanelli' (= glockenspiel) in the 'Slava' and 'campane' (= tubular bells) in the 'Svet'. In *Taras Bulba*, there is no part for glockenspiel (or 'campanelli'), but the tubular bells ('campane') are notated in the bass clef, leaving no room for doubt. The part for 'zvonky' in the third movement of the *Sinfonietta* is more ambiguous as Janáček wrote it as unpitched notes, leading Vogel to speculate that it might have been intended for triangle. While that is possible, in other works Janáček specified a triangle when he wanted one, not least in *Taras Bulba* where it has quite a large part. In the third movement of the *Sinfonietta*, the usual solution is to play these 'unpitched' notes as E flats on the glockenspiel. Elsewhere in Janáček's late music, one of the most telling effects is the combination of glockenspiel and viola d'amore at the moment of Emilia Marty's first appearance in Act I of *The Makropulos Affair* – a wonderfully apt musical equivalent of the 'strange light' indicated at this point in the printed stage directions.

Harp

The harp has a smaller part in the *Sinfonietta* than in some of Janáček's other pieces, with contributions in the second and third movements and a brief but telling appearance in the fourth movement; its role in all three movements is to play ostinato figures. This is rather different from Janáček's usual style of harp writing: playing richly chordal or arpeggiated passages in music that could loosely be described as 'aspirational' in places such as the coda of *Taras Bulba*, the prominent part (for two harps) in the hymn-like passages of the *Ballad of Blaník* and at several places in *Brouček*. As Káťa and Boris meet for one last time in Act III of *Káťa Kabanová*, the harp and celesta are doubled for several bars[15] – a combination Janáček used again to magical effect at the opening of the 'Svet' in the *Glagolitic Mass*.

Extras and Oddities

Janáček's mature works include a number of unusual instruments or additional requirements. In the *Sinfonietta*, this comprises an entire *banda* of nine trumpets, two bass trumpets, two tenor tubas and timpani, and the third movement was originally intended to include a viola d'amore. Other examples of unusual or additional requirements include:

a) On- and offstage music: The stage music in *Jenůfa* comprises a xylophone, 'zvonky' (unpitched), a child's toy trumpet, two horns and single strings; in *Fate* Janáček called for a toy trumpet and small drum on stage; *Brouček* requires three trumpets and a horn as well as bagpipes (see below); *Makropulos* has an important part for offstage *banda* (two horns, two trumpets, timpani), starting in the Prelude and bringing down the curtain at the end. *From the House of the Dead* has a *banda* of three flutes (two doubling piccolo), two clarinets, tenor tuba, three trombones and tuba along with triangle, small snare drum and bass drum, all of which can be performed by musicians from the orchestra. In addition to these, the deep bells in Act II are described as 'within the fortifications' of the prison. As already noted, the clarinets are marked to play offstage in part of the 'Věruju' in the *Glagolitic Mass*. And the large *banda* in the *Sinfonietta* provides another theatrical element, arrayed behind the orchestra.

b) Non-standard instruments include an organ in *Fate* and *Brouček*; an important piano part in Act II of *Fate*; bagpipes and a glass harmonica (or celesta) in *Brouček*; castanets and children's toy drums (at different pitches) in *Makropulos*; and a startling array of chains, saws, shovels and other

---

[15] Fig. 28.

implements in *From the House of the Dead*. The expanded version of the *Nursery Rhymes* calls for an ocarina and a toy drum.

Janáček's enthusiasm for the viola d'amore probably began when he saw Charpentier's *Louise* in 1903. It had become an endangered species in instrumental music but occasionally appeared in the opera house, not least in *Louise* and in Puccini's *Madama Butterfly* (1904), another Janáček favourite. He originally included parts for two violas d'amore in *Fate* and came to associate the instrument with his romantic infatuations: the 'viola of love' was a kind of erotic code. In *Káťa Kabanová* (inspired by Kamila Stösslová) it has prominent solos in several scenes, starting with the Prelude. Janáček used the instrument again in *The Makropulos Affair* (its heroine again associated with Stösslová), and here its sound enhances the otherworldly effect of Emilia Marty's first entry, with another solo at the start of the opera's closing scene.

As noted above, the viola part for the whole of the third movement of the *Sinfonietta* was originally written for viola d'amore. The only association with Kamila Stösslová and the *Sinfonietta* was the work's 'Písek inspiration' (see Chapter 1): the fanfares that Janáček and Kamila heard at an outdoor military band concert in 1924. Perhaps the use of a viola d'amore was Janáček's symbolic way of including something of Kamila in the piece. However, he changed his mind about using it before the premiere, assigning the part instead to the orchestral violas. His final use of the viola d'amore has clear erotic associations: the viola part of the *Intimate Letters* Quartet was first written for it, but after hearing a private run-through, he wisely reverted to using a conventional viola. Particularly in *Káťa* and *Makropulos*, Janáček does seem to have had its distinctive tone quality in mind, suggesting that his use of it was more than purely symbolic.

Orchestral strings

Janáček's string writing is another facet of his unconventional orchestration, particularly in his later works. While he could (and often did) use the strings for highly expressive passages, he also required them to play numerous rapid, repeated figurations or ostinatos – a feature of the string parts throughout the *Sinfonietta*. In the second movement this ranges from filigree violin writing (from bar 46) to angular repeated motifs (from Fig. 9, bar 80), and a variety of ostinato figures from bar 163 to the end of the movement. The same movement also includes a characteristic example of Janáček's fondness for impassioned high-lying string interjections (notably from Fig. 5 onwards). The third movement opens with smooth, flowing phrases for the violins and cellos, accompanied by arpeggio-like ostinatos in the violas, which move to the cellos when the music modulates into C flat major. At Fig. 3, fragments of the arpeggio figure are given to the violas, exposed and in a very high register: a moment that continues to present challenges to even the finest orchestras. The fifth movement opens with rapid string figurations answering the melody on the flutes; and starting at bar 48, Janáček shows no mercy to the cellos, giving them continuous demisemiquaver ostinatos for more than forty bars.

Throughout Janáček's later music, a particular difficulty for the strings arises from his choice of keys. This was especially true in his own time when, traditionally, string players generally preferred playing in sharp keys. His own marked preference was for flat keys, particularly D flat major (the key in which the *Sinfonietta, Taras Bulba, The Excursions of Mr Brouček, The Cunning Little Vixen, From the House of the Dead* and the *Intimate Letters* Quartet all end). He also used B flat minor (not least at the start and finish of *Káťa Kabanová*), A flat minor (at the end of the First String Quartet) and more extreme keys such as C flat major (parts of the third movement of the *Sinfonietta* and Káťa's first entrance in *Káťa Kabanová*) and G flat minor (the third movement of the First Quartet). This idiosyncratic range of keys – and Janáček's sudden shifts from extreme flat to extreme sharp keys – can create difficulties in performance, but they are an essential component of his musical language. A further potential challenge is that Janáček abandoned key signatures in his mature concert works and later operas. This is understandable given that he moves so freely (and often rapidly) through a series of keys, but it can create difficulties for players until the music is thoroughly familiar (though it should be noted that others actually find it easier to play from parts with the accidentals in front of each note). Pieces often begin and end in different keys, and Janáček's choices – notably A flat minor and D flat major (both prominent in the *Sinfonietta*) – seem to be determined by their particular resonance and sonority. The string sections in the best of today's orchestras demonstrate levels of virtuosity and adaptability that were unimaginable a century ago, but even so, Janáček's extreme requirements continue to test even the most skilled instrumentalists.

Implications for performers

Janáček's unusual orchestral palette raises an important question for any performer of his music. Rising orchestral standards mean that passages that were considered exceptionally difficult as recently as the 1970s are now navigated more confidently by players familiar with the music. But that in itself raises a different problem: performances that sound too 'comfortable', smoothing out too many of the hard edges by downplaying some of Janáček's most startling instrumental effects, or playing with a glossy sheen closer to the aesthetic of Rimsky-Korsakov or Richard Strauss than to Janáček. Preserving the boldness of his music – and delighting in its idiosyncrasies – is an essential aspect of any successful and idiomatic Janáček performance.

That prompts a broader question: Can a performance of the *Sinfonietta*, or *Taras Bulba*, or one of the great operas be *too* beautiful? If the contours of the music are softened in the interests of a homogenous orchestral sound, there is a risk of sacrificing some of the character and individuality of the music. It was a quest for this kind of 'beautification' that prompted Karel Kovařovic to reorchestrate *Jenůfa*, and Václav Talich to tamper extensively with *Káťa Kabanová* and *The Cunning Little Vixen*. Musical sensibilities in the second half of the twentieth century became more acclimatised to the idea of understanding – and relishing – the wild spirit of Janáček's language, and its unusual instrumentation. That evolution of a playing style that was not only increasingly accurate but also reflected the character of the music itself, developed in tandem with the first serious attempts at making Janáček's music available in reliable editions: half a century ago, only one Janáček opera was available in orchestral score (in a corrupt version). Now we have access to full scores of most of the operas in carefully edited editions, alongside critical editions of other major works, including the *Glagolitic Mass, Taras Bulba* and the *Sinfonietta*.

Never have Janáček's interpreters had access to more accurate texts, so it comes as a surprise to discover that even when players have far greater familiarity with the music and immeasurably better editions from which to perform it, some conductors still choose to ignore Janáček's detailed markings. A conspicuous example, directly relevant to this book, is the instruction for the timpani to be played with 'wooden sticks' in the *Sinfonietta*. Decades after editions included this marking, it is disappointing to encounter recordings and performances that ignore it. What does this tell us? It suggests that there were (and still are) some conductors who can't quite bring themselves to trust Janáček and who want his music to sound closer to the opulent orchestral writing of his contemporaries.

But there is cause for optimism: The pioneering work done in Brno by Břetislav Bakala and František Jílek, in Munich by Rafael Kubelík, in Prague by Karel Ančerl, and in Britain, the United States and beyond by Charles Mackerras has been followed by a new generation. Conductors such as Tomáš Hanus and Jakub Hrůša have shown the same commitment and determination to bring all of Janáček's originality off the page and to realise his intentions unflinchingly. Successful Janáček conductors need to recreate – and celebrate – the extraordinary boldness of vision that was such a defining feature of his greatest music and, above all, to trust the composer. As Jaroslav Vogel said in 1926, reviewing the world premiere of the *Sinfonietta*, the key is to 'let Janáček be Janáček.'

What inspired Janáček to compose the *Sinfonietta* is considered in detail in the next chapter. But what did he make of the finished work? A few weeks after the premiere, he was in Hukvaldy to celebrate the unveiling of a plaque at his birthplace. Ludvík Kundera reported on the occasion for *Národní osvobození*, quoting from Janáček's speech which rooted the *Sinfonietta* firmly in Moravian soil, and as an expression of the spirit of the honest, sincere Czech man:

> Toasts were made by the mayors of Kopřivnice and Hukvaldy, an old classmate of Janáček's from primary school, by the postmaster Uhlíř on behalf of local musicians, and by the director of the [Brno] conservatory [Jan] Kunc on behalf of the visiting musicians. Then Janáček spoke. Why was it so important to him that his work, well performed, should be heard here, in his native region? After all, his entire output is so closely connected with the region that gave birth to it, with the people from whom it came. Anyone who knows this region with its rapidly changing weather, frequent storms after which a golden sun often shines, anyone who knows its people, vigorous but good-natured, its language, its soul, will also understand the connection between Janáček's works and his native region. He wants his music to be as close as possible to the soul of the Czech people – *Youth, Concertino, Sinfonietta*. Janáček singled out the work that had resounded with such splendour just three weeks earlier, at the Sokol congress: 'I think I have succeeded best in coming close to the mind of the simple[16] Czech man in my latest work, the *Sinfonietta*.[17] I would like to continue on the same path. Although I am getting on in years, it seems to me that a new vein or a new branch is starting to grow in my work – just like when we see a new branch sprouting on those four- or five-hundred-year-old Hukvaldy trees. My latest creative period is a new outpouring of the soul which has reckoned with the rest of the world and wants to be as close as possible to the simple Czech man.'

---

[16] 'Simple' here meaning down to earth, modest and straightforward.
[17] Assuming that Kundera is quoting verbatim, it is worth noting that Janáček called the work 'Sinfonietta' rather than 'Military Sinfonietta', the title he usually preferred at the time.

1
Inspiration – Composition – Publication

The year 1926 was an exceptionally happy and productive year for Janáček. His works enjoyed great success with *Káťa Kabanová* produced in Berlin, the revised *Mr Brouček's Excursion to the Moon* given in Brno, and world premieres of the *Concertino* and *The Makropulos Affair*. Janáček was invited to London, where he was warmly welcomed (in spite of his visit coinciding with Britain's General Strike) and his music was generally well-received there. His native village of Hukvaldy unveiled a commemorative plaque at his birthplace – the Hukvaldy school – which pleased him greatly. New compositions that year included the *Capriccio* and the expanded version of *Nursery Rhymes* (*Říkadla*), alongside two large-scale works: the *Glagolitic Mass* and the *Sinfonietta*.

As discussed in the Prologue, Janáček had only completed four works for full orchestra before 1926 (apart from his early folk music arrangements): *Jealousy* (*Žárlivost*) and three symphonic poems – *The Fiddler's Child* (1913), *Taras Bulba* (composed during the war years in 1915–8) and the *Ballad of Blaník* (1919–20). All four have some kind of programmatic, extra-musical element. *Jealousy* was based on a folk ballad, 'The Jealous Man'; *The Fiddler's Child* took its inspiration from Svatopluk Čech's poem about a deceased fiddler and an abandoned orphan; the 'Slavonic rhapsody' *Taras Bulba* is based on Gogol's novella about a Cossack leader and his sons; and the *Ballad of Blaník* was inspired by Jaroslav Vrchlický's poem about the legendary Knights of Blaník. Programmatic or narrative elements were also to be significant for the unfinished *Danube* Symphony and the abandoned Violin Concerto, 'The Wanderings of a Little Soul', though there is little detail about what their precise inspiration might have been, literary or otherwise. Janáček also drew on extra-musical programmes for several of his chamber music pieces, including the *Fairy Tale* (*Pohádka*) for cello and piano and both string quartets.

Although Janáček had been an enthusiastic supporter of Josef Durdík (and of formal aesthetics in general) in his early years, his own dramatic instincts and a desire to create musical narratives meant that he was often drawn to composing with an extra-musical programme in mind. Janáček usually avoided conventional symphonic forms, perhaps because of a reluctance to work within their more extended structures, perhaps because he regarded the symphony as a romantic emblem of times past – or, most probably, because larger instrumental forms simply didn't suit his intentions as well as opera. In 1923, there was a sign that Janáček's thinking was starting to evolve as he embarked on the *Danube* Symphony, but work on this did not come easily, and its score became something of a repository for unused operatic fragments rather than an organically conceived work. He abandoned the *Danube* in 1925. However, the following year – in a matter of weeks – he completed the *Sinfonietta*, a work of compact dimensions (in terms of duration) that apparently had no programmatic backstory. Its innovative and flexible form is typical of Janáček's conciseness, in sharp contrast to the monumental late Romantic symphony (which was a far cry from Janáček's quest for powerful musical expression achieved with the greatest economy of means). Moreover, the form of the sinfonietta had been popular with Czech composers in the early 1920s, with examples by Emil Axman (1887–1949), Jaroslav Řídký (1897–1956) and Otakar Ostrčil (1879–1935), as well as Janáček's pupil Osvald Chlubna (1893–1971). Janáček even heard Ostrčil's *Sinfonietta* in a concert at the Brno National Theatre on 11 January 1925, though it is most unlikely that this bleak and rather disillusioned score provided any direct inspiration.

'Brother' Janáček and 'some notes' for the Sokol Rally

The impetus for the composition of the *Sinfonietta* was an event of particular significance for the young Czechoslovak nation: the Eighth All-Sokol Rally[1] in Prague in 1926. Since its establishment in 1862, the Sokol[2] Gymnastics Association had become the country's most important sports organisation. Its founders, Miroslav Tyrš and Jindřich Fügner, intended it as non-political, with the aim of promoting the physical, mental and moral growth and well-being of Czech society. The Sokol recognised no social distinctions, and members addressed each other as 'brother' and 'sister'. Its character is well captured by slogans such as 'Let us be strong!', 'A healthy body in a healthy mind!', 'Strengthen your arms, serve your country!' or 'Your homeland in your heart! Strength in your arms!'. Within a few years

---

[1] The Czech word is 'slet' meaning 'rally', 'festival', or 'gathering'. For consistency, we have translated it throughout as 'rally'.
[2] 'Sokol' means 'falcon'.

of its foundation, the Sokol spread throughout cities in Bohemia, Moravia and Silesia, and it found early support from Czech cultural figures such as the writers Jan Neruda and Karolína Světlá, the linguist Josef Jungmann, and the painter Josef Mánes. Many visual artists shared the Sokol's ideals, including František Ženíšek, Mikoláš Aleš, Alfons Mucha and Jakub Obrovský, all of whom designed posters for Sokol rallies.

The Sokol became one of the pillars of the liberated Czech nation – something underlined by the fact that Tomáš Garrigue Masaryk had been an active Sokol member long before he became the first President of the Czechoslovak Republic. Membership represented not only a commitment to the ideal of a 'healthy body in a healthy mind' but also served as a declaration and celebration of Czech identity. The large public gymnastic displays at rallies held in cities around the country were a particularly important aspect of the Sokol programme, and the entire Sokol community then came together for All-Sokol Rallies in Prague.

Janáček himself enjoyed attending Brno Sokol rallies as a spectator. The Sokol Gymnastics Union in Brno was founded in 1862, and after the construction of the Besední dům in 1872, regular events were held there. Janáček was a member of Sokol Brno I from the age of 22 until his death, and in 1893 he composed *Music for Club-Swinging* as an accompaniment for Sokol exercises, dedicated to (and first published by) the Sokol Gymnastic Association in Brno. But seven years before joining the Sokol, at the age of 15 and at the very end of his time as a chorister in the Augustinian monastery, Janáček wrote to his uncle Jan to send him some money for 'a nice light Sokol suit'.[3] Marie Stejskalová, the Janáčeks' housekeeper recalled his involvement with the Sokol in her memoirs, noting that 'he did not exercise, nor did he work for the Sokol in any particular role, but he was interested in all its work and supported the Union in every way'.[4] Zdenka Janáčková recalled that as a younger man, Janáček had been more active in the Sokol, though he was never a devotee of gymnastic exercises.

Czech communities throughout Europe and the United States also founded Sokol branches, and during World War I, many Sokol members were involved in foreign resistance, notably in the Czechoslovak Legions; by 1918, the Sokols were firmly established as a non-political force for independence.

With the founding of the new nation of Czechoslovakia in 1918, the Sokol became more important, and in 1918–20 it even took on a quasi-military

---

[3] Letter to Jan Janáček, 6 August 1869, BmJA, A 4930.
[4] Sarka Zahrádková and Jiří Zahrádka, ed.: *Mářiny paměti. Zapsala Marie Trkanová, podle vyprávění Marie Stejskalové, hospodyně v rodině Leoše Janáčka* (Brno: TIC Brno, 2023), p. 147.

role, helping to establish the new Czechoslovak Army. It is therefore not surprising that the Seventh All-Sokol Rally in 1920 – the first to be held during the new republic – represented a declaration of the young nation's strength. A competition for a rally march was announced, and one Sokol brother – the distinguished composer Josef Suk – entered under the pseudonym of Josef Emanuel Skrýšovský. His march *Towards a New Life* duly won the competition, and its well-crafted music, full of enthusiastic optimism, was in strong contrast to the lyrical but rather melancholic Czech national anthem *Kde domov můj*, the character of which had been criticised by many, including President Masaryk. Although some Sokol members were initially cautious about accepting Suk's new march – preferring an older one by František Kmoch – it eventually gained in popularity and was even equipped with lyrics in the 1930s. Since then, its opening fanfare has sometimes been used, alongside the fanfares from Smetana's *Libuše*, as part of the ceremonial music for the Czech president (the start of the finale of Dvořák's Eighth Symphony and the Fanfares from Janáček's *Sinfonietta* have also been used for the same purpose).

The Eighth All-Sokol Rally in 1926 promised to be another notable event. It was held at the enormous new purpose-built stadium in Prague's Strahov district, attended by 140,000 gymnasts and 800,000 spectators. Expectations were high during the preparations for this huge gathering, so it is no surprise that the newspaper *Lidové noviny* asked Janáček for a musical contribution. The critic and composer Boleslav Vomáčka (1887–1965) wrote about the impetus for the creation of the *Sinfonietta* in his review of the premiere, stating that Janáček had been invited by the editorial staff of *Lidové noviny*

> to write 'some notes' to commemorate the Sokol festivities. Janáček thought for a moment until the idea flashed through his mind: Sokols – red shirts – that means fanfares! So he sketched several fanfares, and from these, more music began to grow in his imagination, phrase by phrase, until in the short space of about three weeks he had the finished score of the *Sinfonietta* in front of him.[5]

Vomáčka almost certainly received much of this information directly from the composer, and it is also likely, as noted by John Tyrrell, that the request to write something for the Sokol Rally was made at a meeting in the Prague offices of *Lidové noviny* on 21 February 1926, which was mainly to discuss *The Makropulos Affair*.[6] It should be noted that the *Sinfonietta* was

---

[5] Boleslav Vomáčka ['B.V.']: 'O Janáčkově symfoniettě', *Lidové noviny*, vol. 34, no. 329, 1 July 1926, p. 7.
[6] JYL2, p. 592. This meeting was announced by Janáček to UE in a letter dated 30 January 1926. WBR, 329; copy in BmJA, A 5991. LJUE, no. 245.

not written at the instigation of those organising the Sokol Rally: it was only offered to the Sokol after its completion in April 1926.[7] It had been customary to announce a composition competition before previous All-Sokol Rallies, but the organisers did not do so in 1926. The Czech Composers' Club objected, regretting that 'the Sokol has not involved qualified Czech composers this year and hopes that at future gatherings Czech composers will be invited to cooperate through a properly organised competition.' The Sokol committee explained that there would be no competition on this occasion because Suk's *Towards a New Life* was to be performed again.[8] However, the indignation of the Composers' Club may also have been fuelled by the rumour spreading in musical circles that Janáček's fanfares had been accepted without any competition.

The Písek inspiration

The composer chose fanfares to honour the Sokol Rally, but Janáček's explanation quoted in Vomáčka's review ('Sokol – red shirts – that means fanfares!') needs considerable amplification. Janáček was a regular visitor to the South Bohemian town of Písek. He had friends there, above all the muse of his later years, Kamila Stösslová (1891–1935) and her family. It was in a letter to Kamila that Janáček later wrote in connection with the *Sinfonietta*, 'I remember those Písek fanfares! They were nice back then.'[9] Vomáčka provided some more details (from Janáček) in his review: 'According to the composer, it all began in Písek, where he was told about the performance of some fanfares. A sceptical Janáček went to hear them and he saw soldiers in historical costumes, playing fanfares unlike any he had heard before.'[10] Each year on 1 May in Písek, fanfares were traditionally played from the top of the church tower, and summer concerts of military music were given in Palacký Park as a regular feature of the town's musical life. But an important question remains: *When* did Janáček hear this Písek military band? It was not in 1925; that year, the promenade concerts in the park took place every Friday from 5:30 p.m. between 8 May and 25 August,[11] a time when

---

[7] Correspondence concerning the Eighth All-Sokol Rally is in the Czech National Archives, Prague, Czechoslovak Sokol organisation, no. 1062, file no. 785.
[8] Ibid., file no. 786. The letter dated 23 April 1926 was signed on behalf of the Czech Composers' Club by Alois Hába (1893–1973) and Josef Bohuslav Foerster (1859–1951). The Sokol's reply is contained in the same folder.
[9] Letter of 29 March 1926, BmJA, E 360. HŽ/IL, no. 373.
[10] Boleslav Vomáčka ['B.V.']: 'O Janáčkově symfoniettě', *Lidové noviny*, vol. 34, no. 329, 1 July 1926, p. 7.
[11] 'Promenádní koncerty', *Otavan*, vol. ix (1925), nos. 7–9, p. 127.

the composer was not in Písek. Janáček's encounter with the local military band must therefore have been earlier.

However, at the end of June 1924, a week before his 70th birthday, Janáček spent a pleasant weekend in Písek. On Friday, 27 June, he arrived on the 3.22 p.m. train from Prague,[12] where he had just attended the final performances of the Prague Conservatory's master class.[13] In the congenial company of the Stössl family, especially the cheerful and solicitous Kamila, the tired composer spent 'three beautiful days that had no shadows'.[14] With Kamila, he attended a concert by a military band in Palacký Park on the Friday evening, performed in the newly built music pavilion.[15] It was there that he heard the fanfares, jotting down a motif from them in his notebook, dated 28 June 1924 (plate 1).[16]

The band of the Eleventh Czechoslovak Infantry Regiment 'František Palacký' was a prominent Písek institution, and as well as military repertoire, its concert programmes included arrangements of music by Smetana, Dvořák, Mozart, Beethoven and Liszt.[17] Apparently, the skilful arrangements and the high quality of the performances were due to the bandmaster, Staff Captain Jaroslav Pacovský. The band's Písek programme also included fanfare marches in which, to the delight of the audience, 'a solo trumpeter, or group of trumpeters, stood up for greater effect when playing their instruments, raising up the bells which were decorated with flags.'[18] In this context, the *Jedecký Pochod* (*Equestrian march*) by Pacovský deserves a special mention. In it, 'the four fanfare trumpets always stood up during their solos.'[19] As Janáček told Kamila two years later,[20] he remembered enjoying the band's fanfares at a concert given on a warm evening in

---

[12] Janáček to Stösslová, 25 June 1924, BmJA, E 224. HŽ/IL, no. 236.
[13] Janáček to Zdenka Janáčková, 25 June 1924, BmJA, A 4989. TCV, no. 480.
[14] Janáček to Stösslová, 30 June 1924, BmJA, E 225. HŽ/IL, no. 237.
[15] The music pavilion can still be seen in Palácký Park today and has recently been restored.
[16] Janáček's notebook, BmJA, Z 59, p. 82. Janáček wrote down the wrong date (Saturday, 28 June 1924), as the concerts always took place on Friday evenings. The Sunday concert on 29 June is not documented and probably didn't take place since on 4 July large gala concert was given in Písek by the combined forces of the local band and of the Infantry Regiment No. 1 'Master Jan Hus' from České Budějovice.
[17] See 'Hudba čsl. pěš. pluku č. 11 Františka Palackého v Písku Janáčka', in: *Otavan*, vol. viii (1924), no. 6–7 (5 August 1924), p. 107.
[18] Jaroslav Mácha: 'Písecké fanfáry', *Hudební nástroje*, vol. 14, no. 3 (1977), pp. 67–9.
[19] Tomáš Hančl: 'Několik glos k problematice exponovaných partů dechových nástrojů v díle Leoše Janáčka', *Leoš Janáček ac tempora nostra* (Janáčkova společnost and ČHF, Brno, 1983), pp. 215–9.
[20] Letter of 29 March 1926, BmJA, E 360. HŽ/IL, no. 373.

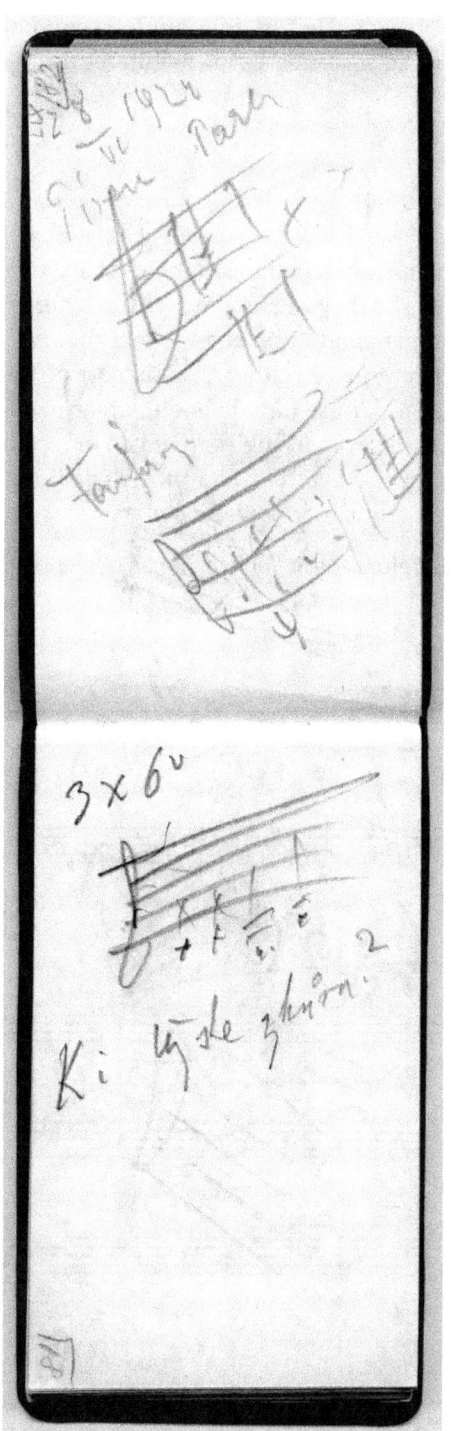

Plate 1. Entry in Janáček's notebook for 28 June 1924 with his jottings of fragments from the military band concert in Písek including 'Fanfáry' (Janáček Archive, Brno, Z59).

the park with his beloved muse at his side. He certainly had the sound of a military band in mind when he began to sketch his own fanfares for the Sokol Rally.

From Fanfares to the *Military Sinfonietta*

Janáček began by sketching some independent fanfares, but these have very little in common with the finished work. They were scored for three horns, three trumpets, five trombones, timpani and harp, and the fact that they were originally conceived as a separate piece (rather than as part of the *Sinfonietta*) is also confirmed by Janáček's use of a different, larger paper type.[21] These sketches have survived on seven pages, reproduced in Ex. 1.1 in their entirety. On the final page (p. 7) there is a hint of the composer working towards the style of his music for the *Sinfonietta* fanfares.

Ex. 1.1. Janáček's sketches for fanfares before the *Sinfonietta* (BmJA, A 7444).

Page 1:

[21] BmJA, A 7444; another sheet written on both sides is at BmJA, A 52 723.

Page 2:

Page 3:

Page 4:

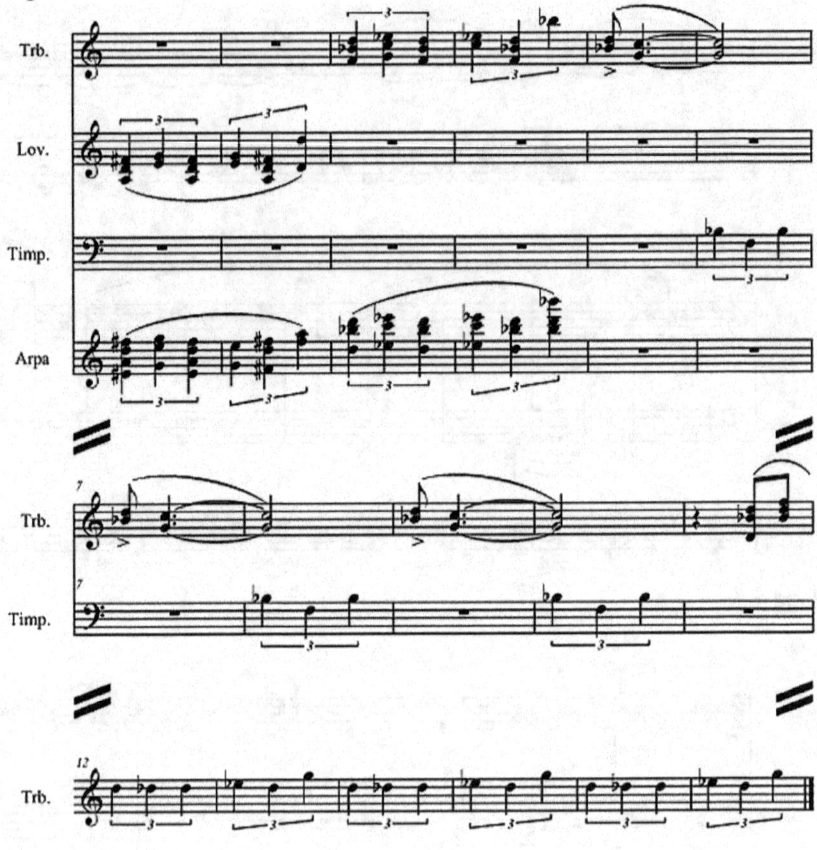

Page 5:

Page 6:

Page 7:

Janáček subsequently cut these sketches into smaller sheets, and on the backs of them he sketched the main ideas for some new fanfares which are essentially the ones we now know from the *Sinfonietta* (plate 2). Janáček then seems to have inserted the fanfare sketches at the end of the last movement of the autograph manuscript of the complete work, adding layers of

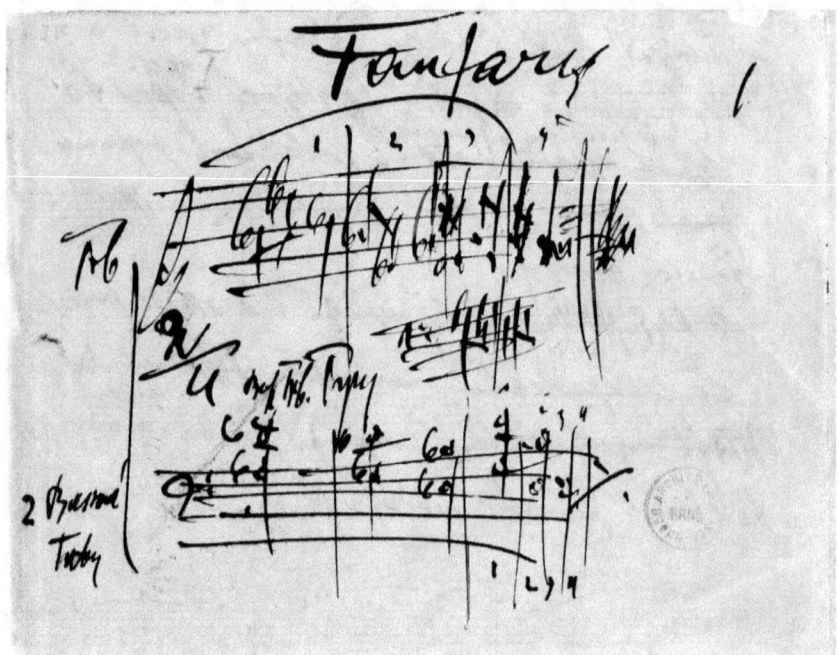

Plate 2. Janáček's earliest sketch for the Fanfares of the *Sinfonietta* (Janáček Archive, Brno, A 7444).

orchestral decoration around them.[22] This is also indicated by the numbering of the pages in the autograph of the *Sinfonietta*, where pages 1–28 of the last movement are followed by the fanfares, starting again at page 1. In this sketch, the composer indicated the order of the movements in red crayon and noted the repetition of the fanfares at the end of the work. Only after this did Janáček write out the Fanfares in their final form: the manuscript from which extracts were subsequently reproduced in *Lidové noviny* (plates 3a and 3b).[23] It is possible that Janáček initially intended the Fanfares

[22] The first sketch page of the Fanfares is now misbound at the start of the volume, even though it was originally placed by Janáček in the last movement. This sketch gives the first three trumpet notes as a minor third (B flat–D flat–B flat). In the later autograph manuscript written out for *Lidové noviny*, Janáček miscopied these three notes as a perfect fourth (B flat–E flat–B flat). The perfect fourth was an error on Janáček's part, corrected in Sedláček's authorised copy, which has B flat–D flat–B flat, as do all the UE and Philharmonia editions derived from it. For discussion of this intriguing question, see Miloš Štědroň: 'Jak vlastně začíná Janáčkova Sinfonietta?!?', *Opus musicum*, vol. 20, no. 3 (1988), p. xxi.

[23] A complete facsimile was issued in 1963; see Supplement to Chapter 1.

Plate 3a, b. The first two pages of Janáček's autograph of the Fanfares, in the manuscript submitted to *Lidové noviny*, with the first three trumpet notes on p. 2 miscopied as B flat–E flat–B flat (Leoš Janáček Foundation, Brno, Ar 3-2, A-1).

(as a single movement) not for performance but purely for publication in *Lidové noviny* as a greeting to the Sokol Rally.

Janáček's original movement plan suggests that in the initial phase of composition, the *Sinfonietta* was meant to begin with the present second movement to which the Fanfares were only added later (at which point the composer renumbered the second movement as 'Ib'). Janáček settled on this final order in the autograph score,[24] and he then handed the entire composition to his favourite copyist, Václav Sedláček (1879–1944),[25] who later copied the orchestral parts, too.[26] It is clear from Sedláček's score that he copied the opening Fanfares shortly before the rest of the work since the original title page was headed, 'Military Sinfonietta/Fanfares', with Sedláček's signature at the foot. The likely explanation is that Janáček wanted to submit the autograph of the Fanfares to *Lidové noviny* as quickly as possible, so that they had it ready for publication.

According to information Janáček later sent to Universal Edition in Vienna, he composed the *Sinfonietta* between 2 March to 15 May 1926.[27] In his letter to Kamila Stösslová on 29 March 1926, Janáček described work on several projects, adding, 'That's enough for me to put down my pen – once I've finished a nice little *Sinfonietta* with fanfares.'[28] He most probably finished it on 1 April, as confirmed in a short message to the conductor František Neumann: 'Everything is finished today! Happy holidays!'[29] On 3 April, Janáček travelled to Štrbské Pleso with his wife, Zdenka, returning home on 5 April. A week later, on 12 April, the ceremonial committee of the Eighth All-Sokol Rally received information about Janáček's newly completed work from Dr Karel Heller, chairman of the organising committee, who reported that 'Leoš Janáček has composed rally fanfares, which he would be willing to dedicate to the Č.O.S. [Sokol].'[30] Those planning the rally had to decide how to use this composition, so they requested more details from Antonín Krejčí (1884–1955), a teacher and an official of the Brno Sokol, actively involved in the organization of the rally and in regular contact with Janáček. On 22 April 1926, he gave the committee more information:

---

[24] This manuscript is in BmJA, A 7444. The first page of the second movement is in the Archive of the Czech Academy of Sciences, Prague.
[25] Sedláček's authorised copy of the full score, ÖNB, L1. UE. 777 GF.
[26] Sedláček's copied orchestral parts, WBR, Janáček 004.
[27] Letter of 19 November 1926, WBR, 329; copy in BmJA, B 2047. LJUE, no. 279.
[28] HŽ/IL, no. 373.
[29] BmJA, A 6097.
[30] Czech National Archives, Prague, Czechoslovak Sokol organisation, no. 1062, file no. 786.

At the request of *Lidové noviny*, the composer Dr Leoš Janáček composed his rally fanfares. The work grew into a *Sinfonietta*. I mentioned this composition to brothers Dr K. Heller and Schwarz, who requested that I should ask Dr Janáček if he would allow his composition to be performed by the Czech Philharmonic on the eve of the festival. The composer Dr Janáček was very pleased with the offer, he declared that the composition was finished and was being copied, and that he would be very happy for the first performance to be given at the All-Sokol Rally. I recommend the fraternal committee to send the composer (whose address is the Organ School, Smetanova, Brno) an official request, asking for permission to perform the work. Please do this as soon as possible, because Dr Janáček leaves for England on about 28 May.[31]

On 26 April, a letter from the Sokol organisers to the rally committee proposed that the *Sinfonietta* should be performed on two occasions:

In response to your order no. 1691 that we should submit a proposal by 30 April indicating when it would be possible to perform the festival fanfares composed by Leoš Janáček, we inform you of the decision of the organising committee. It would be most appropriate to perform it at the gala concert for youth on 26 June, before Smetana's *Má vlast* played by the Czech Philharmonic; then at the opening of the Sokol tribute in the Old Town Square on the day of the parade, 6 July, from the tower of the Týn Church.[32]

The next day, the chairman of the rally committee, Dr Josef Scheiner, asked Krejčí to contact Janáček[33] to make arrangements for sending the score and, at the same time, to hand over a letter of thanks in which Scheiner expressed his gratitude 'that you are willing to allow your *Sinfonietta* with the Rally Fanfares to be performed at the Eighth All-Sokol Rally.'[34] In the same letter, he asked Janáček to discuss practical arrangements with Krejčí. Janáček probably did nothing about this immediately: he fell ill with a painful inflammation of his left ear, causing temporary hearing loss, and was preoccupied with planning his trip to London, setting out on 28 April.

[31] Ibid.
[32] Ibid.
[33] Ibid.
[34] Ibid.

First Sokol performance: the 'Rally' Sinfonietta

The earliest published report of Janáček's new work was by Boleslav Vomáčka in *Lidové noviny* on 29 April 1926: 'Leoš Janáček has just completed a five-movement *Sinfonietta* for a military orchestra. The impetus for creating this work was a request to write fanfares for the Sokol rally, and the idea grew in the master's imagination into a large symphonic work.'[35] Janáček probably told Vomáčka about the completed work just before he left for London (he set out from Prague's Wilson Station on 28 April 1926 at 2:28 p.m.),[36] by which time he had been able to submit the autograph manuscript of the Fanfares to the Prague office of *Lidové noviny*. A similar report appeared in *Lidové noviny* on 1 May 1926.[37] Janáček's own title – *Symfonietta vojenská* (*Military Sinfonietta*) – was only revealed in the *Prager Presse* on 18 May, during an interview about the composer's stay in London.[38]

After his return from London on 12 May, Janáček was expected in Brno for the separate premiere of *Mr Brouček's Excursion to the Moon*. Waiting for him was a letter from the rally committee dated 27 April (delivered by Krejčí) and another dated 5 May in which they announced when and where the Fanfares would be performed and requesting the loan of the score and parts.[39] At this point a misunderstanding arose: the Sokol committee mentioned a 'Symphony with Rally Fanfares', a title that only led to confusion. The committee probably believed that it was a short work for orchestra with fanfares, similar in scope to Suk's *Towards a New Life* (which takes around six minutes to perform). On 13 May 1926, only a day after returning to Brno, Janáček wrote at once to the organising committee:

> Gentlemen!
>
> After my return from London, I am immediately responding to your letter of 5 May. There is probably some misunderstanding about the 'Fanfares'. They are part of the *Military Sinfonietta*, which I wanted to dedicate to the Sokol membership for the Eighth Rally. The fanfares

---

[35] Boleslav Vomáčka ['B.V.'], *Lidové noviny*, vol. 34, no. 218, 29 April 1926, p. 7.
[36] 'Skladatel Janáček jede do Anglie', *Československá republika*, vol. 3, no. 117, 28 April 1926, p. 7.
[37] Gracian Černušák ['–k.']: 'Janáčkovo jaro', *Lidové noviny*, vol. 34, no. 222, 1 May 1926, p. 9.
[38] 'J. R.': Leoš Janáček über eine Londoner Eindrücke', *Prager Presse*, vol. 6, no. 136, 18 May 1926, p. 6.
[39] Czech National Archives, Prague, Czechoslovak Sokol organisation, no. 1062, file no. 786.

can be played on their own, but I would like the entire work to be played at the gala concert. It is not long and could perhaps be heard alongside Smetana's *Má vlast*.

Please reply quickly.[40]

No answer came immediately. So, on 15 May, Janáček sent a copy of the score to Antonín Krejčí with a covering letter:

> Dear friend!
>
> 1. I enclose a letter in which I object that only the Fanfares are to be played.
>
> 2. I ask that the entire *Sinfonietta*, of which the Fanfares form a part, should be performed at the gala concert.
>
> 3. I want to be present at the Philharmonic's final rehearsal for the *Sinfonietta*.
>
> 4. The Fanfares should be played by a military band: that will be the most suitable scoring given the number of trumpets.
>
> 5. If points 1, 2, 3 and 4 are acceptable, I would like a ticket for the concert where I can see and hear the work.
>
> With best regards,
>
> Drph. Leoš Janáček
>
> Brno 15/V 1926
>
> PS. Four copyists can transcribe the parts in four days. Let each of them take care of one movement. The Fanfares are already written out. I must have the score back after the Rally. Don't lose it as it's the only copy!![41]

Janáček grumbled about this situation in a letter to Kamila Stösslová the same day: 'I probably won't go to the Rally; they only want the Fanfares, and I want to hear the whole *Sinfonietta*.'[42] But Krejčí soon had better news: he wrote to Janáček on 18 May informing him that he had handed over the score to the Sokol's ceremonial committee. He apologised on behalf of the organisers for their confusion about the scope of the work, emphasising that the *Sinfonietta* would be performed in its entirety.[43] In another letter

[40] Ibid.
[41] Ibid.
[42] BmJA, E 378. HŽ/IL, no. 390.
[43] BmJA, D 594.

dated 22 May, the organisers themselves apologised for the misunderstanding and provided specific information about the premiere: the complete 'Rally Sinfonietta' would be performed on 26 June by the Czech Philharmonic, conducted by Václav Talich. The separate Fanfares would then be played from the tower of the Týn Church on 6 July when the Sokol procession entered the Old Town Square.[44] The committee also recommended that Janáček should discuss rehearsal arrangements directly with Talich.

In the meantime, the orchestral parts had been copied by Václav Sedláček, and Janáček needed the score back to make checks and revisions. Among the more substantial corrections made in his hand was the expansion of the trumpet parts in the second movement to include the extra players from the *banda* (originally, he intended only the three orchestral trumpets to play in this movement; several months later, this is also how the passage was printed in the first edition of the score); and an important performance instruction was added in the Fanfares – that the timpani should be played with wooden sticks. Since the orchestral parts had already been copied, these changes were not included in them, and Janáček probably did not see the parts; had he done so, he would no doubt have reacted to Sedláček's misreading of the *banda* and orchestral trumpets (which he amalgamated into one group of nine, rather than two distinct groups of nine and three). The parts also carry the incorrect title of 'Sletová symfonietta' (Rally sinfonietta) rather than Janáček's own title of *Military Sinfonietta*.

The management of the Czech Philharmonic announced on 20 May 1926 that it would be giving three concerts during the Sokol Rally, but no details were available until after Talich and the orchestra had returned from a foreign tour.[45] The Czech Philharmonic published its definitive programmes on 4 June, while Talich (who had decided only to perform three movements from *Má vlast* rather than the whole work) had to familiarise himself with Janáček's new score. Janáček wanted to discuss the *Sinfonietta* with Talich in Brno, where the Czech Philharmonic was due to give a concert, but this was cancelled through lack of public interest.[46] Janáček had to travel to Berlin on 28 May for the premiere of *Káťa Kabanová* at the State Opera, then to Hukvaldy to discuss the planned celebrations that were to take place in July for unveiling a plaque at his birthplace. As a result, he had no opportunity to visit Talich in Prague. So, on 27 May he wrote to the conductor:

---

[44] BmJA, D 595.
[45] Czech National Archives, Prague, Czechoslovak Sokol organisation, no. 1062, file no. 786.
[46] Gracian Černušák ['–k.']: 'Česká filharmonie nepřijede do Brna', *Lidové noviny*, vol. 34, no. 254, 20 May 1926, p. 8.

Dear friend!

I am told by the Sokol Rally office that the Czech Philharmonic will play my *Military Sinfonietta* on 26 June. I would have liked to talk to you about this in Brno – unfortunately that did not happen. So, I am passing on some notes to you:

1) The fanfares in numbers I and V (3 [*recte* 9] trumpets in C, 2 tenor tubas, 2 bass trumpets, timpani) would be better with the harsher timbre of a military band.

2) In number II [*recte* III] there is a viola d'amore part. It would be preferable if all orchestral violas play this part.

Please let me know when I can come to the rehearsals.

After returning from Berlin[47] I will be staying from 4 June at Hukvaldy, near Příbor, Moravia.

I wrote the work at white heat, and even the copyist was in a hurry. You will notice the mistakes.[48]

Janáček waited in vain for an answer and he asked Jan Mikota (1903–78)[49] if he had any more information. On 6 June, Mikota wrote that Talich could not reply because he was visiting the new Czech ambassador in Stockholm.[50] Janáček commented ruefully on this situation in a letter to Max Brod (1884–68) on 10 June:

My *Military Sinfonietta* is supposed to be performed in Prague (by the Philharmonic Orchestra) on 26 June. But I don't know if it will happen. Mr Talich is away in Stockholm and then goes to Zurich – while the orchestra is in chaos in Prague![51]

As late as 17 June, nine days before the premiere, Janáček wrote despairingly to Kamila Stösslová: 'I have not had any news from Prague. Who knows if there will be anything for me there?'[52] Janáček returned to Brno

---

[47] Janáček and his wife, Zdenka, travelled to Berlin on 28 May for the local premiere of *Káťa Kabanová* on 31 May. Janáček was delighted with the production, and he met Schoenberg, Schreker and Erich Kleiber at the reception afterwards. See JYL2, p. 614.
[48] Museum of the Bohemian Karst, Beroun, T 756. Copy at BmJA, B 2365.
[49] Mikota worked for HM and accompanied Janáček on his London visit.
[50] BmJA, B 646.
[51] Jan Racek and Artuš Rektorys, ed.: *Korespondence Leoše Janáčka s Maxem Brodem*. Janáčkův archiv vol. 9 (Prague: SNKLHU, 1953), no. 190.
[52] BmJA, E 385. HŽ, no 397. This sentence is omitted in IL.

from Hukvaldy on 21 June, and two days later he finally received a telegram with the longed-for news from Hudební matice: rehearsals would take place on the mornings of 24, 25 and 26 June.[53] He set off at once for Prague. Janáček was not present at the first rehearsal but told his wife, Zdenka, that he had met a conservatory student who had been there and who told Janáček that the *Military Sinfonietta* sounded magnificent.[54] This impression was confirmed by Janáček himself the next day when he attended the rehearsal, telling Zdenka, 'This is not a sinfonietta, but a *Military Symphony*! It works wonderfully and sounds splendid. Tomorrow, Saturday, I will be at the morning rehearsal. As for the performance, I would like to stay but had better not take the risk. I know that already.'[55] Fortunately, Janáček's enthusiasm overcame any qualms about his health and he stayed for the evening concert. At the final rehearsal, he jotted down a correction for one of the trombone parts in his notebook, as well as noting the importance of sticking to the *Prestissimo* tempo indication in the third movement (from Fig. 11, bar 153). Janáček thought then (and later) that it was played too slowly.[56]

Three decades later, in 1954, Talich himself recalled Janáček's visits to the rehearsals for the premiere:

> The composer attended the Philharmonic rehearsals of the new work with remarkable regularity and determination... . As a rule, he was seated in his place before the morning session even began and ... followed the progress of our work with the keenest interest and obvious pleasure. He didn't correct us – instead he gave us advice, sharpening rhythmic articulation here and there, highlighting the dramatic elements, and asking us to avoid unduly lyrical effusiveness. There was a wonderful rapport between us during those few days, devoted as they were to an artistic quest for the ideal interpretation of a score that was far from our usual repertoire at the time.
>
> Only once did Janáček lose his calm self-assurance. In order to clarify some point, he needed to consult the [only] copy of the score, and on the first page ... he found to his amazement that an unknown hand had written 'Rally Sinfonietta'. While protesting in his brusque Lašsko accent, he energetically crossed this out. 'Never "Rally Sinfonietta!" It's *Military, Military!*' This was Janáček's original title for the work, but when the composition appeared in print it had the simpler title of

---

[53] BmJA, B 641.
[54] BmJA, A 3715. TCV, no. 552.
[55] BmJA, A 5016. TCV, no. 553.
[56] BmJA, Z 62, p. 89. He noted a similar issue in Klemperer's Berlin performance on 29 September 1927, discussed in Chapter 2.

Sinfonietta. Why, I wonder? The greater detail of the original title told us something that was historically significant.[57]

Although Talich was remembering these rehearsals almost thirty years after they had taken place, his observations remain very valuable. In later years, Talich interfered extensively with Janáček's orchestration (particularly of his operas), but during the composer's lifetime he largely resisted the temptation to do so. As can be seen from the Sedláček score and parts, Talich made a few small modifications during rehearsals, but these were intended to reinforce important thematic lines and were presumably done with the composer's approval. Talich also ignored Janáček's revision in the second movement (made in May 1926), when Janáček had added the fanfare trumpets, probably because that change was only made after the parts had been copied. He was no doubt relieved to adopt the composer's suggestion that the viola d'amore in the third movement should be replaced by the orchestral violas. The conductor did make one important change at the end of the work, reinforcing the last seven bars with horns, orchestral trumpets and timpani. Janáček did not originally intend the *Sinfonietta* to finish in quite such a flamboyant way, imagining something more restrained after the triumphant climax at the end of the fanfares. However, Janáček readily agreed to Talich's suggestions here and included these changes in the printed edition. The composer's wish that the fanfares should have the brighter timbre of military instruments was granted at the premiere, when it was played by '14 military trumpeters'[58] – though Max Brod mentioned eighteen players, so perhaps there was some doubling.[59] No specific military band is mentioned on the programme, but it is likely that players were selected from the military bands provided by the Ministry of Defence to play at the Sokol Rally.

According to Janáček's notebook, Max Brod and the conductors František Stupka and Břetislav Bakala were also present at the dress rehearsal – and the composer added a touching note that 'the orchestra applauded'. Janáček was evidently delighted with the performance, no doubt glad to have reversed his original plan to leave for home straight after the final rehearsal. This premiere is discussed in Chapter 2, including significant reviews of it.

---

[57] Jaroslav Šeda: *Leoš Janáček* (Prague: SHV, 1961), pp. 379–80, quoting from Talich's speech 'Leoš Janáček a Praha', given at the Prague National Theatre on 18 June 1954.

[58] Jaroslav Vogel ['J. V.']: 'Hudba. Z pražské koncertní síně. Janáčkova "Vojenská symfonieta"', *Československá Republika*, vol. 3, no. 177, 29 June 1926, p. 7.

[59] Max Brod ['M. B.']: 'Janáček-Uraufführung'. *Prager Tagblatt*, vol. 51, no. 152, 27 June 1926, p. 9.

Perhaps the spirit of the *Sinfonietta* is best encapsulated by the speech that Janáček gave at the Czechoslovak Club in London just after he had completed the work:

> I come with the youthful spirit of our republic, and with youthful music, I am not someone who likes to look back, but instead I prefer to look forward. I know that we must grow and I don't see that growth emerging from remembering the years of suffering and oppression. Let's get rid of that! Let's not think about times long gone – and let's realise that we must look to the future! We are a nation that has to mean something in the world! We are the heart of Europe! And that heart must be heard beating throughout Europe![60]

The 'Brno inspiration'

At the dress rehearsal before the premiere, Janáček shared with Max Brod the outline of a non-musical programme for the *Sinfonietta*, providing titles for the individual movements which Brod published in his review of the premiere (see Chapter 2). The composer jotted down these movement titles for himself on the back of the printed programme (plate 12b).

Military Sinfonietta
1. Fanfares
2. The Castle
3. The Queen's Monastery
4. The Street
5. The Town Hall[61]

Janáček certainly remembered this note when he later wrote the feuilleton 'My Town', first published in German by the *Prager Presse* (4 December 1927), then in Czech by *Lidové noviny* (24 December 1927):

> One day I saw the city transformed, as if by a miracle. My aversion to the gloomy Town Hall vanished, and my hatred of the hill [of the Špilberk Castle] in whose dungeons so much misery had been suffered disappeared, as did my aversion to the street and its teeming crowds.
>
> On that day, the lights of freedom burned brightly above the town: it was the rebirth of 28 October 1918!

---

[60] Jan Mikota: 'Leoš Janáček v Anglii'. *Listy hudební matice*, vol. 5, nos. 7–8 (25 May 1926), p. 260.
[61] BmJA, D 165 LJ.

> I was part of it. I belonged to it.
>
> The blaze of victorious trumpets, the solemn silence hovering over the lane to the Queen's Monastery, night shadows and the gentle breeze blowing from the green hill.
>
> It was a vision of the greatness of our city – and it was from understanding this that my *Sinfonietta* was born – from my city of Brno![62]

It's possible that there was a further Brno inspiration related to the events of October and November 1918 – and one tied specifically to the Town Hall. On 7 November 1918, the front page of *Lidové noviny* reported on events that had taken place the previous day. Under the headline 'České Brno', the article – by the paper's editor in chief, Arnošt Heinrich – described the handover of power to Brno's first Czech mayor of 6 November and began with a description of the celebrations:

> Yesterday at noon, a red-and-white banner flew from the tower of Brno's Town Hall, and the fanfares from *Libuše* rang out to the four corners of the world. Crowds thronged in front of the Town Hall. At times they sang national songs, but at others a strange and indescribable silence fell. The great enemy – the hated oppression of centuries – was falling into ruins. But among the Czechs present there was no anger or any trace of vengeful retribution. There was an almost religious mood in the crowd, marking a victory for justice, and gratitude to the people who had overcome the oppressors.[63]

Aside from the pivotal importance of this moment in terms of the city's longed-for freedom from Habsburg rule, Heinrich's mention of the fanfares from Smetana's *Libuše* being played from the Town Hall tower is something that would surely have lodged in Janáček's memory. He was in Brno at the time – and if he didn't witness the celebrations in person, he would certainly have read about them in the next day's newspaper.

Janáček was essentially a dramatist, so it is not surprising that many of his compositions have extra-musical connotations. However, the *Sinfonietta* is an unusual case. It can, at first glance, be regarded as absolute music, but behind that, it has a programmatic narrative deeply rooted in Janáček's hometown. Regardless of whether the links to specific Brno

---

[62] Leoš Janáček 'Meine Stadt', *Prager Presse*, 4 December 1927; 'Moje město', *Lidové noviny*, vol. 35, no. 648, 24 December 1927, p. 5. In April 1928, the German version of this article was reprinted in an anthology of articles from the *Prager Presse* issued as *Brünn: die Hauptstadt von Mähren* (Prague: Orbis, 1928), pp. 43–6.

[63] Arnošt Heinrich: 'Česká Brno', *Lidové noviny* vol. 26, no. 306, 7 November 1918, p. 1.

locations occurred to Janáček earlier in the composition process or only when he heard the *Sinfonietta* in rehearsal with the Czech Philharmonic, the character of the individual movements corresponds well to their programmatic designations. However, after the appearance of Brod's review, the composer's brief note jotted down on the programme and his more fully developed account in 'My Town', the idea of the *Sinfonietta*'s non-musical content was a subject to which Janáček never returned – and there is no mention of it in any early editions of the score.

The last day of the Sokol Rally: Fanfares from the Týn tower

The Sokol Rally had opened with the gala concert including the premiere of the *Sinfonietta* and it continued successfully towards its climactic final days. On 4 July 1926, a partial facsimile of the fanfares was published in *Lidové noviny* under the title 'Leoš Janáček's Rally Fanfares', fulfilling the newspaper's original request for a celebratory contribution.[64] The last day of the rally was on Tuesday, 6 July. On the Sokol's behalf, Antonín Krejčí had invited Janáček to the closing event,[65] but he did not attend. Contemporary photographs demonstrate that this was a grand occasion, culminating in a 'Procession of guests and Sokol members through Prague', which started on Sokolská Street, continued through Wenceslas Square, Národní Street and the Masaryk Embankment, and ended in the Old Town Square, where it was greeted by President Masaryk in front of the Old Town Hall and the grandstand (plate 13). It was here that the opening Fanfares from the *Military Sinfonietta* were played from the gallery of the Týn Church tower as the immense procession entered the square. A detailed report in *Lidové noviny* described the scene:

> Shortly before half past nine, a platoon of mounted police set off from Mikulášska and the procession reached the square. At that moment, fires were lit at the sides of the Hus monument, the lights dotted around the Town Hall were illuminated, and the President of the Republic appeared on the Town Hall balcony, accompanied by members of his family, the Romanian Prince Nikolai, government officials headed by the Prime Minister, representatives of the National Assembly, Chancellor Dr Šámal, etc. Festive fanfares sounded from the gallery in the tower of the Týn Church, and the crowds gave a jubilant welcome to

---

[64] 'Sletové fanfáry Leoše Janáčka', *Lidové noviny* vol. 34, no. 335, 4 July 1926, pp. 5–6. A complete facsimile was published by SHV in 1963.
[65] Letter from Krejčí, 1 July 1926, BmJA, D 760.

the president. The Sokol band stopped in front of the grandstand and the great procession continued on its way.[66]

About two hours later, after speeches and a memorial tribute to Jan Hus, the music from the Týn Tower sounded again:

> The Sokols faced the monument, the guests in the grandstand stood up, and from the tower gallery of the Týn Church, the military band played 'Kdož jsú boží bojovníci' [Ye who are God's warriors].[67]

That Janáček's Fanfares were played during these celebrations is confirmed by a request made to the Prague city council by the Sokol organisers for use of the Týn Tower to accommodate twenty musicians 'to play "Ye who are God's warriors" and "Fanfares by Dr L. Janáček, dedicated to the VIII. Rally."'[68] (Incidentally, in the same letter, the Sokol also undertook to 'prohibit the musicians from smoking in the areas where they will be seated'.) It is likely that the Fanfares were performed by the same military musicians who had performed them at the premiere.

There was little reaction to this unusual outdoor performance. Janáček was no longer in Prague as he had gone to the spa at Luhačovice to regain his strength and to compose the *Glagolitic Mass* in peace and quiet. The only testimony came from the composer's niece, Věra Janáčková, who reported on the events a little differently from the newspaper account: 'I heard that it was a great occasion, including your fanfares which were very effective played from the Týn Tower, after the Sokol procession. Unfortunately, I did not hear them: I had a very nice seat reserved on the stage by the Town Hall, but I was tired from a lot of rushing around with my mother and the very trying conditions during the rally. So I fell asleep, and at 9:30 it was too late to get to the Old Town Square.'[69] Věra wrote that the Fanfares were heard after the procession, but since she admitted that she couldn't get there in time to hear them, her report is all at secondhand. Her letter does, however, confirm that the performance from the Týn Tower took place in spite of the cumbersome logistics of getting nine trumpets, two bass trumpets, two tubas, several timpani and a conductor to the top of the Týn Tower.[70]

[66] J. V.: 'Pochod padesáti tisíc', *Lidové noviny*, vol. 34, no. 337, 7 July 1926, p. 4.
[67] Ibid., p. 5. A report of festive fanfares playing from the Týn tower also appeared in *Sletový zpravodaj*, no. 10 (7 July 1926), a supplement to the daily *Národní osvobození*.
[68] Czech National Archives, Prague, Czechoslovak Sokol organisation, no. 1062, file no. 798.
[69] Letter from Věra Janáčková to Janáček, 16 July 1926, BmJA, A 3619.
[70] Given that the bass trumpets double the timpani part throughout, it is possible that the Fanfares were performed without timpani on this occasion.

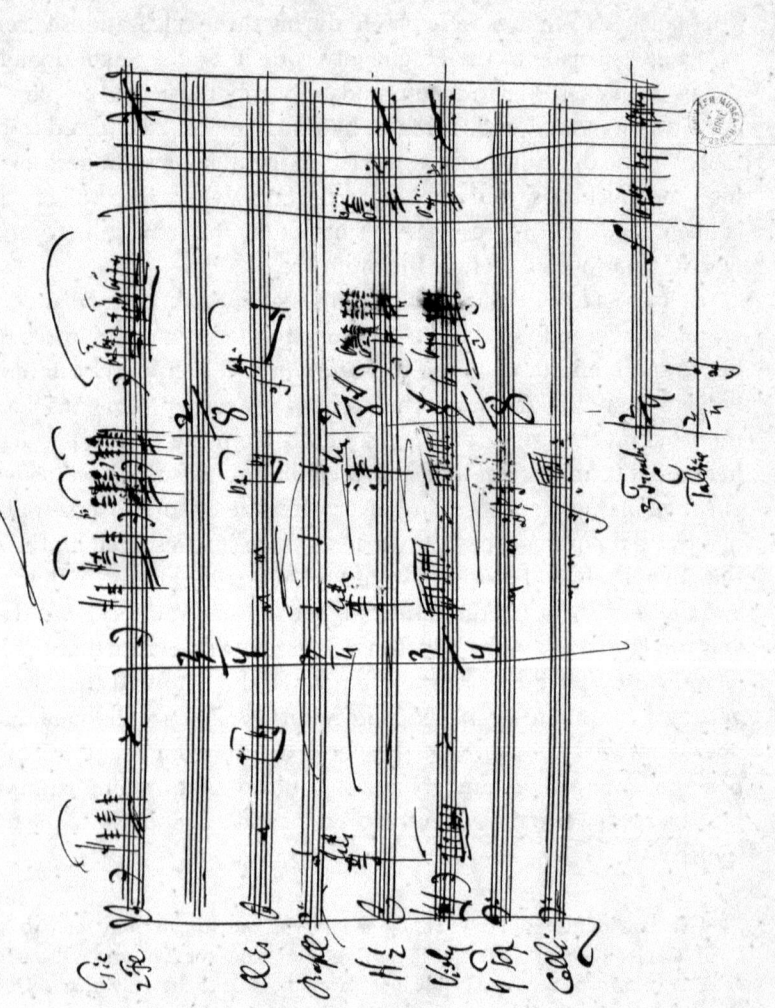

Plate 4. Janáček's autograph manuscript of the *Sinfonietta*, fifth movement, bars 149–56, with the cymbal clash ('Taliře', on the bottom stave) in bar 151, one bar before the entry of the fanfare trumpets (Janáček Archive, Brno, A 7444).

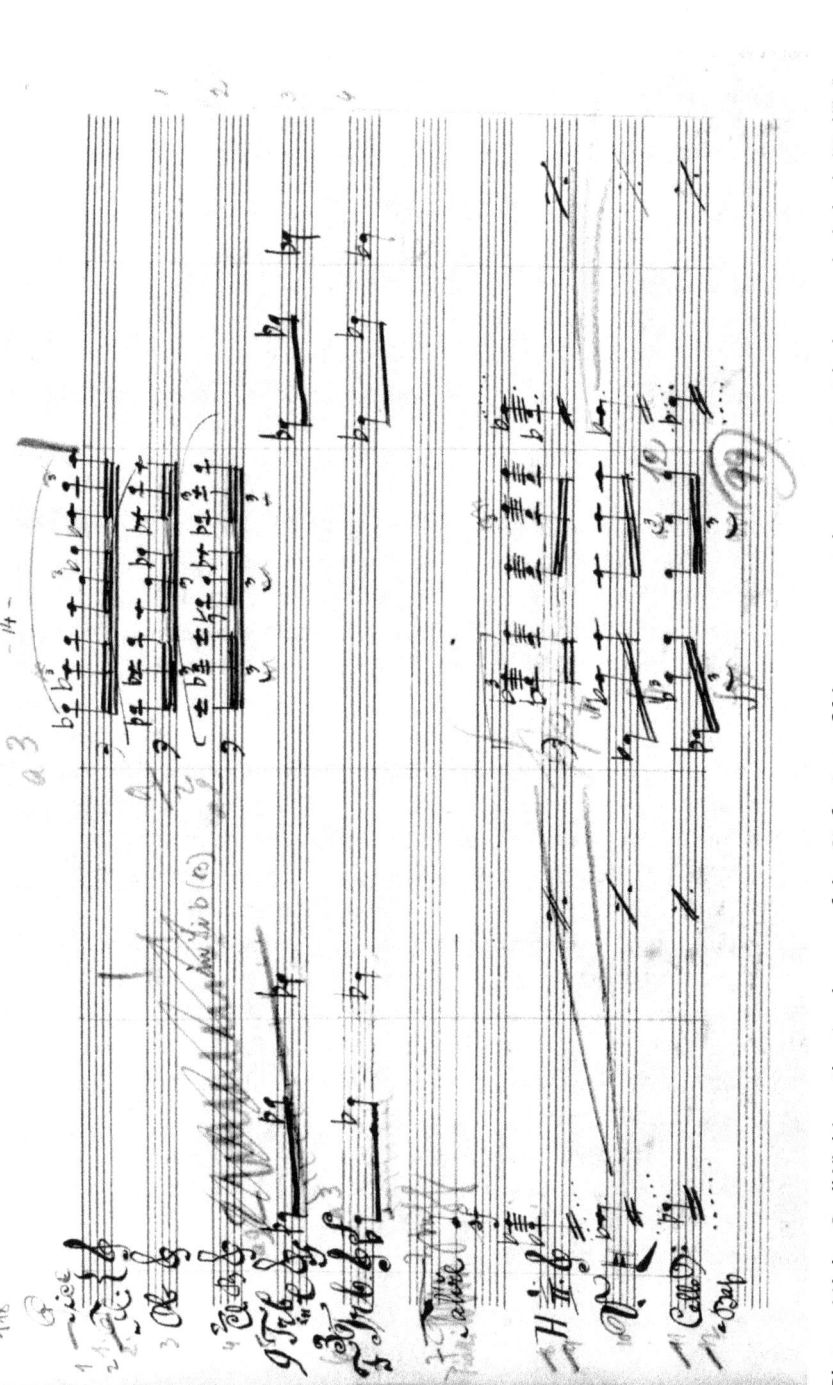

Plate 5. Václav Sedláček's authorised copy of the *Sinfonietta*, fifth movement, bars 152–6, with the cymbal clash ('Talíře') in bar 152, at the same time as the entry of the fanfare trumpets (Austrian National Library, L1. UE. 777 GFOL)

Publishing problems

At least two publishers were keen to publish Janáček's newest composition, and protracted negotiations followed between Universal Edition (UE) in Vienna and Hudební matice in Prague about publication of the score and representation of the work (worldwide and in Czech markets). This situation had arisen two years earlier when similar discussions had taken place in 1924 about *The Cunning Little Vixen*. On that occasion, with a major musical-dramatic work, the Viennese firm (with its international reputation as a publisher of new operas) won over its Prague rival. But in general, Hudební matice had been Janáček's publisher of choice for his non-operatic music including many piano, chamber and choral works, *Taras Bulba* (which UE had rejected on account of its overtly Russian subject matter) and the *Lachian Dances*. But matters were much less straightforward when it came to the *Sinfonietta*.

When Janáček left for London at the end of April 1926, *Lidové noviny* published a report about the composer's new work by Boleslav Vomáčka, who also wrote for the journal *Listy hudební matice*; and Janáček was accompanied on his London trip by Jan Mikota who worked with his brother Václav Mikota (1896–1982) at Hudební matice. In other words, the Prague firm knew all about the *Sinfonietta*, mostly from Janáček himself. Based on an informal undertaking Janáček had given two years earlier that his non-operatic works would be published by Hudební matice, the firm no doubt assumed that it could count on publishing the *Sinfonietta*, but this was not the case. In later negotiations (after the *Sinfonietta* had been taken on by UE), Janáček reassured Hudební matice that it would be able to publish a pocket score of the work in collaboration with UE.

On 3 June 1926, the composer informed UE about the upcoming premiere of the *Sinfonietta*, wondering whether they would publish it. He also expressed doubts about Hudební matice's ability to find the finances needed to issue a pocket score independently of UE.[71] The next day, Emil Hertzka, director of UE, wrote to Janáček expressing interest in the new work, noting that he was prepared to consider cooperation with Hudební matice; however, he wanted time to study the score before coming to a final decision.[72] Although Janáček promised to send the score to Hertzka immediately,[73] he did so only after the Prague premiere (Talich needed the only copy as his conductor's score). Meanwhile, Hudební matice had

---

[71] WBR, 329. Copy in BmJA, B 2047. LJUE, no. 253.
[72] Hertzka to Janáček, 4 July 1926, BmJA, D 1073.
[73] WBR, 329. Copy in BmJA, B 2029. LJUE, no. 254.

invited another Viennese publisher, Wiener Philharmonischer Verlag,[74] to cooperate in publishing a pocket score, an approach which caused some consternation given Janáček's existing relationship with UE.[75] At the same time, Janáček hoped that he might persuade UE to come to an agreement with Hudební matice.[76] He sent the score of the *Military Sinfonietta* to UE on 3 July, reporting on the successful premiere and mentioning the interest of Wiener Philharmonischer Verlag.[77] Hertzka at UE proposed a similar arrangement with Hudební matice to that for *The Cunning Little Vixen* – namely, to offer them rights to the *Sinfonietta* in Czechoslovakia. In a letter of 11 July, Hudební matice countered with a very different proposal, informing UE that Janáček had entrusted Hudební matice with the rights to the new work and that it was therefore negotiating from a position of strength. It asked that UE should contribute financially to publication of the full score, pocket score, orchestral parts and a piano arrangement; and it suggested that it would offer UE distribution in Austria and Germany, while Hudební matice would distribute the work in Czechoslovakia; worldwide distribution would be shared between both companies. The same arrangement was suggested for hire fees: in Czechoslovakia it would be the responsibility of Hudební matice, in Austria and Germany of UE, and in other countries revenue from them would be shared equally. When Hudební matice sent a copy of this letter to Janáček on 11 July, the composer was furious:

> Why are you still claiming that 'I gave you the publication rights for the *Sinfonietta*?' All I ever suggested was that you might publish it jointly with Universal Edition.
>
> I am sure that Universal Edition will reject such an improper proposal. You, Mr Mikota, told me in front of Dr Löwenbach[78] that Hudební

---

[74] Wiener Philharmonischer Verlag was founded in April 1923 by Alfred Kalmus, who established the company after fourteen years at UE. From the start there was a close relationship between the two firms, though at the time of these negotiations, Wiener Philharmonischer Verlag was an independent company in which UE were shareholders. Best known for its series of Philharmonia pocket scores, the firm was bought by UE in 1927, after which Philharmonia became an imprint of UE. The close interrelationship between the two firms explains the simultaneous appearance of two different first editions of the pocket score, one from UE and the other from Wiener Philharmonischer Verlag, in January 1927 (see the Supplement to Chapter 1 for further details).

[75] Wiener Philharmonischer Verlag to Janáček, 16 June 1926. BmJA, D 1076.

[76] Janáček to UE, 20 June 1926. WBR, 329. Copy in BmJA, B 2031. LJUE, no. 267.

[77] WBR, 329. Copy in BmJA, A 5998. LJUE, no. 258.

[78] Jan Löwenbach (1880–1972) was a lawyer specialising in copyright and a friend of Janáček.

matice would have distribution of the work in the Czech Republic and Universal Edition the rest of the world. Why was this not clear? Universal Edition also suggested this to you in the letter which I sent you, and which needs to be returned to me.

And now we have all this messing about! It doesn't help us reach any useful conclusion. You need to settle the matter with Universal Edition of jointly publishing the pocket score of the *Sinfonietta* and do nothing else.

And do this as soon as possible, otherwise I will simply give the whole work, unconditionally, to Universal Edition.

And I must repeat that you, i.e. Hudební matice, have no 'publishing rights' to the *Sinfonietta* from me![79]

The same day, Janáček reiterated to Hertzka at UE that he had not entrusted any rights to Hudební matice.[80] Having looked at the score (and read Brod's review, an abridged version of which appeared in UE's house journal *Musikblätter des Anbruch*), Hertzka was enthusiastic about the new work. He would prefer UE to be the sole publisher but was willing to come to an agreement with Hudební matice if Janáček had an obligation to them. However, Hertzka and the composer both understood the need to act quickly: conductors were already expressing an interest in performing the work[81] including Otto Klemperer (1885–1973)[82] and Fritz Zweig (1893–1984).[83] After Janáček's strongly worded letter to Hudební matice, Václav Mikota and Jan Löwenbach went to the Donaueschingen Festival where they met representatives from UE and Wiener Philharmonischer Verlag. Janáček was initially unaware of this meeting and suspected Hudební matice of drawing out the negotiations for no good reason. He was starting to lose patience, deciding that he would cede all the rights to UE. On 31 July, he fired off another tetchy letter to Hudební matice:

> The negotiations about the *Military Sinfonietta* have been dragging on for a whole month!
>
> It could have been printed by now.
>
> Today I received a letter from Universal Edition which said:

---

[79] Copies of letter from HM to UE (11 July 1926), and Janáček to HM (21 July 1926) in BmJA, D 1130.
[80] Janáček to Hertzka, 11 July 1926, BmJA, B 2032.
[81] Hertzka to Janáček, 14 July 1926, BmJA, D 1078.
[82] Telegram from Klemperer to Janáček, 12 July 1926, BmJA, B 923.
[83] Zweig to Janáček, 10 September 1926, BmJA, A 3597.

1. That they are happy with my proposal for a joint publication of the score of my *Military Sinfonietta*.

2. That the proposal by Hudební matice is unclear.

3. That they want to conclude a contract quickly – satisfactory to all parties – which Hudební matice can sign on the following basis:

a) It will give the publishing rights to Universal Edition (because it is absurd to share such rights).

b) All editions of the *Military Sinfonietta* will be produced at Universal Edition's expense.

c) Hudební matice will have exclusive rights in the Czech Republic on condition that it will make reasonable profits from sales.

d) The title page will state that Hudební matice has exclusive rights to sales in the Czechoslovak Republic.

e) Hudební matice will receive a commission from the hire fees of orchestral parts sent out within the Czechoslovak Republic. You will note that this is an extraordinary gift to Hudební matice, as it will incur no expenses.

That way, my work will find its way quickly into the world, which is what is needed for a composition like this.

I ask you to accept these conditions immediately – or reject them immediately.[84]

Two days later, UE sent the same conditions to Hudební matice, which now said it was ready to come to an agreement.[85]

On 14 August, Janáček sent the signed contract from Luhačovice to UE in Vienna (plate 7). It stipulated that he would receive a 15% royalty on sales of scores and on hire fees for performance material, once an agreement was concluded with Hudební matice for the Czech rights.[86] The Prague firm was no longer minded to argue over details: after Hertza sent the draft agreement to them, Václav Mikota wrote to Janáček on 21 August 1926:

> I would like to inform you, dear master, that a letter arrived yesterday from Director Hertzka at UE in which he informed us of the conditions for the exclusive representation of the *Sinfonietta*. I have to

---

[84] Janáček to HM, 31 July 1926, JA BmJA, D 1643.
[85] Letter from HM to Janáček, 2 August 1926, BmJA, D 738.
[86] WBR, 329. Copy in BmJA, B 2035. LJUE, no. 265. The official copy of the contract for the *Sinfonietta* is in the Leoš Janáček Foundation, Brno, no call no.

Plate 6. Janáček with Jan Mikota outside the Prague offices of Hudební matice Umělecké besedy in 1926 (Janáček Archive, Brno).

KOPIE.

Abtretung des Urheberrechtes

Hiedurch übertrage ich zugleich für meine Erben und Rechtsnachfolger der Firma:

Universal-Edition A. G., Leipzig – Wien
und deren Rechtsnachfolgern

das unbeschränkte und übertragbare Urheberrecht einschließlich des Aufführungsrechtes und des Rechtes zur Wiedergabe durch mechanisch-musikalische Musikwerke an meinem Werke:

"Militärsymphonietta"

von Leoš Janacek

mit der Befugnis der ausschließlichen Vervielfältigung und gewerbsmäßigen Verbreitung jeder Art für alle Zeiten, für alle Auflagen und für alle Länder, gleichviel, ob mit denselben literarische Verträge bestehen oder nicht, kurz, mit allen Rechten, die das Gesetz dem Urheber eines solchen Werkes einräumt oder vorbehält, auch in Zukunft einräumen oder vorbehalten wird, insbesondere auch mit allen bestehenden oder künftigen Rechten bez. der Benutzung auf mechanischen Musikinstrumenten oder ähnlichen Vorrichtungen und z~~~~~~~~~~~~~~~~~~~~~~~~~~~~~~.

Ich erkläre, daß ich in dem angegebenen Umfange allein über das Urheberrecht an dem Werke zu verfügen berechtigt bin und daß ich jenes weder ganz noch teilweise anderweitig übertragen habe. Die Universal-Edition A. G. ist allein berechtigt, an dem Werke sowohl wie an dem Titel sachgemäße Zusätze, Kürzungen und Änderungen vorzunehmen oder vornehmen zu lassen sowie die üblichen Bearbeitungen, Auszüge und Einrichtungen für einzelne oder mehrere Instrumente oder Stimmen mit vorhe-~~~~~~~~~~~~~~~~~~~~~~~Übersetzungen in andere Sprachen und Übertragungen nehmigung ~~~~~~~~~~~~~~~~herauszugeben. Ich überlasse ihr die Bestimmung über den Zeit- des Autors punkt der Herausgabe, die Festsetzung und spätere Veränderung des Verkaufspreises und verzichte auf das Recht, Melodien erkennbar dem Werke zu entnehmen und einer neuen Arbeit zugrunde zu legen.

Wird die Schutzfrist des Urheberrechtes gesetzlich verlängert, oder wird der Schutz auf neue Formen der Benützung des Werkes ausgedehnt, so bleibt dieser Vertrag für die Dauer der Verlängerung und für die Erweiterung des Schutzes in Kraft.

Die Niederschrift des Werkes verbleibt im Besitze der Verlagshandlung als deren Eigentum.
Für die Abtretung meines Urheberrechtes erhalte ich: ~~~~~~~~~~~~~~~~~~~~~~~~~~~~~~
~~für die erste Auflage von~~ ~~~~~~~~~~Exemplaren ein festes Honorar, zahlbar bei Unter-~~
~~schrift~~ ~~nach Verkauf über den ich separate Empfangsbestätigung ansiele.~~
b) eine Tantième in der Höhe von 15% des österreichischen Ladenpreises — ~~xxx~~
~~Bruttoprinzbrnx~~ — eines jeden verkauften und bezahlten Exemplares in halbjährlicher Abrechnung. Falls die Halbjahresabrechnung einen geringeren Betrag ergibt als ~~~~~~~~~~~~, wird dieselbe auf neue Rechnung vorgetragen.
~~~~~~

Erfüllungsort für beide Teile ist Wien.

1%
Tow~~~~ aus den Einnahmen für verliehenes oder verkauftes Orchester-
material.

Wien, am 4. August 1926
Dr.ph.Leos Janacek m.p.
Luhacovice,14/VIII.1926.

Diese Abmachung tritt in Kraft,sobald die
Universal-Edition mit der Hudebni Matice
über den Alleinvertrieb für die Cechoslov.
republik eine Abmachung getroffen haben wird.

Plate 7. Janáček's contract with Universal Edition for the *Militärsymphonietta*, dated by him on 14 August 1926 (Leoš Janáček Foundation, Brno).

submit this to our committee, but I can already say that the conditions are completely acceptable and that the whole letter was written in a very friendly tone, assuring us that UE values its association with H[udební] m[atice]. That will surely form the basis for closer cooperation between the two companies, particularly in the joint promotion of your works.[87]

Incredibly, there was still more delay because Hudební matice's committee was unable to give prompt consideration to the matter. On 11 September, Janáček had to nag them once again, demanding a quick response:

> I have just received a letter from Universal Edition in which they inform me that they have still not, to date, had a decision from you. That date is 11 September 1926! This is no way to run business affairs and Hudební matice should be ashamed of itself. If you do not conclude negotiations for the *Sinfonietta* within a week, I will delete the agreement [i.e. for Hudební matice to have the Czech rights] in the contract with Universal Edition.[88]

Finally, this ultimatum had the desired effect and an agreement was concluded between Vienna and Prague in mid-September.[89]

Preparing to print the *Sinfonietta*

UE had been in possession of Sedláček's copied score since early July, but it also needed the copied orchestral parts. Janáček asked Hudební matice to arrange this, and they duly collected the parts from the Czech Philharmonic and sent them to Vienna.[90] Before starting production, UE needed to compare the parts with the score – and since some of the composer's changes had been made after the parts were copied, revisions needed to be added to them.[91] As discussed above, UE also needed to finalise the agreement with Hudební matice before engraving the work.[92] As a result, it was only in late September and early October that UE began to prepare the score, asking Janáček to clarify any doubtful points.[93] Although the com-

---

[87] BmJA, D 737.
[88] Museum of Czech Literature, Prague, G 4889. Copy in BmJA, D 1645.
[89] HM to Janáček, 14 September 1926, BmJA, D 754.
[90] HM to Janáček, 21 August 1926, BmJA, D 737.
[91] Janáček to UE, c. 21 August 1926. WBR, 329. Copy in BmJA, A 6005. LJUE, no. 266.
[92] UE to Janáček, 9 September 1926, BmJA, D 1030.
[93] UE to Janáček, 29 September and 2 October 1926, BmJA, A 4255 and A 4254.

poser was busy finishing the *Glagolitic Mass*, he returned the proofs of the *Sinfonietta* promptly.[94] There was a pressing need to prepare the orchestral parts as soon as possible, as the Czech Philharmonic, conducted by František Stupka, intended to perform the work in Prague on 5 December 1926 and needed the material no later than 15 November.[95] In addition, delivery of the orchestral material for the performance on 9 December in Wiesbaden under Otto Klemperer was another matter of urgency. Given this time pressure, UE urged Janáček to send any corrections by 9 November 1926 so that all the changes could be included in the material before these projected performances.[96]

The dedication

A further delay was caused by Janáček's wish to dedicate the work to four members of the London committee who had arranged his visit and looked after him during his stay. Hertzka took the view that a dedication to four individuals was impractical and instead suggested dedicating it to the committee as a whole and that the composer should seek advice about the form of words from Jan Mikota.[97] But in order not to delay publication any longer, Janáček quickly made up his mind to dedicate the piece to Rosa Newmarch, his most devoted English advocate, who had led the committee.[98] All the early editions have the same dedication: 'Věnováno paní R. Newmarchové' (Dedicated to Mrs Rosa Newmarch).

There's no ambiguity here, but even so, it has often been suggested, erroneously, that the *Sinfonietta* was dedicated to the Czechoslovak armed forces. Jaroslav Vogel, usually the most reliable of biographers (and someone who had known the work since its first performance), made this claim, presumably extrapolating a dedication from the work's original title of *Military Sinfonietta*[99] (or perhaps conflating it with Janáček's dedication of *Taras Bulba* 'To our troops' in a 1923 article).

Janáček's letter to the Sokol on 13 May 1926 (quoted above) added a quite different layer of confusion: in it he told the organisers of the rally about his '*Military Sinfonietta*, which I wanted to dedicate to the Sokol membership

---

[94] Janáček to UE, 15 October 1926. WBR, 329. Copy in BmJA, A 6007. LJUE, no. 270.
[95] HM to Janáček, BmJA, A 3600.
[96] BmJA, D 1025.
[97] UE to Janáček, 23 November 1926, BmJA, D 1022.
[98] Janáček to UE, 23 November 1926. WBR, 329. Copy in BmJA, B 2048. LJUE, no. 281.
[99] Vogel 1981, p. 322.

for the Eighth Rally,[100] but this suggestion was never mentioned again – and Rosa Newmarch remains the sole dedicatee of the *Sinfonietta*.

Publication of the score

Despite UE's efforts to prepare material in time for Stupka's Czech Philharmonic concert on 5 December, the *Sinfonietta* had to be replaced on that occasion by *Taras Bulba*,[101] but provisional material did reach Wiesbaden in time for Klemperer's performance on 9 December (see Chapter 2). Printing of the pocket score was ordered on 15 December 1926, and copies were available in January 1927 in a joint enterprise by UE and Wiener Philharmonischer Verlag (see Supplement to Chapter 1), with Hudební matice listed as the representative for the Czechoslovak Republic.[102] The initial print run totalled 600 copies (200 of the UE issue, 400 of the Wiener Philharmonischer Verlag issue),[103] and orchestral parts were printed at the same time. Printing of the full score was slightly delayed by corrections to the title page,[104] but it was ordered on 4 January 1927 and published on 28 January in an edition of 100 copies.[105]

Janáček received a copy from Vienna the next day and wrote at once to Hertzka at UE with instructions about others who should be sent copies as soon as possible: 'I have received the score of the *Sinfonietta*. But only one complimentary copy? Mrs R[osa] Newmarch must be sent a copy; F[rantišek] Neumann, who prepares my premieres here, has also asked me for a copy. He wants to perform the *Sinfonietta* here.'[106] Presumably, UE acted on these instructions.

On this full score, UE is given as the sole publisher (with no mention of Wiener Philharmonischer Verlag), but the title page does mention representation for the work in the Czechoslovak Republic by Hudební

---

[100] Czech National Archives, Prague, Czechoslovak Sokol organisation, no. 1062, file no. 786.
[101] Jan Mikota to Janáček, 11 December 1926, BmJA, B 908.
[102] UE to Janáček, 21 January1927, BmJA, D 1102.
[103] Information from UE print book, entry for U.E. 8680, 'Janáček: Sinfonietta, 16⁰ Partit[ur]'. Another 400 copies of the Wiener Philharmonischer Verlag edition were printed in September 1928.
[104] UE to Janáček, 25 February 1927, BmJA, A 4307.
[105] Information from UE print book, entry for U.E. 8679, 'Janáček: Sinfonietta, Partitur'. See also Nigel Simeone: *The First Editions of Leoš Janáček* (Tutzing: Hans Schneider, 1991), p. 179.
[106] Janáček to UE, 29 January 1927, BmJA, B 2054.

matice.[107] It also lists Dr P. A. Pisk as the editor of the 'Konzert-Revision', presumably because he saw the score through the press. All three published scores give the title as *Sinfonietta* instead of Janáček's original title, *Symfonietta vojenská* (*Military Sinfonietta*). It is uncertain when this change was made or by whom. The UE house editor corrected 'Symfonietta' to 'Sinfonietta' on Sedlaček's copy, which was used as the printer's model, but the same editor left 'vojenská' unchanged and untranslated. The contract with UE had called the work *Militärsymphonietta*, but Janáček himself used the shortened form of 'Symfonietta' in his correspondence with UE from August 1926 onwards. Even so, it's unclear exactly when the title was simplified to its more neutral form, when it was adopted as the official title, and whether the change was Janáček's idea or had been made by UE (which had the right to alter the title according to its contract). It is probable that the idea of removing 'Military' came from UE, and it may have occurred at the proofreading stage. From an Austrian perspective, the removal of military connotations was understandable: the wounds from its defeat in the Great War had still not fully healed.

UE's attempts to persuade Janáček to make a version that would not require the participation of a military band were perhaps motivated by similar considerations, though this could equally have been a purely commercial and pragmatic decision: In terms of promoting the work to an international market, *Sinfonietta* was a simpler (and potentially less contentious) title, while the additional demands of the *banda* could be seen as a potentially expensive disincentive to performing organisations.

UE certainly had a success on their hands with the *Sinfonietta*, and Janáček benefitted financially. Over a two-year period – between August 1926 (when the contract was signed) and Janáček's death in August 1928 – UE paid him royalties of 2,878 CZK from hire fees and sales of the score. While his earnings from operas were much higher, this was still a substantial sum (for context, a loaf of bread cost 3.40 CZK at the time, a kilo of butter 25 CZK and a good men's suit 650 CZK). In addition, there were royalties collected on Janáček's behalf by the Czech copyright protection agency (Ochranný svaz autorský), which cooperated with similar organisations in other countries to collect foreign performing rights. It should also be noted that Janáček's royalties from sales and performances in Czechoslovakia were sent through UE, which explains why no payments for the *Sinfonietta* are to be found in Hudební matice's accounts.

---

[107] UE to Janáček, 28 January 1927, BmJA, A 4312.

Without a military band?

As early as February 1927, UE encouraged Janáček to adapt the score for performance without the thirteen extra brass players of the *banda*, arguing that only a few German orchestras could afford to assemble such a large ensemble.[108] Janáček suggested that it would be possible to perform the work with one tenor tuba and one bass trumpet, that the fourth flute part could be assigned to the other flutes, and that the third clarinet could be put in the bass clarinet part. However, these minor adjustments were hardly what UE had in mind. For the fanfares, Janáček recommended inviting military bands, which could be found in every large Czech city.[109] UE persisted, explaining that there had been very few military bands in Germany since the Great War, and those that remained were sometimes of a low standard. Furthermore, professional orchestras were often unwilling to cooperate with military musicians, making it difficult for a military band to play in a symphony concert. UE asked Janáček either to write an adaptation for performance without the *banda* or to give his permission to have one made.[110] At first, the composer refused to do this himself and recommended that UE should find someone else.[111] However, when UE sent him the reduced version of the Fanfares in the first and fifth movements made by Erwin Stein (1885–1958),[112] Janáček responded with his own suggested changes. He did this reluctantly, noting that 'the first and fifth movements of the *Sinfonietta* really cannot be rescored; the clarity and the instrumental colours would be lost!'[113] His suggestions can be summarised as follows:

1. Instead of the first and second tenor tubas: two French horns
2. Instead of the first and second bass trumpets: one tenor trombone
3. Replace the nine trumpets with four trumpets; in places where there are more parts, replace trumpets 4, 5 and 6 with two oboes and one cor anglais

The reduced instrumentation for the Fanfares was therefore four trumpets, two oboes, one cor anglais, two French horns, one trombone, and timpani, and Janáček noted that 'the oboes and cor anglais will act like an

---

[108] UE to Janáček, 16 February 1927, BmJA, D 1098.
[109] Janáček to UE, 18 February 1927, WBR, 329. Copy in BmJA, B 2058. LJUE, no. 296.
[110] UE to Janáček, 22 February 1927, BmJA, D 1096.
[111] Janáček to UE, 25 February 1927, WBR, 329. Copy in BmJA, B 2061. LJUE, no. 300.
[112] JYL2, p. 686. See the letter from UE to Janáček, 17 March 1927 asking for comments on Stein's version, BmJA, D 1094.
[113] Janáček to UE, 22 March 1927, WBR, 329. Copy in BmJA, B 2063. LJUE, no. 303.

echo group!'[114] Based on Janáček's instructions, Stein modified his score, and on 24 August 1927, UE ordered fifty copies of a fourteen-page score ('Beilage für kl. Orch' according to the UE print book), receiving them on 3 October 1927.[115] This contained the rescored Fanfares and the conclusion of the fifth movement (from Fig. 9 to the end). It was only much later that UE integrated the 'Beilage' with the rest of the work to produce a complete score of the Stein version for hire purposes.

* * *

The *Sinfonietta* has come to be regarded as one of the most distinctive orchestral works of the interwar period, above all through its highly original fusion of symphony and suite, combined with an element of cyclic form with the Fanfares and their exact reprise with orchestral elaborations in the final movement. The Fanfares themselves – performed by military musicians accompanied by timpani which are directed to be played with wooden sticks – form an almost 'profane' or rustic counterpart to the more 'cultured' sonorities of the symphony orchestra in the rest of the work. When these two worlds come together at the end of the *Sinfonietta*, two layers of sound are combined, representing the worlds of folk music (or military brass music) and the more 'polished' artistry of the symphony orchestra simultaneously.

The instrumentation of the whole work is extraordinary. Although Janáček used the viola d'amore in three operas (*Fate, Káťa Kabanová* and *The Makropulos Affair*), his use of it as an important musical element in the third movement of the *Sinfonietta* marked its first appearance in one of his purely orchestral works.[116] In his remarks to Talich before the premiere, it seems he changed his mind about its practicality (and audibility), and in Sedláček's copy, the designation 'viola d'amore' has been deleted throughout the movement, replaced by orchestral violas. The writing for woodwind is also unusual: the bassoons played only in the second movement (and four bars in the fourth), while the extreme-high and -low registers of other instruments (such as the clarinets in the finale), and the use of striking colouristic effects (such as the rasping muted trombones in the second movement), give the whole work a distinctive sound. Its qualities seem to stem in part from Janáček's recent experience of writing for unconventional chamber ensembles in the *Concertino* and the expanded *Nursery Rhymes*. From

---

[114] Ibid.
[115] Information from UE print book.
[116] He had planned to use a viola d'amore in the *Danube* Symphony and specified it again in his incidental music for *Schluck und Jau*.

the start, the *Sinfonietta* was described by critics as a work full of optimism, determination and a kind of 'constructive enthusiasm'. In this context, it is worth noting that on 31 January 1926 – just before starting work on the *Sinfonietta* – Janáček attended a Czech Philharmonic concert, conducted by Konstantin Saradzhev, of music by modern Soviet composers.[117] That the *Sinfonietta* was intended as a celebration of Czech independence and freedom is clear from comments by Boleslav Vomáčka which could well have stemmed from conversations with the composer himself. They seem to underline that notion of 'constructive enthusiasm': 'Janáček's *Sinfonietta* is a celebration of today's free Czech man, his spiritual beauty and joy, his strength, courage and determination to fight for victory.'[118]

---

[117] The works performed were Alexander Goedicke's Symphony No. 3, the *Epitaph* by Dmitri Melkich and Lev Knipper's suite *Tales of the Plaster Buddha*, BmJA, JP 562.
[118] Boleslav Vomáčka ['B.V.']: 'O Janáčkově simfoniettě', *Lidové noviny*, vol. 34, no. 329, 1 July 1926, p. 7.

Supplement
Sources: Manuscripts and Editions

This is a summary of all the significant sources and editions of the *Sinfonietta* from Janáček's earliest sketches to complete manuscripts; copies annotated by conductors for performances during Janáček's lifetime; correspondence; and published editions from the first edition in 1927 to the most recent critical edition. It includes brief descriptions of important manuscripts, followed by descriptions (with diplomatic transcriptions of title pages) of significant editions, notably the first printings of the full and pocket scores, and the important revised printings which appeared in 1937 (full score) and 1951 (pocket score) incorporating some of Janáček's final revisions as well as those of his most trusted conductor, František Neumann (see Appendix). Interestingly, there is no mention of corrections or revisions on the editions themselves.

Later editions are described with brief comments on the sources consulted for each one. Particular attention has been paid to the edition by Barvík and Zimmermann (one of the first to examine a range of manuscript and printed sources) and the critical-practical edition by Zahrádka, which drew on all available sources.

Three versions for reduced instrumentation are described. Of these, the most interesting is the one customarily attributed to Erwin Stein. This reduction reflects Janáček's own instructions (in letters to UE) about how the work might be performed without the additional instruments of the *banda*. Even so, it should never be considered as a version fully sanctioned by Janáček: he made the suggestions under pressure from UE, and it was never his intention that the *Sinfonietta* should be played without the full complement of instruments.

Sources
The sources for Janáček's *Sinfonietta* have been preserved almost in their entirety in various institutions. Only the composer's corrected proofs, made in the autumn of 1926, have not survived.

1. Manuscripts
- The earliest source is Janáček's sketch for fanfares, reproduced in Chapter 1 (**ex. 1.1**). The composer then cut five sheets into quarters and used the blank verso pages for sketching the second and third movements. BmJA, A 7444.
- A single page sketch of the original fanfares. BmJA, A 52 723.
- Sketch for movements 2–5. BmJA, A 7444.

- Complete eighteen-page autograph of movement 1, partly published as a facsimile in *Lidové noviny* under the title 'Sletové fanfáry Leoš Janáček' (*Lidové noviny*, vol. XXXIV, no. 335 [4 July 1926]). Leoš Janáček Foundation, Brno. Ar 3-2, A-1. Complete facsimile published by Státní hudební vydavatelství, Prague, 1963. Title page: LEOŠ JANÁČEK: FANFARÝ ZE SINFONIETTY. No PN, [18]pp., unnumbered.
- Autograph score of movements 2–5 (without the first page of movement 2). BmJA, A 7444.
- Autograph of the first page of movement 2. Archives of the Academy of Sciences of the Czech Republic, Prague, call no. B 3439.
- Authorised copy made by Václav Sedláček in April and May 1926, ÖNB, call no. L1. UE. 777 GFOL. Used as the conducting score by Václav Talich for the world premiere on 26 June 1926, then as the printer's model (Stichvorlage) for the first edition. In addition to corrections by Janáček, it also includes corrections and revisions by Václav Talich.
- Manuscript orchestral parts made by Václav Sedláček, used for the world premiere on 26 June 1926, then as the printer's model for the first edition of the parts (UE, 1927). WBR, UE Janáček 007.

2. Annotated copies

- Full score (UE 1927), corrected by František Neumann (who conducted both Brno performances during Janáček's lifetime). This score served as the basis for the revised edition by UE issued in 1937. WBR, UE Janáček 004 (D). This is an important source, containing Neumann's corrections, probably sent to UE in 1928. The score contains another sheet with corrections from a later date by an unknown author.
- Full score (UE 1927), used by Otto Klemperer for the Berlin performance on 29 September 1927 (attended by Janáček). Royal Academy of Music, London, call no. Klemperer Collection: 25 JANACEK. Includes Klemperer's corrections and additions, particularly his extensive retouchings on the final page.
- Full score (UE 1927), used by Henry Wood for the British premiere on 10 February 1928. Royal Academy of Music, London, call no. Henry Wood Collection: HW JANACEK. Includes extensive performance markings by Henry Wood.
- See Appendix for detailed descriptions of the annotations in all three of these scores.

3. Correspondence

- Janáček's letters about the *Sinfonietta*, including proof corrections, before and after publication of the work:
Letter from Janáček to Václav Talich, 27 May 1926, with interpretative suggestions: Museum of the Bohemian Karst Beroun, call no. T 756. Copy at BmJA, B 2365.
Letters from Janáček to UE, 18 February 1927, 22 March 1927, 4 April 1927, 10 April 1927, including corrections. WBR, Korrespondenz Leos Janacek–UE (Archiv UE). Copies at BmJA, B 2058, B 2063, B 2064, A 6018.
Letters from Janáček to UE from 6 April 1927 and 16 April 1927 containing corrections. BmJA, D 1092, B 1128.

4. Printed editions

- First edition of the pocket score: Universal Edition and Wiener Philharmonischer Verlag, January 1927. Two different issues were published simultaneously in January 1927. Variant 1 is in UE's pale green covers with dark green lettering, within a decorative border and a large UE logo in the centre. Apart from the printing date, the back cover is blank. Variant 2 is in the Wiener Philharmonischer Verlag's 'Philharmonia' series in grey covers with black lettering. The inside and outside back covers include an advertisement for Philharmonia pocket scores. According to the UE print books, both editions were printed in December 1926, and the mark 'Weag' on the last music page indicates that the printer was Waldheim-Eberle A.G.

Variant 1:
Title page [within a double rule]: Věnováno paní R. Newmarchové / LEOŠ JANÁČEK / SINFONIETTA / für Orchester / pour Orchestre for Orchestra / pro orchestr / (1926) / PARTITUR / PARTITION SCORE / PARTITURA / Aufführungsrecht vorbehalten. Droits d'exécution réservés. / UNIVERSAL-EDITION A.G. / Wien [rule] New York / Pro Republiku Československou Hudební Matice, Praha / Copyright 1927 by Universal Edition / Printed in Austria. PN U.E. 8680, W. Ph. V. 224, 115 pp. Printer's date on back cover: XII.1926. 200 copies printed (information from UE print book). This edition contains a preface (analysis) by 'Dr. A. P.' [Paul A. Pisk]. Janáček was actively involved in the publication.

Variant 2:
Title page: PHILHARMONIA / PARTITUREN • SCORES • PARTITIONS / Věnováno paní R. Newmarchové / LEOŠ JANÁČEK / SINFONIETTA / Für Orchestr Pro orchestr / For Orchestra Pour

Orchestre / (1926) / [ornament] / Eigentum der UNIVERSAL-EDITION A.G. Wien–New York / und mit deren Genehmigung in die / „PHILHARMONIA"-Partiturensammlung aufgenommen / Pro Republiku Československoú HUDEBNÍ MATICE, Praha / Aufführungsrecht vorbehalten – Performing rights reserved – Droits d'exécution réservés / No. 224 / [rule] / WIENER PHILHARMONISCHER VERLAG A.G. / WIEN 1927. PN U.E. 8680, W. Ph. V. 224, 115 pp. Four hundred copies printed in December 1926, with a further 400 copies printed in September 1928 (information from UE print book). Like variant 1, this also contains the preface (analysis) by 'Dr. A. P.' [Pisk].

- First edition of the full score. Universal Edition, January 1927. Title page [within a double rule]: Věnováno paní R. Newmarchové / LEOŠ JANÁČEK / SINFONIETTA / für Orchester / pour Orchestre for Orhcestra / pro orchestr / (1926) / PARTITURA / Konzert-Revision: Dr. P. A. Pisk / [decorative rule] / Aufführungsrecht vorbehalten – Droits d'exécution réservés. / UNIVERSAL-EDITION A.G. / Wien [rule] New York / Copyright 1927 by Universal Edition Inc., New York / Pro Republiku Československoú Hudební Matice, Praha / Printed in Austria. PN U.E. 8679, 72 pp. Printer's date on back cover: I.1927. One hundred copies printed (information from UE print book). As with the pocket score, Janáček was actively involved in the publication. The claim on the title page of the full score that it is a 'Konzert-Revision' by Pisk is incorrect, since the musical text is Janáček's own. It is possible that Pisk was involved in preparing the *Sinfonietta* for publication, and he was the author of the introduction to the pocket score.

- First edition of the orchestral parts. Wien and New York: Universal Edition. PN U.E. 8681. Forty-five separate parts. Copies received by UE on 21 January 1927. The parts were for hire only, though UE's performance records, noted on their internal 'Werke-Kartothek', show that under exceptional circumstances (usually for large orchestral libraries) parts were also available for purchase (plate 9).[119]

---

[119] The UE work cards for the *Sinfonietta* have columns for 'Kauf' (purchase) and 'Leih' (hire). Those who purchased sets of the orchestral parts between 1927 and 1937 included Hudební matice, Prague, for New South Wales, Australia (16 March 1928); [Franz] Jost, Leipzig (5 July 1928); Benjamin, Hamburg (10 July 1928); Münster (28 July 1928); Los Angeles (5 October 1928); Stuttgart Landestheater (17 October 1928), Arbós [Madrid Symphony Orchestra], (30 October 1928); Fritz Reiner, Cincinnati (6 August 1929); Praeger & Meier, Bremen (9 October 1929), Curwen, London (6 September 1930); Czech Philharmonic, Prague (17 March 1932); Otto Klemperer, Berlin

Plate 8a, b, c, d. Front covers and title pages of the two simultaneously issued pocket scores of the *Sinfonietta*, both published in January 1927 (variant 1 above; variant 2 below). The note-text is identical, with the double plate number U.E. 8680 W.Ph.V. 224 (Nigel Simeone, private collection).

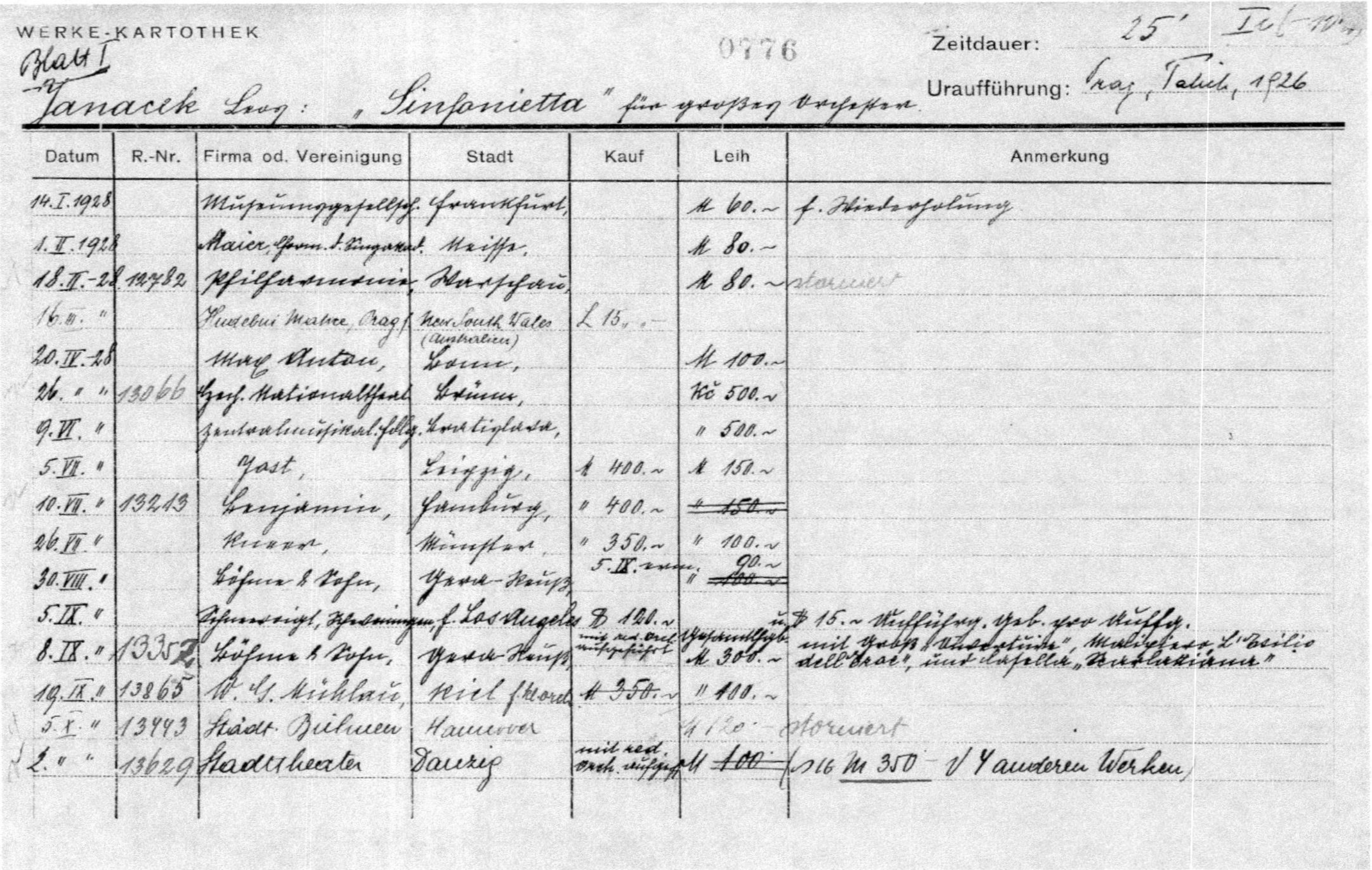

Plate 9. The first card for the Sinfonietta in Universal Edition's Werke-Kartothek showing performance, hire and purchase records between January and October 1928 (UE Archive, Vienna).

- Second edition of the full score. Universal Edition, December 1937. Corrected reprint of the first edition. PN U.E. 8679, 72 pp. Printer's date on back cover: XII.1937. Sixty copies printed (information from UE print book). This revised edition was edited (anonymously) by Benno Sachs and Erwin Stein. It incorporates Janáček's later corrections, errors discovered during rehearsals and after publication, and, especially, the corrections by the conductor František Neumann. The original plates of the first edition – appropriately corrected – were used for this printing. A reprint was issued in 1959.
- Second edition of the pocket score. Universal Edition, May 1951, in its Philharmonia series. Corrected reprint of the first edition. PN U.E. 8680, W. Ph. V. 224, 115 pp. One thousand copies printed (information from UE print book). This includes corrections and additions from the revised 1937 full score.
- Full score. Muzyka, Moscow, USSR, 1964. Title page: L. ЯАНАЧЕК/ L. Janáček/ СИМСФОНИЕТТА / SINFONIETTA / ДЛЯ БОЛЬШОГО СИМФОНИЧЕСКОГО / ОРКЕСТРА / FOR SYMPHONY ORCHESTRA / ПАРТИТУРА / FULL SCORE / ИЗДАТЕЛЬСТВО МУЗЫКА STATE PUBLISHERS MUSIC / МОСКВА 1964 MOSCOW. PN M. 31187 Г., 108 pp. Preface by Igor Belza. A newly typeset score based on the 1927 Universal Edition full score.
- Pocket score. Supraphon, Prague and Bratislava. Title page: VĚNOVÁNO PANÍ R. NEWMARCHOVÉ / LEOŠ JANÁČEK / SINFONIETTA / (1926) / Pro ČSSR, Německou demokratickou republiku, / Maďarsko, Rumunsko, Bulharsko a Polsko / EDITIO SUPRAPHON, PRAHA–BRATISLAVA 1967 / [rule] / PHILHARMONIA PARTITUREN / in der Universal Edition, Wien–London / Printed in Austria. PN U.E. 8680, W. Ph. V. 224, 115 pp. Printed from the plates of the original 1927 UE/Wiener Philharmonischer Verlag pocket score with corrections from the 1951 reprint. It also contains the original preface (analysis) by Dr P. A. Pisk. It was intended for sale in what was then the Eastern Bloc.
- Revised full score. Editio Supraphon, Prague, 1979. Editor: Jarmil Burghauser. Title page: LEOŠ JANÁČEK / SINFONIETTA / PARTITURA / (Jarmil Burghauser) / 1979 / EDITIO SUPRAPHON PRAHA. PN H6231a, 108 pp. There is no preface, and the note text is based on the 1927 UE score. Some errors have been corrected, and some metronome markings that the editor found problematic are solved

---

(20 January 1933); Fortin, for Radio Paris (29 January 1936); and Radiojournal Prague [i.e. Prague Radio] (30 November 1937).

by omission. Other sources used by the editor cannot be determined from the edition.
- Revised pocket score. Eulenburg, London, 1979. Editor: Jarmil Burghauser. Title page: Leoš Janáček / Sinfonietta / Edited by Jarmil Burghauser / [logo] / Ernst Eulenburg Ltd., London / Edition Eulenburg, Zürich / Ernst Eulenburg & Co. GmbH., Mainz / Edition Eulenburg Inc., New York. Edition number 1369, PN EE 6669, 116 pp. This edition contains a brief preface in which the editor outlines the changes to the edition without specifying them in detail. It largely matches Burghauser's 1979 Supraphon full score (above) but incorporates changes from the revised 1937 UE score. As in the 1979 Supraphon edition, problematic tempo or metronome markings are resolved by omission. The sources consulted by the editor cannot be determined from the edition. The changes often match those of the edition by Karl Heinz Füssl issued by UE in 1980 (see below), who consulted Burghauser.
- Revised full score. Universal Edition, 1980. Editor: Karl Heinz Füssl. Title page: Věnováno paní R. Newmarchové / LEOŠ JANÁČEK / SINFONIETTA / für Orchester / pour Orchestre for Orhcestra / pro orchestr / (1926) / PARTITUR / Nach den Originalquellen / herausgegeben / von / Karl Heinz Füssl / (1980) / UNIVERSAL EDITION / Pro Republiku Československoú Hudební Matice, Praha. PN U.E. 8179, 72 pp. Based on the 1927 full score and its 1937 corrected reprint, with additional corrections by Füssl. The editor adds a critical report describing the sources he worked with and the principles of the edition, comparing the 1937 corrected edition with the original printed version, Sedláček's authorised copy from 1926, and the composer's autograph. Füssl resolved some ambiguities concerning the fourth trombone and tuba, bells, and especially tempo markings, while omitting metronome markings that he finds problematic, apparently after consulting Jarmil Burghauser.
- Revised full score, later issue. Universal Edition. Editor: Karl Heinz Füssl. Title page: [UE logo] / Leoš Janáček / Sinfonietta / für Orchester (1926) / herausgegeben von Karl Heinz Füssl. PN UE 30 586, 115 pp. A large-format score based an enlarged version on the original UE pocket score plates from 1927 and its 1951 corrected reprint, with additional corrections by Füssl (see previous item).
- Revised pocket score. Universal Edition, 1980. Editor: Karl Heinz Füssl. PN U.E. 8680, W. Ph. V. 224, 115 pp. One thousand five hundred copies printed (information from UE print book). With the original preface by Dr P. A. Pisk from 1927.

- Revised full score and pocket score. Edition Peters, 1980. Editors Miroslav Barvík and Reiner Zimmermann. Title page: LEOŠ JANÁČEK / SINFONIETTA / FÜR ORCHESTER / (1926) / Herausgegeben von / Miroslav Barvík und Reiner Zimmermann / PARTITUR / EDITION PETERS · LEIPZIG. Edition number 9875 (conductor's score), 9875a (pocket score), both with PN E.P. 13060, 166 pp. This edition includes an afterword, critical report, and notes on interpretation. The editors compared Janáček's manuscript, Sedláček's copy from 1926, and the first edition of the pocket and orchestral scores from 1927. They corrected errors and pointed out some ambiguities, but they do not reflect Janáček's later revisions. The score also includes additions based on the performance practice of Jaroslav Vogel and Břetislav Bakala (identified in the critical report). The critical report presents the sources and describes the differences between them. In the notes on interpretation, the editors offer solutions for performing some contradictory or ambiguous passages based primarily on the experiences of Vogel and Bakala. The editors also deal with the problem of articulation, phrasing and Janáček's tempo and metronome marks and suggest adjustments according to the performance practice of Vogel and Bakala.
- Critical practical edition, pocket score. Universal Edition, 2017. Editor: Jiří Zahrádka. Title page: [UE logo] / Leoš Janáček / Sinfonietta / für Orchester (1926) / herausgegeben von Jiří Zahrádka. PN UE 36 503, lxxiii, 116 pp. This edition evaluates all known sources and is primarily based on the Sedláček copy used by Talich at the premiere and subsequently used as the printer's model by UE. The copy was compared with the first printed edition, the handwritten orchestral parts used at the premiere, the autograph score and corrected proofs. The edition aims to present the work as performed by Talich and the Czech Philharmonic in 1926, while also adopting the corrections that Janáček subsequently sent to UE, as well as further corrections sent to UE by František Neumann, conductor of the Brno performances in 1927 and 1928. The edition also takes into account some of the composer's wishes that were not adopted at the premiere for practical reasons and that consequently did not make it into the 1927 edition (e.g., using twelve trumpets – the three orchestral trumpets and the nine from the *banda* – in the second movement). In the notes to the musical text, the editor draws attention to the modifications and additions made by Václav Talich at rehearsals, and removes errors that arose during the copying, when Václav Sedláček mistranscribed or misunderstood Janáček's almost illegible autograph. The editor also added dynamics,

specified tempos, and corrected errors based on a fresh examination of the sources. The score also contains additions that Janáček approved (e.g., the addition of timpani, horns and trumpets by Talich for the last seven bars and the addition by František Neumann of the *banda* trumpets for the last three bars) as well as possible solutions to problematic passages regarding orchestral balance adopted by the leading Janáček authority, Charles Mackerras. The edition includes a preface with sections on the genesis of the work and on the critical edition of the score and its sources. A detailed critical report is available from UE on request (PN UE 37 871).

- Critical practical edition, full score. Universal Edition, 2017. Editor Jiří Zahrádka. Title page: [UE logo] / Leoš Janáček / Sinfonietta / für Orchester (1926) / herausgegeben von Jiří Zahrádka. PN UE 35 865, xlvii, 116 pp. A large-format edition of the pocket score described above.
- Critical edition of the full score. Bärenreiter, Prague, 2025, as part of the Complete Critical Edition of the Works of Leoš Janáček, SKV D/9. Editor: Jiří Zahrádka. PN BA 11580-01. Adapted from the 2017 UE score, updated and including a detailed critical report.

5. Arrangements

- Full score of the reduced instrumentation by Erwin Stein. Universal Edition, October 1927. PN U.E. 8679A, 14 pp. (lettered A–N), comprising the first movement and the fifth movement from Fig. 9 to the end. Fifty copies printed (information from UE print book). Soon after publication of the first edition in 1927, UE requested a version of the Fanfares in the first and last movements to be adapted for the main orchestra, enabling performance without the *banda*. Initially, Janáček did not want to make the arrangement, leaving it to Erwin Stein. But he was not satisfied with Stein's first version and sent new instructions which were adapted by Stein in time for publication of the 'Beilage' for reduced orchestra first issued by UE in October 1927. The publisher thus issued this arrangement of the Fanfares and final section of the work (from Fig. 9 of the finale onwards) according to Janáček's instructions, rescored for four trumpets, two oboes, cor anglais, trombone and timpani.
- Reprint of the reduced instrumentation by Stein, integrated into a complete full score of the work. Universal Edition, undated. Title page: Leoš Janáček / Sinfonietta / für Orchester (1926) / reduzierte Fassung von Erwin Stein. PN UE 30 584, 72 pp.

- Full score of the reduced instrumentation by Josef Keilberth, published by Universal Edition, undated. Title page: Leoš Janáček / Sinfonietta/ für kleines Orchester (1926) / bearbeitet Josef Keilberth / Partitur UE 30 588 / Universal Edition. PN UE 30 588, 76pp. In Keilberth's arrangement the *banda* is replaced in the first and last movements by three flutes, three oboes, three clarinets, two bassoons, four horns, four trumpets, three trombones, tuba and timpani.
- Full score of the reduced instrumentation by Heinz Stolba. Universal Edition, 2017. Title page: Leoš Janáček / Sinfonietta / für Orchester (1926) / reduzierte Fassung von Heinz Stolba (2017). PN UE 37 634, xii, 118 pp. Based on the critical-practical edition published by UE in 2017, this version not only reduced the *banda* but also the orchestral forces while aiming not to lose the character of Janáček's original. The total number of wind instruments is reduced from thirty-seven to twenty-two. Unlike the versions by Stein and Keilberth, Stolba has arranged the fanfares for brass alone, maintaining the original colour of Janáček's orchestration. This version contains an introduction in which the arrangement is explained in detail.
- Arrangement for piano four hands. Bärenreiter Editio Supraphon, 1996. Title page: Leoš Janáček / SINFONIETTA / Pro klavír na čtyři ruce upravil František Jílek / Für Klavier zu vier Händen bearbeitet von František Jílek / The four-hand piano arrangement was made by František Jílek / BÄRENREITER EDITIO SUPRAPHON PRAHA. PN H 7741, 67 pp. This arrangement, made in 1985 by the Czech conductor and Janáček specialist František Jílek, is a transcription of the complete work.

Plate 10. Postcard reproduction of a poster by Karel Šimůnek for the Eighth Sokol Rally, Prague, 1926 (Jiří Zahrádka, private collection).

Plate 11. Václav Talich in the late 1920s. The photograph is signed and dated 18 May 1930 (Janáček Archive, Brno).

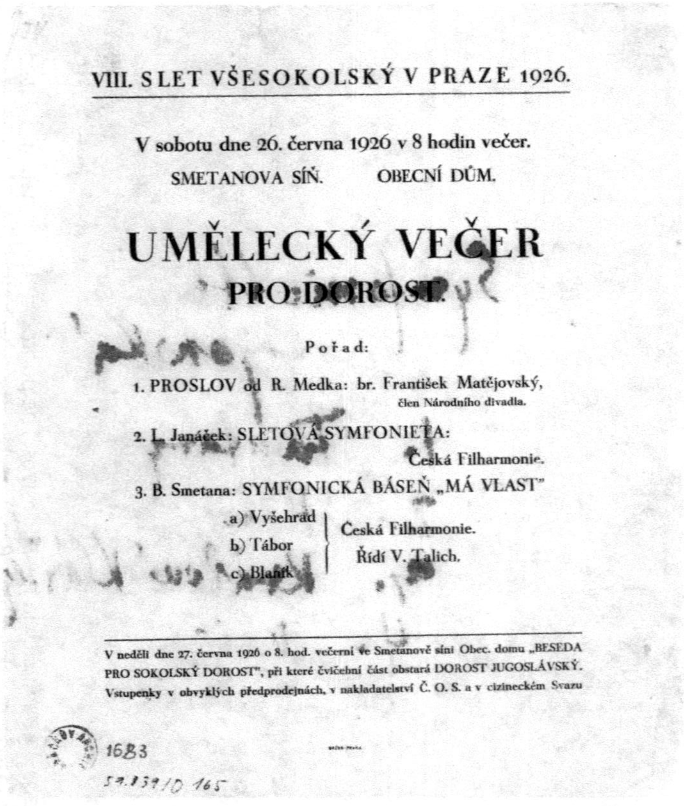

VIII. SLET VŠESOKOLSKÝ V PRAZE 1926.

V sobotu dne 26. června 1926 v 8 hodin večer.
SMETANOVA SÍŇ.   OBECNÍ DŮM.

UMĚLECKÝ VEČER
PRO DOROST

Pořad:

1. PROSLOV od R. Medka: br. František Matějovský,
   člen Národního divadla.

2. L. Janáček: SLETOVÁ SYMFONIETA:
   Česká Filharmonie.

3. B. Smetana: SYMFONICKÁ BÁSEŇ „MÁ VLAST"
   a) Vyšehrad | Česká Filharmonie.
   b) Tábor | Řídí V. Talich.
   c) Blaník

V neděli dne 27. června 1926 o 8. hod. večerní ve Smetanově síni Obec. domu „BESEDA PRO SOKOLSKÝ DOROST", při které čtvrtní část obstará DOROST JUGOSLÁVSKÝ. Vstupenky v obvyklých předprodejnách, v nakladatelství Č. O. S. a v cizineckém Svazu

Handwritten annotations:

Symfonietta
vojenská
1. fanfary
2. Hrad
3. Královo Klášter
4. ulice
5. Rocnice

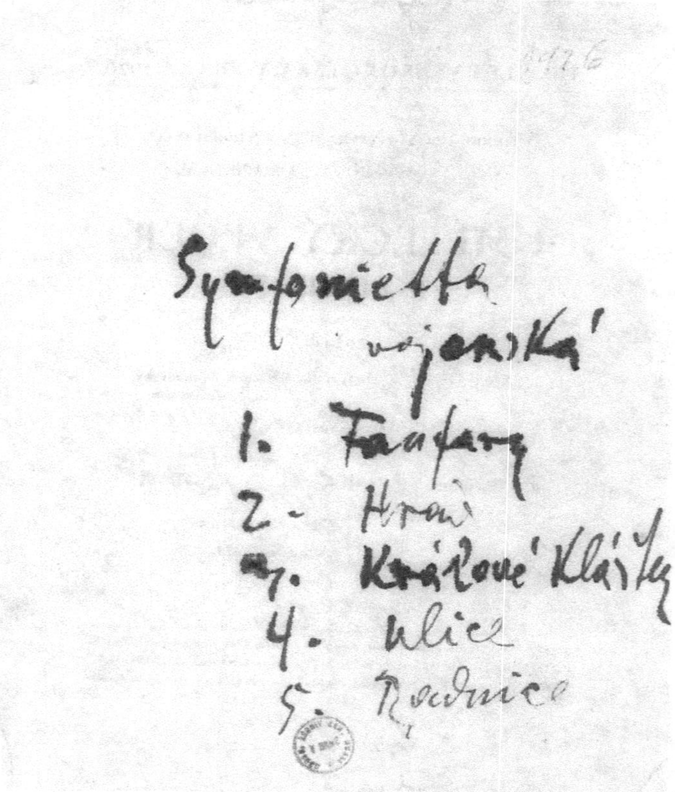

Plate 12a, b. Janáček's copy of the programme for the world premiere, 26 June 1926, with his annotations on the verso (Janáček Archive, Brno, D 165 LJ).

Plate 13. President Tomáš Garrigue Masaryk greeting the ceremonial procession of the Sokol Rally on 6 July 1926 in Prague's Old Town Square. This was the occasion when the Fanfares were played from the tower of the Týn church (Jiří Zahrádka, private collection).

2

The *Sinfonietta* in Janáček's Lifetime: A Chronicle

This chapter chronicles performances of the *Sinfonietta* given during Janáček's lifetime, including press reviews and extracts from relevant correspondence. Except where stated otherwise, the work was given under the title *Sinfonietta* (or *Symfonietta* in Prague and Brno). Wherever possible, and to provide context, complete programmes are listed. The following performances are documented:

26 June 1926, Prague. Czech Philharmonic, Václav Talich
9 December 1926, Wiesbaden. Wiesbaden Staatskapelle, Otto Klemperer
4 March 1927, New York. New York Symphony Society, Otto Klemperer
6 March 1927, New York. New York Symphony Society, Otto Klemperer
3 April 1927, Brno. Brno National Theatre Orchestra, František Neumann
29 September 1927, Berlin. Berlin Staatskapelle, Otto Klemperer
14 October 1927, Frankfurt-am-Main. Museums-Konzert, Clemens Krauss
16 October 1927, Frankfurt-am-Main. Museums-Konzert, Clemens Krauss
18 November 1927, broadcast, Munich Radio Orchestra, Franz Adam(?)
19 December 1927, broadcast, Munich Radio Orchestra, Franz Adam(?)
15 January 1928, broadcast, Munich Radio Orchestra, Franz Adam
6 February 1928, Darmstadt. Opera orchestra, Karl Böhm
6 February 1928, Magdeburg. Walther Beck
10 February 1928, London. BBC National Symphony Concert, Henry Wood
12 February 1928, Vienna. Vienna Symphony Orchestra, Jascha Horenstein
1 March 1928, Halle. Berlin Philharmonic Orchestra, Georg Göhler
6 March 1928, Karlsruhe. Badische Landestheater Orchestra, Josef Krips
16 March 1928, Dresden. Dresden Staatskapelle, Fritz Busch
27 May 1928, Brno. Brno National Theatre Orchestra, František Neumann
10 June 1928, Cologne. Gürzenich Orchestra, Hermann Abendroth

World premiere:
26 June 1926, as Sletová symfonietta ['Rally Sinfonietta']
Prague, Smetana Hall. Czech Philharmonic, conducted by Václav Talich. Janáček present.
Broadcast live on Czech Radio.

> Spoken address by Rudolf Medek, read by František Matějovský
> Janáček: *Sletová symfonietta*
> Smetana: *Má vlast:* Vyšehrád, Tábor, Blaník

This important premiere was broadcast live on Czech Radio. The event is described in *Radio-Journal*[1] as an 'artistic evening for the youth of Sokol', and it is interesting to note that the title of Janáček's new work is given simply as *Symfonietta* (rather than 'Rally Sinfonietta' or 'Military Sinfonietta').

Several leading critics were present at the concert, none of them more important or influential than Max Brod (1884–1968). For a decade, Brod had been one of Janáček's most ardent champions as well as a close collaborator. His pioneering biography of Janáček had appeared in 1924 (in a Czech translation) and 1925 (in the original German),[2] and his German translations of the operas[3] were of fundamental importance in securing productions in German-speaking theatres, finding audiences far beyond Brno and Prague. On 27 June 1926, the day after the premiere, Brod's review of the *Sinfonietta* appeared in the *Prager Tagblatt*. His reaction was extremely enthusiastic, and from some of his comments about the work's programmatic elements, it's clear that he had discussed the new piece with the composer himself – almost certainly at the dress rehearsal which they both attended:

> Yesterday the Czech Philharmonic played Janáček's latest work, a symphony, under Talich's rousing direction. Its title is 'Military Symphony'. It cannot be denied that Janáček's masculine, combative nature has often produced war-like fanfares. But this time, with its happy, jubilant character, the work could just as well be called a 'Symphony of Joy' or 'People's Symphony'. A direct path leads from Janáček's latest chamber music – the wind sextet *Youth* and the *Concertino* – to this new work, which is testimony to his unflagging zest for life. It is scored

---

[1] *Radio-Journal*, 19 June 1926, p. 6.
[2] *Leoš Janáček: život a dílo* [trans. Alfred Fuchs] (Prague: Hudební matice, 1924); and *Leoš Janáček: Leben und Werk* (Vienna: Wiener Philharmonischer Verlag, 1925).
[3] Brod's German-language librettos of Janáček included *Jenůfa* (1918), *Katja Kabanowa* (1922), *Das schlaue Füchslein* (1925), *Die Sache Makropulos* (1928) and *Aus einem Totenhaus* (1930), all published by Universal Edition.

for large forces, in five movements, and yet very concise in its development. The unblended colours of the orchestration create a youthful *al fresco* feeling. This time, however, they are almost outdone by the interesting figurations (including the daring, lightning-like flashes of the flute runs in the third movement), vigorous rhythms, and dance-like swirling motifs, which demand the listener's attention. Yes, in this symphony, which represents the pinnacle of Janáček's instrumental music to date, the master succeeds in being both original and popular at the same time.

This is not music intended for specialists, only accessible to a few, but rather it deserves to be played for the benefit of everyone, and to have a direct impact on their nerves and muscles, just as it is born of nerves and muscles.

I have a feeling that this work will make its way into the repertoire of the great symphony orchestras in Berlin, Vienna and Rome, and that it will make a particularly strong impact in Moscow. For it is a real symphony of the masses, of the teeming crowds whose whole life is portrayed in the three middle movements. The composer calls the second movement 'The Castle', in which gleaming trombones (at first in a cheerful folk mood) represent an Easter stroll. In the third movement, an enemy attack breaks out against the walls of a monastery (Janáček is thinking of the Swedish War and the Queen's Monastery in Brno). And in the fourth movement, 'The Street', its high-spirited motifs and effervescent noise of daily life are a celebration of freedom. In the two outer movements, a separate band of 18 military musicians appears with the blaring sound of their high-pitched instruments. At the beginning, this band plays alone, in some utterly distinctive fanfares, at first accompanied by parallel fifths; then the timpani also join in. And in the final movement the band joins the large orchestra in a triumphant orgy of sound, the like of which we have not experienced for a long time. Janáček – who wrote this work in a very short time and (as he himself has said) with unusual ease – has started a new symphony which he plans to call *The Danube*.[4]

A shorter version of Brod's review subsequently appeared in *Musikblätter des Anbruch* (September 1926, p. 335) but that omitted several interesting details from his original *Prager Tagblatt* article, including the revelation about the Brno inspiration which Janáček revealed at the time, jotting the movement titles on the back of his copy of the programme (plate 12b).

---

[4] Max Brod ['M.B.']: 'Janáček Uraufführung', *Prager Tagblatt*, vol. 51, no. 152, 27 June 1926, p. 9.

Brod's *Prager Tagblatt* review appeared the day after the premiere, so it constitutes the first published mention anywhere of the 'Brno inspiration'.

Boleslav Vomáčka – already familiar with the work's prehistory, as we have seen in Chapter 1 – reported on the first performance for *Lidové noviny*. For him, the *Sinfonietta* was 'further proof of the master's vibrant creative powers and startling originality. The very creation of the work bears the mark of a brilliant but mysterious birth. Seemingly out of nothing, from tiny fragments and ideas which had remained in the composer's subconscious, a great work suddenly awakened and grew.'[5] Vomáčka went on to describe the origins of the work and discussed the title – concluding that Janáček had been right to object to the Sokol's description of it as a 'Rally Sinfonietta' since his own title of 'Military Sinfonietta' had a far broader significance. Vomáčka concluded that the new work was a vibrant affirmation of Czech nationhood:

> Janáček's *Sinfonietta* is a celebration of today's free Czech man, his spiritual beauty and joy, his strength, courage and determination to fight for victory. In the opening fanfares, manly strength and harmonic balance are apparent; in the middle movements, the joy of a free spirit is translated into delightful folk dances, while towards the end, there arises the strength to fight and the will to win victory – emphasised by the combination of the fanfare band with the full orchestra. This powerful conclusion, so full of passion, faith and moral strength, raises Janáček's work on to the level of the finest compositions created in our liberated homeland. At the same time, Janáček's work bears all the characteristic hallmarks of his style and compositional technique, especially in the formulation of themes, in rhythmic intensity, and in the very original orchestration. However, the most striking feature is the extraordinary generosity of this music, and the melodic richness in which the work is steeped – breathing the very air of the new Czech spirit. A work which is not only a sublime conception but also immediately captivating, there is no doubt that its impact will keep growing as it becomes more widely known.[6]

In his review for *Československá Republika*, the conductor Jaroslav Vogel was every bit as enthusiastic as Brod and Vomáčka, with some detailed comments about the music, and interesting remarks on Talich's performance.

---

[5] Boleslav Vomáčka ['B.V.']: 'O Janáčkově simfoniettě', *Lidové noviny*, vol. 34, no. 329, 1 July 1926, p. 7.
[6] Ibid.

Saturday's festival concert in the Smetana Hall was memorable because it was the first performance of Janáček's latest orchestral composition, his *Military Sinfonietta* for large orchestra and a special brass ensemble. According to Janáček himself, the impetus for this work was the challenge he received to write festive fanfares for the Eighth All–Sokol Festival. However, Janáček's volcanic musicality did not stop at those fanfares: instead, the work grew into a complete five-movement symphony, which begins and ends with fanfares, but in between it illuminates themes of defiance, strength and joy in various ways, with music that is lyrical, heroic and dance-like. Alongside *Taras Bulba*, what Janáček has created here represents the pinnacle of his orchestral music to date, and one of the most joyful (in any sense you like) Czech works ever written. The impetus for it was certainly the Sokol but not only the Sokol. The organisers were completely wrong when they renamed it 'Rally symphonietta' for this concert. However, because Janáček's creative and imaginative spirit translated the Sokol's idea of strength into its most important symbol – as defender of the homeland – the *Sinfonietta* became a true paean to the Czechoslovak soldier, his ruggedness and dedication. (The affinity with the aforementioned *Taras Bulba*, his great hymn to Slavic strength in general, is obvious). In doing so, Janáček took an important step forward [because] until now in Czech art, the Czech soldier had only been portrayed as a member of an occupied nation.

Talich recognised that Janáček's lion's claws should not be dressed in the silk gloves of the Suk-like sound world in which Talich himself grew up, and he played Janáček, quite simply, as Janáček. The result is, of course, unusual, but only in the sense that there is, as Janáček says, not a hint of 'business as usual' anywhere in it. On the other hand, the *Sinfonietta* is full of brilliant new ideas, such as the excited dialogue between trombones and flutes in the third movement, or the lively muted trumpet solo over the falling cello pizzicatos in the fourth movement, or, finally the completely extraordinary place in the last movement where piccolos and high clarinets anxiously intertwine over the strange roar of trombones and low strings. In Janáček's hands, even simple and familiar elements can take on a new and powerful effect, best demonstrated by the beautiful, mellow A flat minor chord, into which the unyielding D flat major fanfare suddenly flows towards the end of the work.[7] The performance of this splendid new piece, to which the conductor and the orchestra of the Czech Philharmonic, reinforced by 14 military trumpeters, devoted their best efforts, was

---

[7] A reference to the chord change at bar 280, six bars before the end of the piece.

received with great and spontaneous applause, which erupted when the master was called on to the stage several times.⁸

Janáček had evidently not shared his 'Brno inspiration' with Vogel; instead, Vogel made an interesting comment about the work's (apparent) depiction of the Czech armed forces and, in the headline, he used Janáček's own title 'Military Sinfonietta' rather than 'Rally Sinfonietta' as given on the printed programme. His short but telling observation on Talich's conducting – playing 'Janáček as Janáček' – suggests that this was a stylish and idiomatic performance – though Talich never conducted the piece again. Vogel's review also confirms that Janáček attended this premiere in spite of the composer's original (and inexplicable) intention to leave Prague after the final rehearsal. Plans for a second Prague performance on 5 December 1926, with the Czech Philharmonic conducted by František Stupka, had to be abandoned as the performing material was not ready in time, and Stupka conducted *Taras Bulba* in its place.

As for Janáček himself, it has already been noted (in Chapter 1) that he was irritated by the Sokol committee changing the title to 'Rally Sinfonietta' on the printed programme.⁹ But he had nothing to say about the performance in his letters to Kamila following the concert (or even any reminder of the Písek-Kamila inspiration); instead, he fussed over plans for her to come to the unveiling of a plaque in his honour at Hukvaldy three weeks later (which she did not attend). He offered no opinion on the premiere to UE either: instead he seems to have been preoccupied with trying to broker a co-publishing arrangement between UE in Vienna and Hudební matice in Prague (see Chapter 1).

Radio was still an exciting novelty in 1926. The BBC in London was inaugurated in November 1922 and Czech Radio (Československý rozhlas) soon followed, established in May 1923. Three years later, it provided extensive outside broadcast coverage of events at the 1926 Sokol Rally. The considerable technical challenges of this were outlined in *Radio-Journal* in its issue of 26 June 1926. The broadcast that night enabled the *Sinfonietta* to be heard by radio listeners far beyond Prague. One of them was Janáček's friend Jan Löwenbach who wrote to the composer from the South Bohemian town of Strakonice the day after the concert:

> I must write to tell you what pleasure I had from your great success, and from the fact that I was lucky enough, after all, to hear your

---

⁸ Jaroslav Vogel ['J.V.']: 'Hudba. Z pražské koncertní sine. Janáčkova Vojenská symfonieta', *Česká republika*, 29 June 1926, p. 29.
⁹ See JYL2, p. 624.

> **Staatstheater Wiesbaden**
> Grosses Haus
>
> Donnerstag, den 9. Dezember 1926.
>
> **IV. Symphonie-Konzert**
> der Staatskapelle
> Leitung: Otto Klemperer.
> Solisten: Josef Peischer (Violine)
> August Eichhorn (Cello)
>
> Programm:
> I. Teil:
> 1. **Händel**: Viertes Concerto grosso in A-moll
> 2. **Johannes Brahms**: Doppelkonzert für Violine und Violoncell mit Begleitung des Orchesters
> Josef Peischer und August Eichhorn
> II. Teil:
> 3. **Richard Strauss**: Don Juan
> 4. **Leos Janacek**: Militärsinfoniette (Deutsche Uraufführung)
>
> Anfang 7.30 Uhr.   Ende gegen 9.30 Uhr

Plate 14. Announcement of the German premiere in the *Wiesbadener Bade-blatt*, 9 December 1926.

> *Sinfonietta*. Although not present, I heard everything very well, from the atmosphere in the hall, the orchestra tuning up, the monumental introduction of the first movement, the richness, freshness and rhythmic variety of the middle movements, and culminating in the blazing and victorious final movement. And then that applause: at first it was spontaneous and intense, then calmer, and finally tremendous when they called you on to the platform. I 'saw' all that while listening to it here in Strakonice, thanks to the excellent *radio* station! Although I regret that I could not stay in Prague – because of the children – I was delighted to hear the enthusiasm for you and above all for your work, before which I stand in admiration! I thank you very much for it, and congratulate you on your latest success.[10]

---

[10] BmJA B00640. Published in Ivo Stolařík: *Jan Löwenbach a Leoš Janáček: vzájemná korespondence* (Opava: Slezský studijní ústav, 1958), p. 39.

The Sinfonietta in Janáček's Lifetime: A Chronicle   77

German premiere:
9 December 1926, as Militärsinfoniette
Wiesbaden, Staatstheater. Wiesbaden Staatskapelle, conducted by Otto Klemperer.

Handel: Concerto Grosso No. 4 in A minor
Brahms: Double Concerto (Josef Peischer, August Eichhorn)
Janáček: *Militärsinfoniette*
Strauss: *Don Juan*[11]

The first performance outside Czech lands – and the first anywhere in a regular concert rather than as part of a special occasion for the Sokol Rally – was given in Wiesbaden on 9 December 1926, in the fourth concert of the Wiesbaden Staatskapelle (the opera orchestra), conducted by Otto Klemperer. He had first made contact with Janáček about the work a couple of weeks after Talich's premiere: on 12 July 1926, he sent a telegram asking for permission to give the American premiere[12] and followed this up on 13 July with a letter:

> I took the liberty of sending you a telegram today about your *Military Symphony*, with the request that you allow me to give the first performance in New York. I don't know if you remember my name. I had the honour of being the first to perform your works *Jenůfa* and *Káťa Kabanová* in Germany, at the Cologne Opera House. *Jenůfa* is also in the repertoire at Wiesbaden (where I am currently working for six months of the year at the Prussian State Theatre). As I am conducting the excellent New York Symphony Orchestra in New York for two months, I would like to give your symphony its first performance there. I would be very grateful if you would help me to carry out my plan by agreeing to it. May I hope for a brief reply?[13]

Janáček replied in a letter from Hukvaldy on 15 July:

> As if I don't know you! I am delighted to give you the rights to the first performance of my *Military Sinfonietta* in America – New York. I know that the performance will be excellent. I will send you a copy with some comments after it is published. Just give me your address.[14]

---

[11] The preliminary announcement (plate 14) has the programme ending with the *Sinfonietta*, but reviews indicate that the concert ended with *Don Juan*.
[12] Telegram from Klemperer to Janáček, BmJA, B 923.
[13] Letter from Klemperer to Janáček, BmJA, A 3618.
[14] Letter from Klemperer to Janáček, original in Gesellschaft der Musikfreunde, Vienna.

At the same time, he sent Klemperer a telegram to which the conductor replied at once:

> Your friendly telegram, which I have just received, has given me particular pleasure. Please accept my most heartfelt thanks. From Universal Edition, which I had also contacted, I received a telegram saying 'Decision in eight days'. I think they want to present the matter to Director Hertzka first. I have also written to him in the meantime. If you, for your part, could now also write a few lines to Hertzka, that would certainly promote the matter in the best possible way.
>
> The New York Symphony Orchestra, which I conduct in America, is a truly excellent one. A fine string ensemble with 18 first violins and virtuoso wind players. Rest assured that I will do everything to help your new symphony have a great success in America. I can only repeat that I would consider it an honour to give the first performance over there of your music, which I love so much.[15]

Klemperer wrote again (in a letter this time) on 22 July:

> You would not believe how much joy you have given me with your letter. I am looking forward to getting to know your *Sinfonietta* and I hope that the printing will be finished shortly.... . I would be so happy to make your acquaintance sometime, and I only hope that this will happen soon. Thank you once again for your trust (with regard to the American premiere) and accept my most respectful greetings.[16]

Before giving the *Sinfonietta* in New York (see **Third performance**), Klemperer conducted it in Wiesbaden on 9 December 1926. If he did tell Janáček about this beforehand, no letter or telegram survives. A review appeared in the *Wiesbadener Tagblatt* the day after the concert:

> The second part of the concert brought a novelty: the *Military Sinfonietta* by L. Janáček. Like his opera *Jenůfa*, it is original, natural and lively music. Slavic folk art plays a role in it; a joyous delight in sound, and melodic and harmonic piquancy are prominent elements of the composition. The military character is already established by the presence of almost a dozen brass instruments – trumpets and bass trumpets: they play the entire first movement with fanfares. In the Allegro second movement, the whirling woodwinds play a particularly witty role, but at the climaxes the militarism sets in again. The

---

[15] Telegram from Klemperer to Janáček, BmJA, A 3626.
[16] Letter from Klemperer to Janáček, BmJA, A 1831.

most successful movement is probably the following one, especially its opening, a richly melodic Andante; the accompaniment of the low brass is again very individual. The fourth and fifth movements are characterised by rhythmic liveliness; the full orchestra is involved almost throughout – a wild troop of soldiers seem to be letting off steam, and that becomes a bit nerve-wracking. The *Military Sinfonietta*, for which the conductor demonstrated the most loving devotion, was performed in a correspondingly brilliant manner by the orchestra. This latest import from Bohemia was deservedly applauded with enthusiasm by the audience: Janáček's open-hearted and friendly music deserves such a reception in Germany – and there was no reason for feigned enthusiasm.[17]

The *Wiesbadener Bade-Blatt* also reported on the concert with a review published on its front page:

In the second part of the evening, a *Military Symphony* by Leoš Janáček was played, given its first performance in Germany. The piece begins and ends with an episode for trumpet choir, in which simple motifs adapted to the characteristics of the instruments intertwine more and more, building up to climaxes of sonorous intensity. The work as a whole is captivating due to its strong individuality… . Once again it proves that the musical language of the composer of *Jenůfa* is strongly rooted in folklore in terms of rhythm and melody, though of course, the influence of modern trends in music cannot be denied either… . The State Theatre Orchestra once again performed at a praiseworthy level: it delighted with the sensual beauty and compelling intensity of the music's tone colours, and gripped with the brilliant splendour of its sound. Mr Klemperer conducted with clear intent and with forward-moving momentum, and the artists under his leadership followed willingly. The audience applauded enthusiastically.[18]

Although these positive reviews suggest an enthusiastic reception, Klemperer himself was rather disappointed by the audience reaction in Wiesbaden, writing to UE on 14 December that 'the reception by the public in Wiesbaden public was not quite as enthusiastic as I had hoped. The music and the unusual sound of the orchestra are taken to be too newfangled.'[19] But on the same day, Fritz Zweig – a friend of both Klemperer and Janáček – wrote to the composer to say that he had been enthralled by the

---

[17] O.D.: 'Staatstheater', *Wiesbadener Tagblatt*, 10 December 1926.
[18] Fz: 'Symphoniekonzert im Staatstheater', *Wiesbadener Bade-Blatt*.
[19] Quoted in JYL2, p. 662.

work in Klemperer's performance: 'Mr Klemperer, who, as you will know, has become director of the State Opera on the Platz der Republik (not Unter den Linden, where [Erich] Kleiber is) performed your Symphony [*Sinfonietta*] last Friday and is enthusiastic about the work. We talked a lot about you and how we consider you to be the most esteemed of living composers.'[20] It was not until a few weeks later that Klemperer reported on the Wiesbaden performance to Janáček, in a letter dated 18 January 1927, written soon after his arrival in New York:

> Only today – from New York – have I got around to writing to you about the indescribably deep impression your *Sinfonietta* made on me and all the audience at the Wiesbaden performance. It is a truly magnificent work; it is on the programme of my American concerts, and I will also be giving the first performance in Berlin. The only point that will often be difficult to overcome are the 12 trumpets, the 2 bass trumpets and the 2 tubas. All of these are difficult and expensive to obtain. Perhaps you have heard that I have been appointed in Berlin and, from 27 September, I will become director of the State Opera on the Platz der Republik. I am extremely interested in performing your new work *The Makropulos Affair* in Berlin at the State Opera, which is under my supervision. May I take the liberty of asking whether you would be willing to entrust me with your new work? I would be very happy and proud if it were possible.... I will be here in New York until 9 March, then back in Wiesbaden at the State Theatre.[21]

American premiere:
4 and 6 March 1927
New York, Carnegie Hall. New York Symphony Orchestra, conducted by Otto Klemperer.

> Mozart: Symphony in G minor, K550
> Schubert: Five Deutsche and Seven Trios with Coda, D90
> Janáček: *Sinfonietta*
> Strauss: *Till Eulenspiegel* / Smetana: *The Bartered Bride* Overture[22]

---

[20] Letter from Fritz Zweig to Janáček, BmJA, A 3589.
[21] Letter from Klemperer to Janáček, BmJA, B 619.
[22] Olin Downes's review mentions that the concert on 4 March ended with *Till Eulenspiegel*. An unsigned review of the 6 March concert mentions that it ended with *The Bartered Bride* Overture.

Olin Downes was one of the very few English-speaking critics to have met Janáček in person and to have discussed musical matters with him, notably in an interview published in the *New York Times* in July 1924 to celebrate the composer's seventieth birthday.[23] He viewed Janáček as a refreshingly independent-minded figure and he was receptive to the music, writing a warm review of the *Sinfonietta* and of Klemperer's performance:

> A *Sinfonietta* by Leoš Janáček was played for the first time in America by the New York Symphony Society, Otto Klemperer conducting, last night in Carnegie Hall. This is a charming and original work. Janáček is known in New York by his opera, *Jenůfa*, produced by the Metropolitan Opera Company, without success, two years ago. The *Sinfonietta* is much less pretentious, of course, than the opera, but it seems freer of conventionality or padding, more certain of its workmanship and more original in content.
>
> It employs an unusual orchestra of many wind instruments, including nine trumpets in C, three in F, two bass trumpets, four trombones, bass tuba, the usual horns and reinforced woodwind choir. There are unusual tone colours. There is a pantheistic mood. Janáček knows nature, the forest and its denizens. His opera [*The Cunning Little Vixen*] was performed a season ago in Prague. He himself is of peasant origin, a simple and independent man, whose musical thinking is his own, and who has been largely self-educated as a musician. In the music heard last night are humor and fantasy of a delightful kind. The writing is unconventional. Of development, in the usual sense, there is little, but there is a joyous play of short melodic and rhythmical fragments, a freedom from the shackles of traditional form, and a genuine freshness of feeling.
>
> The unusual character of the orchestra employed is the result of the musical ideas, and not a composer trying to astonish or puzzle and audience. This, in fact, is the music of an honest man, who has allowed neither his opinions nor his standards to be decided for him. Perhaps the *Sinfonietta* is a little long; certainly, it is a work of individuality, inner serenity and laughter. And this work was performed for the first time last May [*recte* June] in Prague, when the composer was 72 years old! Janáček's development as a composer was much retarded by circumstances. He has been late in coming into his own... . The playing of the orchestra ... reflected great credit upon Mr Klemperer, whose earnest rehearsing has materially raised the standards of the New York

---

[23] The interview forms part of Olin Downes: 'The Music of Janáček, Composer of *Jenůfa*, to Be Heard at Metropolitan', *New York Times*, 13 July 1924, Section 7, p. 5.

Symphony's performances this season. The applause that rewarded Mr Klemperer was fully deserved.[24]

Following this Carnegie Hall performance, Klemperer repeated the *Sinfonietta* at the Mecca Auditorium (now the New York City Center) on 6 March. He sent Janáček a telegram on 7 March 1927: 'Two performances of *Sinfonietta*. Enthusiastic audiences and good press. Greetings.'[25] Karel Starý d'Albert, an American musician of Czech origin, wrote to Janáček on 25 March 1927 with his impressions of the second (Sunday) performance:

> I dare to write you a few lines which I hope might please you, about your beautiful *Sinfonietta* which was performed on Sunday afternoon by the Symphony Orchestra here in New York. After such a wonderful concert, the critics followed the next day and made me wonder why God created music critics … a critic is rather like a corpse staggering through life. How memorable that afternoon was, and how the journalists argued with one another over your music which so confused their heads – and none of them could say anything useful. Your notes are like electricity which enters a person's body and never leaves again… . They go straight to the heart. It was a great treat for me to hear your *Sinfonietta* – a magnificent work that is waiting for a conductor who will elevate it even more with its fleeting, wonderfully elaborated motifs. Congratulations to you, Mr Janáček, from the bottom of my heart, and I look forward to hearing your magnificent *Sinfonietta* again.[26]

Brno premiere:
3 April 1927, as Vojenská symfonietta ['Military Sinfonietta']
Brno, National Theatre Orchestra, conducted by František Neumann.
Janáček present.

Suk: *A Summer Tale*
Berg: Three Fragments from *Wozzeck*
Janáček: *Vojenská Symfonietta*

František Neumann (1874–1929), director of the Brno National Theatre, is best remembered for conducting several of Janáček's most important

---

[24] Olin Downes: 'Music: Janacek's *Sinfonietta* Delights', *New York Times*, 5 March 1927, p. 9.
[25] Telegram from Klemperer to Janáček, BmJA, B 271.
[26] Letter from Karel Stary d'Albert to Janáček, BmJA, B 633.

operatic premieres,[27] but he was also active as an orchestral conductor. His earliest encounter with Janáček's music was in 1906 when he conducted the Czech Philharmonic in the premiere of *Jealousy* (originally intended as the prelude to *Jenůfa*). He worked as Kapellmeister at the Frankfurt Opera (where he was known as Franz Neumann) from 1904 until his appointment as head of opera at the Brno National Theatre in 1919. Neumann conducted the world premieres of *The Ballad of Blaník* (21 March 1920), *Taras Bulba* (9 October 1921) and the *Lachian Dances* (2 December 1924), as well as the Brno premiere of the *Sinfonietta*. He was the conductor with whom Janáček worked most closely in the last decade of his life – his most ardent champion at the time and the conductor who performed Janáček's works with the greatest authority and dedication. On 15 August 1928 – following the composer's wishes – he conducted the final scene from *The Cunning Little Vixen* at Janáček's funeral, held in the foyer of the Brno National Theatre. Neumann's early death a few months later, in February 1929, meant that he left no recordings.

The Brno premiere of the *Sinfonietta*, conducted by Neumann, was in the last concert of the Brno National Theatre Orchestra's 1926–7 season on 3 April 1927.[28] It was part of a demanding programme that also included Suk's *A Summer Tale* and three fragments from Berg's *Wozzeck*. The April 1927 issue of the Brno periodical *Hudební rozhledy* included an article by Vladimír Helfert on the *Sinfonietta* in which he noted that Janáček was moving away from programmatic inspiration for his concert works and hints that he was now developing a very individual kind of neoclassicism. It's also worth noting that Helfert makes no mention of the 'military' aspect of the piece or of any Sokol connection:

> The *Sinfonietta* marks a new phenomenon in Janáček's orchestral music: a departure from Romantic programme music and a move towards the more modern concept of absolute music... . In terms of expression, all the characteristic features of Janáček's music are present here – the typical brilliance, passionate temperament, changeability and volatility in rhythm and metre. But all these features appear in this work in an unusually balanced way. There is fierce temperament, but

---

[27] *Káťa Kabanová* (23 November 1921), *The Cunning Little Vixen* (6 November 1924), *Šárka* (11 November 1925) and *The Makropulos Affair* (18 December 1926). On 15 May 1926 he conducted the Brno premiere of *The Excursion of Mr Brouček to the Moon*. On 23 August 1919, Neumann inaugurated the Brno National Theatre at the Mahen Theatre with *Jenůfa*. Janáček was present at all these performances.

[28] JAWO gives the date as 4 April, but this is an error.

not explosiveness. If it didn't sound so contradictory, I would say that Janáček is approaching a kind of classical period in his work.[29]

Helfert also commented on the work's form, concluding that he considered it to be essentially a suite:

> Laid out in five movements, the form of the piece resembles a suite rather than a symphony. The first movement is a prelude, like a ceremonial fanfare, which provided the original impetus for the whole work. The master originally wanted to write a fanfare for brass instruments, but then decided to expand it into a suite. The following movements follow the principle of contrast. However, Janáček wanted to unite these pieces into a musical whole, and this led him to bring back the fanfares in the last (fifth) movement which provides the work's climax.[30]

Janáček's former pupil Vilém Petrželka reviewed the concert in *Moravské slovo*. He noted that the *Sinfonietta* had a great success with the public and was an outstanding demonstration of the composer's 'spiritual youth'. Petrželka had some interesting comments on the work, not least his observation – in striking contrast to Helfert – that the music demonstrated Janáček's skill as a 'symphonic builder'. Like Helfert, Petrželka made no mention of any Brno inspiration but instead detected – as Jaroslav Vogel had at the Prague performance – 'scenes and impressions of military life' in the central movements:

> The *Sinfonietta* is a work of small symphonic format, but [Janáček] characterises the designation 'Military' in an amazingly witty and original way. The first movement opens the whole piece with a sonorously distinctive fanfare for brass, with unusually interesting orchestration. The middle movements, depicting scenes and impressions of military life, are imbued with Janáček's fiery emotional soul, both in opalescent cantilenas and in the originality of the rhythms. The fourth movement, with its ostinato trumpet theme, immediately intrigues the listener. The fifth and last movement astonished with the return of the brass fanfares from the first movement, crowning the entire work and showing us Janáček as a great symphonic builder – a feature of his work that we have not been fully aware of until now.[31]

---

[29] Vladimír Helfert: 'Janáčkovy nové skladby ... II. Symfonietta', *Hudební rozhledy*, vol. 3, no. 7 (April 1927), p. 111. Hereafter Helfert 1927.
[30] Helfert 1927, p. 111.
[31] Vilém Petrželka ['–el']: 'Šestý a poslední symfonický koncert divadelní', *Moravské slovo*, 5 April 1927, p. 3.

Plate 15. František Neumann. Pastel portrait by Eduard Milén, c. 1924 (Nigel Simeone, private collection).

Petrželka concluded his review by saying that Neumann's conducting had 'differentiated the three different musical worlds of Suk, Berg and Janáček, giving each of them their authentic sound... . The entire programme was warmly received by the audience and was a worthy end to this year's series of symphonic concerts.'

Similar opinions were expressed by Gracian Černušák in *Lidové noviny*, but he detected less of the 'symphonic builder', instead sharing Helfert's view of it as a kind of suite:

The sixth symphonic concert of the National Theatre orchestra was perhaps the most interesting of the whole year, because all the pieces were new to Brno and two of them still had a hint of topicality. The greatest success was achieved by Janáček's *Sinfonietta*, formally resembling a suite, the festive mood of its opening returning at the end, sharply different in content to the other sections and yet expressively connected and making a very effective sound.[32]

**Berlin premiere:
29 September 1927
Berlin, Kroll Opera. Berlin Staatskapelle, conducted by Otto Klemperer. Janáček present.**

Bach: Orchestral Suite No. 3 BWV1068
Mozart: Piano Concerto in D minor K466 (Artur Schnabel)
Janáček: *Sinfonietta*

On 17 September 1927, Klemperer sent Janáček a telegram giving advance notice of this concert and hoping that the composer might be able to attend: 'Berlin premiere of *Sinfonietta* planned for 29 September. May I expect you? Yours sincerely, Klemperer, State Opera.'[33]

Janáček replied to say he would be happy to come. Klemperer's response, dated 19 September 1927, gave the composer the rehearsal schedule and had some interesting questions about the musical text of the work (see Appendix for further discussion of these):

> Thank you very much for your kind letter. I am extremely pleased that you want to come. I have a rehearsal on 26 September at 10 a.m., then on 27th at around 11 a.m., and on the 29th (concert day) also at around 11 a.m. Would you allow the last bars to be played by all *12* trumpets? And is it intentional that the bassoons do not play in the last movement? I am delighted that you are coming and only hope that you will be satisfied with the performance. With respect, your most devoted Klemperer.... . Please telegraph your arrival and Berlin address.[34]

This letter was followed by a telegram on 24 September, asking if Janáček could arrive in Berlin by 27 September at the latest to attend the rehearsal

---

[32] Gracian Černušák ['–k']: 'Z brněnských koncertů, Brno 4. dubna', *Lidové noviny*, 5 April 1927, p. 7.
[33] Telegram from Klemperer to Janáček, BmJA, B 1254.
[34] Letter from Klemperer to Janáček, BmJA, D 279.

Plate 16. Janáček and Otto Klemperer after the Berlin premiere, 29 September 1927 (Janáček Archive, Brno).

that day, since little could be changed at the final rehearsal on the day of the concert. In the end Janáček set out for Berlin on 28 September, arriving in the early evening, and he was present at the final rehearsal as well as the performance itself. The visit was recalled by Hans Curjel (1896–1974), Klemperer's dramaturg at the Kroll Opera:

> Janáček arrived for the concert. He got off the train in the morning, a stocky man with a gentle but distinctly sculpted head, naturally wavy white hair and deep blue eyes. We walked from the station to the hotel. Janáček seemed oblivious to the hustle and bustle of the city. In the afternoon he came to the dress rehearsal. It was amazing to watch how he reacted to his own music, standing in an empty auditorium, not correcting anything. Above all, he praised the clarity of the performance, and the fact that Klemperer avoided any exaggeration or undue pathos. The concert was a huge success. Janáček stood on the stage next to the conductor, a representative of the generation that also included Mahler, who was six years younger. The next day Janáček told us about working on his new opera *From the House of the Dead*. Nine months later he died, but we couldn't get out of our heads the idea of staging his opera based on Dostoevsky.[35]

Fascinating as this is – particularly for the description of Janáček at the rehearsal – Curjel's chronology is unreliable. Janáček's diary reveals a somewhat different sequence of events, noting that he was met by Fritz Zweig, and expressing his admiration for Klemperer's thorough preparation:

> Berlin.
>
> 1. Arrived at 5 p.m. Zweig was waiting. To the Askanischer Hof Hotel by walking through the Tiergarten park. Unter den Linden – the opera house not yet finished. Sleep at 9 p.m. Beautiful. Stars falling on to the street!
>
> 2. At 9.30, Zweig and Klemperer arrived. A tall man, severe! We went to the theatre. He sang and played through the whole *Sinfonietta* for me from memory. *From memory!* Tempo – except for the *Prestissimo* at [Fig.] 11[36] – good!! At eleven o'clock, the dress rehearsal:
>
> Bach – shaky (3rd movement poor)

---

[35] Hans Curjel, quoted in Eva Weissweiler: *Otto Klemperer. Ein deutsch-jüdisches Künstlerleben* (Cologne: Kiepenheuer und Witsch, 2010), pp. 201–2.

[36] Third movement, Fig. 11, bar 153. Janáček noted the same problem in rehearsals for the world premiere (see Chapter 1).

Mozart – excellent – Schnabel. Conversation with him before his performance.

Then my piece! – Superbly played!

...

Conversation about the *House of the Dead*. Klemperer wants to do it! Well, they talked me into it, although the stage seems small to me!

To the hotel. Conversation with the embassy. They will come!

3.30 [Emil] Pirchan arrived. The red flood at the end of Act III.[37]

In the café by 6 p.m.

7.30. A car arrived for the concert. [Heinz] Tietjen is the Intendant.

He was pleasant and already knew about the *House of the Dead*.

Mrs Klemperer dropped in. Kissing.

Tietjen astonished!

Prof. Soligen is with Nováková from Brno!

Chat about the German theatre in Brno!

Endless ovations! My piece was victorious!

...

Speeches by Klemperer and me.

Up until 2 o'clock. Signed a declaration for Universal Edition.

Klemperer wants me to orchestrate the *Diary of One Who Disappeared*.

To bed; get up at 6.30.

30 [September]: Leaving. Happy.[38]

The fact that Janáček was genuinely pleased is confirmed by the message he sent Gracian Černušák in Brno after the dress rehearsal: 'I can't believe that I composed the *Sinfonietta*! The performance under Klemperer is unmatched by anyone.'[39] This is high praise indeed, though it should be noted that Janáček was often excited immediately after hearing performances of his work and described several conductors as 'unrivalled' or 'the

---

[37] A reference to Act III of Pirchan's 1924 Berlin production of *Jenůfa* which Janáček had attended.
[38] Janáček's diary, BmJA Z 66, pp. 129–38.
[39] Postcard from Janáček to Černušák, BmJA, A 6518.

best', some of whom he later criticised. Still, he was evidently prepared to sanction Klemperer's reinforcement of the trumpets at the end of the piece and clearly admired Klemperer's thorough knowledge of the work ('from memory!'). Curjel's reminiscence suggests that Janáček was also happy with Klemperer's interpretative approach to the *Sinfonietta*, while Janáček's diary praises his choice of tempi – something that might appear to lend a special interest to Klemperer's two surviving recordings (see Chapter 4). The whole occasion evidently gave the composer real pleasure. Heinrich Strobel reviewed the concert for *Musikblätter des Anbruch*:

> Klemperer's first programme: Bach's first D major suite [i.e. No. 3], the D minor concerto by Mozart and (as a premiere) the *Sinfonietta* by Janáček, given in the densely packed Kroll Opera. Janáček is certainly first and foremost a dramatist. In all of his concert works, you can feel the peculiar motifs of his dramatic technique on a smaller scale. They all have something improvisatory about them. But what we love about him is the folk-like, fresh, cheerful quality. Almost a miracle: the development of the seventy-year-old Czech master leads us ever deeper into the present. In this *Sinfonietta*, which is much more of a dance suite, there are even hints of Stravinsky in the fourth movement with its ostinato trumpet melody. There is all the freshness of a style of music-making deeply rooted in folklore, and the delicate sonorities that always captivate with Janáček. There are lyrical elements too, but the bouncing dance melody of the wind instruments, always reflected in new colours, prevails with the most dazzling variety. At the beginning and end of the work we hear festive fanfares played by a large brass choir, giving the flowing sequence of movements a formal unity. It reaches a pinnacle of splendour, but never becomes excessive – especially when it is played with the vitality Klemperer brings to it. The evening was a tremendous public success: for the conductor, for Artur Schnabel, and for Janáček.[40]

Much the same enthusiasm can be found in the review with appeared in the *Berliner Volks-Zeitung*:

> Otto Klemperer, one of the strongest personalities among living conductors alongside Furtwängler and [Bruno] Walter, appeared on stage for his first symphony concert at the head of the Staatskapelle, which he had reorganised... . He was greeted with loud applause and the audience he has already won over will quickly grow. He is a tall man,

---

[40] Heinrich Strobel: 'Das erste Klemperer-Konzert in Berlin', *Musikblätter des Anbruch*, vol. 9, no. 10 (December 1927), p. 431.

unconcerned with elegant movements but completely devoted to the music. He knows how to captivate his audience and, above all, his orchestra.... The new piece was Janáček's *Sinfonietta*. Its music, which was in part very original, vibrant and with popular appeal, was performed in a virtuoso and effective manner. The composer was present and was able to enjoy a complete success.[41]

The music critic for the *Berliner Tageblatt* was the great Mozart scholar Alfred Einstein; his perceptive comments on the *Sinfonietta* – and his delighted reactions to it – make for particularly interesting reading:

> The novelty of the evening, which was also absolutely perfect for demonstrating the true virtuosity of the conductor and orchestra, was the *Sinfonietta* by Leoš Janáček, composed in 1925 [*recte* 1926], the work of a seventy-two-year-old. Well, there is no sign of age here: it is downright delightful in the youthfulness of its material.... It is called a sinfonietta ... and it does not have the discursive form of a symphony, although it has a certain thematic unity, a cyclical structure – one of the most surprising and pleasing ideas is when the opening, typically suite-like trumpet movement returns at the end in full orchestral splendour. The character of the first [i.e. the second], a 'sonata' movement is followed by a sensitive slow movement, then a scherzo shimmers quietly, just as the personality of Janáček shines through the cheerful objectivity of this musical language. The whole work resembles a kind of folk speech; the spoken dialect is Moravian, perhaps even specifically from Brno, and one listens with delight and amazement to these little turns of phrase with their drollness, quirkiness, and intimacies; they are both strange and yet immediately understandable. The most astonishing and enchanting thing for the musician is the instrumental garb in which Janáček clothes his ideas: from the trumpet and timpani blast of the 'Intrada' to the woodwind trills of the last movement, it is of an originality and freshness that proves Janáček has never read an instrumentation method. Instead, he establishes a new one that is entirely his own. One can no longer speak of the 'uprooting of art in our time' when such a master is still at work: he is a kind of miracle, just as Bruckner was a miracle in the age of Brahms and Wagner.[42]

After Janáček left Berlin, he sent a postcard from Prague thanking Klemperer for the performance. The conductor replied on 11 October, 'We are

---

[41] H.P.: 'Otto Klemperer: der neue Herr in der Kroll-Oper', *Berliner Volks-Zeitung*, Abend-Ausgabe, 30 September 1927, p. 2.

[42] Alfred Einstein: 'Das erste Sinfoniekonzert der Staatskapelle', *Berliner Tageblatt*, Abend-Ausgabe, 30 September 1927, pp. 2–3.

still profoundly impressed by your brilliant work, and delighted that you were here, and happy.'[43]

14 and 16 October 1927
Frankfurt-am-Main, Opera House. Opernhaus- und Museums-Orchester, conducted by Clemens Krauss.

Mendelssohn: *The Fair Melusine* Overture
Chopin: Piano Concerto in E minor (Emil von Sauer)
Janáček: *Sinfonietta*
Strauss: *Till Eulenspiegel*

The Austrian conductor Clemens Krauss (1893–1954) introduced the *Sinfonietta* to Frankfurt in the second Friday and Sunday Museum Concerts of the 1927–8 season. The programme listed the complete orchestration of the Janáček including '14 trumpets, of which two are bass trumpets'. On 19 October 1927, Janáček wrote to Hertka that 'the *Frankfurter Zeitung* is said to have written very nice things about the *Sinfonietta*',[44] and the critic for the *Frankfurter General-Anzeiger* commented that 'Krauss, with the support of the orchestra, achieved a great success with the new work.'[45] A review of musical activities in Frankfurt by Artur Bogen was published in the *Kölnische Zeitung* a few weeks later (17 November 1927) in which he noted, 'In the Frankfurt Museum Society, under Clemens Krauss, modern music is now becoming more and more evident in the programmes... . The second concert was an opportunity for Leoš Janáček's *Sinfonietta* to be heard – and to make an impact with its captivating and powerful sound.'[46]

18 November 1927
Broadcast, Deutsche Stunde in Bayern [Munich].
21:05, 'Sinfoniekonzert'. The performers not identified but were almost certainly the Munich Radio Orchestra, conducted by Franz Adam (see *Radio-welt*, 1927, No. 46, p. 41).
Deutsche Stunde in Bayern was the precursor of Bayersicher Rundfunk.

---

[43] Letter from Klemperer to Janáček, BmJA, D 274.
[44] LJUE, p. 328.
[45] LJUE, p. 329.
[46] Artur Bogen: 'Aus dem Frankfurter Musikleben', *Kölnische Zeitung*, 17 November 1927, p. 8.

19 December 1927
Broadcast, Deutsche Stunde in Bayern [Munich].
20:00, 'Konzert des Rundfunkorchesters', Munich Radio Orchestra, almost certainly conducted by Franz Adam (*Radiowelt*, 1927, no. 51, p. 34).

15 January 1928
Broadcast, Deutsche Stunde in Bayern [Munich].
17:00: 'Konzert des Rundfunkorchesters', Munich Radio Orchestra, conducted by Franz Adam (*Radiowelt*, no. 2, p. 25; *Radio Wien*, vol. 4, no. 16, 13 January 1928).[47]

British premiere:
10 February 1928
London, Queen's Hall. BBC National Symphony Concert, conducted by Henry Wood.

Berlioz: *Carnaval romain* Overture
Debussy: *Prélude à l'après-midi d'un faune*
Janáček: *Sinfonietta*
Wagner: Bridal procession from *Lohengrin*
Haydn: Cello Concerto in D major (Raya Garbousova)
Edward Mitchell: Fantasy-Overture
Strauss: *Don Juan*

Sir Henry Wood conducted the British premiere of the *Sinfonietta* on 10 February 1928 at a BBC National Symphony Concert in Queen's Hall, the first part of which – including the *Sinfonietta* – was broadcast live on the radio (up to the extract from *Lohengrin*). The *Radio Times* offered readers a brief account of Janáček's career, introducing a composer who was unknown to British radio listeners: this was the first work by Janáček ever to be broadcast by the BBC.

---

[47] In *Der Deutsche Rundfunk: Rundschau und Programme für alle Funkteilnehmer*, Franz Adam is identified as the conductor of this broadcast, and he almost certainly conducted the two previous Munich performances on 18 November 1927 and 19 December 1927. Adam was conductor of the Munich Radio Orchestra from 1924 to 1928. An enthusiastic Nazi (who joined the party in 1930), Adam went on to notoriety as founder (in 1931) and chief conductor of the Nationalsozialistische Reichs-Symphonie-Orchester, a position he held until the end of the war.

Janáček (born in 1854) is a Czechoslovakian composer who worked quietly away for a long time writing operas, before he became known outside his circle at Brno ... where he has taught and played the pianoforte and organ for many years. He was over sixty when his opera *Jenůfa* was produced. This has become well known in his own country and in Austria and Germany, and has also been performed in America. Janáček's study of folk music (about which he has written a book) has led him to seek a new type of vocal music for his operas, founded on the natural inflections of the speech and song of the folk, the influence of whose dance and song-tunes is to be found in most of his instrumental pieces.

After meeting the composer during his London visit in 1926 (and subsequently encouraged by their mutual friend Rosa Newmarch), Wood became an enthusiastic advocate for Janáček's music, soon following the *Sinfonietta* with the British premieres of *Taras Bulba* (Queen's Hall, 16 October 1928), the *Lachian Dances* (Queen's Hall, 19 August 1930) and the *Glagolitic Mass* (Norwich Festival, 23 October 1930).

British press reaction to the *Sinfonietta* was mixed, largely because Janáček's musical language seemed to baffle the London critics of the time. Even so, the unnamed reviewer in the *Daily Telegraph* found plenty to enjoy:

> Once more to the British Broadcasting Corporation we owe the first performance in England of an important work by a composer of European reputation. The work was a *Sinfonietta* for full orchestra, produced under Sir Henry Wood's baton in Queen's Hall last night, and the composer, the veteran, Leoš Janáček. In his own country, the Czechoslovakian musician has now great honour, while the other day at Leipzig was celebrated the seventieth performance of his opera *Jenůfa*; in ours his name is yet scarcely known to the ordinary amateur. That such an extremely virile, lively, passionate modern work as this *Sinfonietta* which dates from 1925 [recte 1926] (and is dedicated to Mrs Rosa Newmarch) should have emanated from the brain of an artist who had already passed his allotted span of three score years and ten is surprising, until we remember that Verdi had reached a still greater age when he completed his crowning achievement.
>
> Janáček, for this, requires a big and exceptional orchestra. No fewer than twelve trumpets are demanded, nine in C and three in F; two tenor tubas and one bass trumpet; the tympani including a special military specimen upon which can be sounded a high B flat. The work is in five movements: the first a sort of fanfare in which only the brass and percussion are engaged. It is a brilliant opening, strikingly

individual in idiom and colour and rhythm. Then there follows an Andante (in 4/8 measure), a Moderato, an Allegretto, and a final Allegro, each for the most part in 2/4. The style throughout is extremely terse and abrupt, the composer showing a pronounced partiality not only for a 2/4 measure or multiples of it, but for two-bar phrases, and it is as astonishing as it is amusing to observe how much variety he has been able to pack into a work so composed.

And the movements are practically formless. Each is a little rhapsody.... . Dance motives abound, but never come to much. The whole work, in fact, suggests a ballet. It is the kind of music that makes its appeal at once or not at all, according to the taste of the listener; and as the appeal is decidedly objective, and therefore obvious, it is not at all unlikely that the work will become a popular item in the repertory of full orchestras. But it will be an expensive one if all those trumpets and tubas are to be employed.[48]

In the *Manchester Guardian* the concert was reviewed by its London correspondent, Eric Blom. His criticisms of Janáček's musical style were often echoed in the British press until at least the 1950s. Even so, Blom gave the work a guarded welcome, while concluding that it was probably not of lasting significance.

The meaning of all those disjointed phrases, which are combined into a kind of musical mosaic, is not easily grasped and the lack of structural cohesion of each of the five movements which neither combine nor detach themselves decisively does not tend to make the impression any clearer. But while one is puzzled, one enjoys a bewilderment that comes in a great measure from the extraordinary originality of this veteran composer who ... somehow managed to be more modern and subversive than any of the musical *enfants terribles* in Paris or Vienna. The secret of this inventive freshness may probably be attributed to Janáček's detachment alike from old and new schools and movements. One feels that he is not 'advanced' from choice or by any theoretical reasoning, but simply because he happens to be one of the few truly enterprising and independent spirits among living creative musicians.

This artistic wilfulness is carried to sublimely impractical lengths. Apparently he does not even care whether his works can be readily be performed, for he calmly uses twelve trumpets in his score, which makes it quite impracticable under ordinary conditions... . This

---

[48] 'London Concerts: National Symphony Orchestra', *Daily Telegraph*, 11 February 1928.

work of Janáček's is full of alluring devices and surprising invention, but it is only one of music's minor adventures, not one of its great experiences.[49]

An unsigned review in *The Times* (probably by H. C. Colles) commented on the musical language in much the same way but also reckoned some allowance needed to be made in view of the under-rehearsed performance:

> Janáček's music is defiant. His *Sinfonietta* in five movements begins and ends with a fanfare of many trumpets battering at the ears. Between its two appearances he has said a great many things. He has sported with dance tunes which might have been picked up on the village green, toyed with decorative arabesques on the woodwind, relapsed into a more reflective mood in a slow movement of considerable beauty, and brushed that away in turn with the trombones bursting into a tune that might have come from Verdi's 'worst opera'. Janáček's music sometimes gives one the sensation of listening to a humorous speech in a language that one only imperfectly understands. One misses points; on the other hand, one is afraid of finding humour where none is intended. Janáček is disconcerting because he appears so simple-minded. Can he really be as simple as all that? At any rate, he is a composer who cannot leave the hearer indifferent. His music is never vague; his brusque, disjointed phrases remain in the mind after a first hearing.
>
> Something must be allowed for a rough and rather perilous performance. The BBC had not given the same amount of rehearsal to Janáček that they lavished on Schoenberg before their last concert. The players were grappling with what must have been an entirely new idiom ... and only Sir Henry's untiring alertness brought them safely through.[50]

The critic Michel-Dimitri Calvocoressi (a friend of Ravel and fellow member of *Les Apaches*) was enchanted by the *Sinfonietta*, reviewing Wood's performance for *Musical Times*. After lamenting the neglect of Janáček's music, he wrote, 'He is a most genially imaginative, clever, straightforward composer; and it might be added, considering the fact that the delightful *Sinfonietta* under notice was written in 1925 [*recte* 1926], one whose mind seems endowed with the privilege of never-fading youth. Whether he is as successful in earnest moods as in moods of mere play, I

---

[49] Eric Blom ['E.B.']: 'A Musical Mosaic: *Sinfonietta*, a New Work by Leo [!] Janáček', *Manchester Guardian*, 11 February 1928.

[50] 'National Symphony Concert: Janáček's *Sinfonietta*', *The Times*, 11 February 1928.

cannot say at present; but for lightness and sheer joy ... his music belongs to the most attractive I know.'[51]

One report of this concert is of particular significance: the eye-witness account sent to the composer by the work's dedicatee, Rosa Newmarch, three days after the performance. On 13 February 1928, she wrote to Janáček:

> Dear Mistr,
>
> Well, you have had a great week here! On Tuesday, Feb. 7th your Concertino was played at the Gerald Cooper Concerts... . Then, on Friday, February 10th, Henry Wood conducted your Sinfonietta at the Broadcasting Concert in the Queen´s Hall. *My* Sinfonietta was splendidly played; the trumpets and trombones and tubas were all excellent. Sir Henry, who is very delighted with the originality and freshness of the work took *great* trouble over the performance. *I* felt very proud that it was dedicated to me. The slow movement is beautiful; but the second movement and the last give me most pleasure. It is not true that the performance was 'rough'; for a *first* performance it was remarkably good. The number of players needed for the brass is certainly a difficulty in the way of playing it in the provinces, but I feel sure Henry Wood will repeat it when the opportunity occurs. At any rate it has done a great deal to advance your fame here.
>
> Now I will work to get the *Mass* performed, as soon as Universal Edition sends it to me... . I will send you some more press notices if they are worth having. But critics are a mixture of stupidity and fear. They seemed to enjoy your music very much at the rehearsal, and then, when it was a question of writing about it, none had the courage of his opinion! They are frightened of everything new, these gentlemen! But nevertheless, it has been a victory for you.[52]

Janáček replied to Newmarch five days later, on 18 February: 'I am happy about the performance of the *Sinfonietta*. Be so good and give my warm thanks to Sir Henry Wood. I am very grateful to him... . A week ago [12 February], the *Sinfonietta* was also performed in Vienna and was successful. I am glad of it. I wrote it as if it were a play-thing.'[53] This last sentence suggests that Janáček had genuinely enjoyed composing the work, perhaps because the ideas flowed so quickly and fluently.

---

[51] Michel-Dimitri Calvocoressi: 'BBC National Symphony Concert', *Musical Times*, 1 March 1928, pp. 257–8.
[52] BmJA, D 1382. Not in Fischmann.
[53] Fischmann, pp. 155–6.

6 February 1928
Darmstadt, Hessisches Landestheater. Fifth Symphony Concert, conducted by Karl Böhm.

Beethoven: *The Ruins of Athens* Overture
Mozart: Piano Concerto in D minor K466 (Dorothea Braus)
Ravel: *Le Tombeau de Couperin*
Janáček: *Sinfonietta*

This was one of several performances given in Germany in the early months of 1928: The critic for the *Darmstädter Tagblatt* (identified only as 'F.N.') found nothing to enjoy in the *Sinfonietta* in spite of a well-prepared performance, largely because of Janáček's unconventional handling of form and orchestration: for some Germanic sensibilities his unorthodox writing was evidently beyond the pale. This was certainly not a consistently held view (see, for instance, the reviews of Klemperer's Berlin performance above; or Josef Krips's Karlsruhe performance below), but clearly Janáček was never going to satisfy this Darmstadt critic:

> The last work to be performed was the *Sinfonietta* by Leoš Janáček, whose opera *Jenůfa* was performed here a few years ago. In that, Janáček showed himself to be an artist who was inspired as much by folk music as by a deep understanding of the country and people of his homeland, but he shows a quite different side in the *Sinfonietta*. With a certain stubbornness, themes are set up and developed that, in our opinion, are not suitable for symphonic treatment; they are mostly played on brass instruments, which, when repeated frequently ... become monotonous. Sudden contrasts of the strongest kind confront one another. Typical of his style is the emotional, almost sentimental, slow middle movement, in which, after real warmth, softer trombone sounds alternate with shrill, fast interludes. At times the instrumental groups are sharply differentiated in terms of sound. The beginning and end are connected by the same theme and the same monotonous brass and timpani. We admit that this *Sinfonietta* is completely alien to us, though we thought it would be going too far to disrupt its performance ... and to demonstrate our disapproval by fleeing the theatre before the end of the last movement. But despite objections to the work, it must be admitted that Dr Karl Böhm had prepared it meticulously, with very thorough rehearsal. As far as one can judge from a first hearing, the performance was extremely precise and the orchestra gave of its best to make it a success.[54]

[54] 'F.N.': 'Hessisches Landestheater. Grosses Haus – Montag, den 6 Februar 1928. 5. Sinfonie-Konzert', *Darmstädter Tagblatt*, 7 February 1928, p. 3.

According to Ernst Hilmar,[55] another performance took place on the same day (6 February) in Magdeburg, conducted by Walther Beck.

Vienna premiere
12 February 1928
Vienna, Konzerthaus. Vienna Symphony Orchestra, conducted by Jascha Horenstein.

Haydn: Symphony No. 82 in C ('The Bear')
Mendelssohn: Violin Concerto (Henri Marteau)
Janáček: *Sinfonietta*

Janáček wrote to Kamila Stösslová on 8 February 1928 that 'they' (probably UE) had invited him 'to go to Vienna for Sunday. They're giving my War Sinfonietta there.[56] It's not a first-class orchestra playing it and I don't even know who's conducting it. So I won't be going as I know I wouldn't find heaven there.'[57] On 11 February, the day before the performance, the conductor Jascha Horenstein sent Janáček a telegram about the concert the next day: 'I invite you, dear master, to personally attend the premiere of your *Sinfonietta* tomorrow, Sunday, at the Konzerthaus. Your presence would bring extraordinary joy to everyone. Jascha Horenstein, Neustiftgasse 64.' At such short notice, Janáček was not able to attend – and as he had already told Kamila a few days earlier, he had no intention of going. But this Viennese premiere was intriguing for social as well as musical reasons. It was given at the height of 'Red Vienna' (*Rotes Wien*), shorthand for the social, architectural and cultural policies enacted in the city under the control of the Social Democratic Workers' Party. One of the most enduring monuments of *Rotes Wien* – the immense Karl-Marx-Hof in Heiligenstadt – was under construction at this time. The Arbeiter-Symphoniekonzerte – Workers' Symphony Concerts – were founded in 1905 by David Josef Bach with the aim of presenting serious music to working-class audiences, and from 1922 onwards Anton Webern became a leading figure in the organisation. The concerts were played by the Wiener Symphoniker. A review appeared in the Vienna *Arbeiter-Zeitung*, which played an important role as the semi-official organ of *Rotes Wien* and the Austrian Social Democrats.

---

[55] LJUE, p. 347.
[56] Janáček wrote *válečnou* (war) rather than *vojenskou* (military). This might have been a slip of the pen, but either way it's interesting: after publication of the score in January 1927, he usually referred to it by the shorter title of *Sinfonietta*.
[57] BmJA E00571. HŽ, no. 582.

With that in mind, it is fascinating to read the comments of the paper's critic (identified only as 'pp') about the appeal of the *Sinfonietta* to a working-class audience:

> The public's reception of Janáček's new *Sinfonietta* at the last Workers' Symphony Concert proved as well as ever that the future of new music is closely linked to the cultural rise of the working class. Janáček's work, whose success with a bourgeois audience was by no means a given, immediately found its way to the hearts of workers. This may be because the art of the venerable Czech composer is directly rooted in the people. It is said that in his Moravian hometown, Janáček is often encountered on the street with a musical notebook in which he records the sounds of everyday life, the melodies of his compatriots' speech and their simple and natural ways. From these elements, which are not invented but found, Janáček then creates his great works, his operas, choral music and symphonic pieces.
>
> In the new *Sinfonietta*, a five-movement work, one can detect this natural, elemental motivic material in every movement… . But Janáček does not limit himself to the raw material. He dresses it in the splendid garb of clear but by no means straightforward harmony and envelops it in the intoxicating sounds of orchestral instruments, mixed in a quite extraordinary way. The first movement is scored only for brass and timpani. One has the vision of rustic music, or perhaps the brass band of a Czech legion, which gradually comes together to sing a folk song – one of those tunes that has the softness of the Moravian landscape as well as the ability to build up to triumphant jubilation. There is, of course, also a structure to this movement, not based on the classical models, but on those of French Impressionism. The melodic elements are repeated, simply strung together and not developed into larger units as in the classics. There are also no counter-melodies in the strict sense, but the figures that accompany and play around the melody are derived from the accompanying chords. This means that Janáček's music remains easy to understand, even if the chords and their sequences are not simple. The second movement has a dance-like character. In the third, the strings start an infinitely yearning melody, which is soon replaced by livelier motifs. The fourth movement, similar to the scherzo of a classical symphony, is based on a trumpet motif that might have been overheard from a peasant dance. It whirled past in breathless haste and aroused the thunderous applause of the listeners, who had also received the earlier movements with great interest.[58]
>
> In the final movement, the *Sinfonietta* is crowned by the music of the

---

[58] An intriguing comment which suggests that there was enthusiastic applause after each movement.

large brass ensemble that opened it – now closing it accompanied by all the other instruments.

Kapellmeister Jascha Horenstein conducted the concert. A few years ago, he conducted a Vienna Workers' Symphony Concert, at that time a young, still unknown artist. In the meantime, he has gone to Germany, where he has become well-known and respected in Berlin. Now he has returned to the place where he first worked, matured but still full of youthful passion. With its extreme technical difficulties, he presented Janáček *Sinfonietta* clearly to the audience, and placed particular emphasis on the moods of its individual movements... . He is a conductor who is able to imbue every work he performs with the strong mark of his musical personality.[59]

1 March 1928
Halle, Stadtschützenhaus. Berlin Philharmonic, conducted by Georg Göhler.

Bruckner: Symphony No. 3
Janáček: *Sinfonietta*
Wagner: *Tannhäuser* Overture

This was the hundredth Philharmonic concert in Halle – the fifth of the 1927–8 season – but one local critic, Martin Frey, did not consider any of the works on the programme to be appropriate choices for a celebration, though he found a few things to admire in the new work.

> The *Sinfonietta* by Leoš Janáček, the leading Czech composer, makes it clear that he is a passionate admirer of folk song. His love for these national treasures is understandable, but in the *Sinfonietta* they do not quite fit into the formal framework, appearing somewhat uneasy in this environment. The contrasts and opposites sometimes clash sharply, but the unique instrumental colour of the five movements – each with its own characteristic instrumentation – ensures a rich variety. Light, witty ideas predominate, and some are extremely interesting. But the true Janáček is revealed in his long singing themes which leave the listener with a feeling of regret – they seem to disappear too soon, never to be heard again... . The whole piece is something of a musical kaleidoscope and the designation *Sinfonietta* is questionable: its

---

[59] 'pp': 'Arbeiter-Symphoniekonzert', *Arbeiter-Zeitung*, 14 February 1928, p. 9.

characteristics are partly national, partly impressionistic. The work was very well played and well received by the audience.[60]

Rudolf Donath in the *Hallische Nachrichten* was extremely enthusiastic about the *Sinfonietta*, and he clearly relished the features of Janáček's music that many critics struggled with, particularly the 'secret beauty' of his hard-edged orchestral sonorities and the unquenchable energy of the music:

> Janáček's *Sinfonietta* is a phenomenal work – by a seventy-two-year-old, but not a work of old age full of fatigue and resignation. Janáček is still a fighter in the front rank of European composers. In him, the struggle for a new, lively style has no problematic aftertaste. For it is fed by the fresh springs of Czech folklore, without straying into the banal. If we wanted to label Janáček, we could call him a Stravinsky (from the period of *Petrushka*) liquefied by melody. The formal element is much less important in his work. Basic elements are concise rhythms ... and vibrant colours – not painterly impressionistic ones but composed of pure instrumental tones. Some shrill sounds may not immediately reveal their secret beauty, but as in real life, things are sometimes unruly in the *Sinfonietta* – made up of people for whom the countryside is still healthy working soil rather than a holiday destination. And we can only hope that at 72, we might have the same freshness, energy and – above all – frank humour and *joie de vivre* of Janáček... . In Georg Göhler's performance, the work sparkled with colour and joy, basking in warm lyricism for the more expansive passages.[61]

6 March 1928
Karlsruhe, Landestheater. Badische Landestheater-Orchesters, conducted by Josef Krips.

Janáček: *Sinfonietta*
Braunfels: Piano Concerto (Walter Braunfels)
Beethoven: Symphony No. 2 (in place of Berg's Orchestral Pieces which
    were originally announced)

Originally this programme was to have started with Janáček and ended with Alban Berg, either side of Walter Braunfels playing his piano concerto.

[60] Martin Frey: '5. Philharmonisches Konzert', *Saale-Zeitung: Allgemeine-Zeitung für Mitteldeutschland*, 3 March 1928, p. 4.
[61] Rudolf Donath: '100. Konzert der Philharmonie: Göhler und die Berliner Philharmoniker', *Hallische Nachrichten*, 2 March 1928, p. 2.

The Berg was changed to Beethoven late in the day, but Janáček remained on the programme. One critic offered an interesting corrective to those who questioned Janáček's unorthodoxy and his handling of form:

> Janáček comes directly from Mussorgsky, the composer of *Boris Godunov*... . The orchestration of the *Sinfonietta* is extraordinarily expressive, but despite the brilliant and sometimes exaggerated splendour of instrumental colours, the form is never unclear or blurred in its contours. Janáček is not a composer who scorns form. Sharply defined rhythms, with many variations, work as a natural binding agent. Despite some of the complexities, these five movements have many captivating moments. The power which emanates from Janáček's music is full of boldness, natural power and distinction.[62]

16 March 1928
Dresden, Semper Opera House. Dresden Staatskapelle, conducted by Fritz Busch.

Janáček: *Sinfonietta*
Mozart: Sinfonia concertante K364 (Francis Koene, Alfred Spitzner)
Brahms: Symphony No. 2

Described in *Musikblätter des Anbruch* (May 1928) as a 'sensational success', this Dresden performance, under one of the finest conductors of the interwar years, was very warmly received in the local press, though Janáček was not present and no correspondence survives between Janáček and Busch. John Tyrrell noted that they met in Prague in the spring of 1926 to discuss the possibility of staging the German premiere of *The Cunning Little Vixen* in Dresden (a plan that came to nothing).[63] A long review by Karl Schönewolf in the *Dresdner neueste Nachrichten* gave the work an enthusiastic welcome, adding some perceptive comments on Janáček's stylistic development.

> Fritz Busch performed the *Sinfonietta* by the Czech composer Leoš Janáček yesterday with every sign of a great success and greeted with vigorous acclaim. The work deserves it... . The forces that flow into Janáček from folk song (they flow particularly richly in Bohemia and Moravia), spare the composer from resorting to theoretical

[62] 'St.': 'Badisches Landestheater, Achtes Sinfoniekonzert', *Der Volksfreund*, 9 March 1928, p. 4.
[63] JYL2, p. 585.

experiments. They are the lifeblood of his work... . Janáček wrote this *Sinfonietta* four [*recte* two] years ago. It has unbelievable youthfulness, unbelievable boldness, and is elemental in its invention and design. Only Verdi's genius could still be so youthful at such an age. And who – among his contemporaries from any country – is as forward-looking as the Moravian Janáček?

He draws his elemental power (not unlike the Hungarian Bartók) from his national folk tradition – and his international importance comes from the uniqueness of that tradition... . Elements of folk music are everywhere in this *Sinfonietta*, which represents an enormous and significant step beyond the style of *Jenůfa*. The folk tunes become the themes of the symphony, and they are integrated into the work's architecture, becoming the natural ornaments of an impressive building. There is no dead space in this *Sinfonietta*. It compels attention from first note to last. It begins grandly with a festive, extremely splendid movement for brass and timpani... . There then follow tone paintings which seem to evoke a more bitter mood. This is always done by purely musical means, never 'programmatically', in dazzling colours – and it is always an expression of a brilliant personality. A sure sign of this is the slow movement. Disciples of jazz have forgotten how to write an *Adagio*. But here it becomes music of lavish inner richness. It is here above all that a new synthesis of Classicism and Romanticism is achieved. The grandiose climax in the finale, in which the opening theme returns, confirms this. This is a rare work, the importance of which will perhaps only be recognised in years to come.

In Fritz Busch the *Sinfonietta* found a congenial interpreter. He understands the immense orchestral sonorities that performing this work requires. And he enjoys the bold, far-flung harmonies that makes this piece so appealing. Fritz Busch's performance should have aroused great delight in every listener, and it certainly did so in those who recognise the genius of this Czech composer. Is it a coincidence that this great musician is only now beginning to make a name for himself?[64]

This very warm response was echoed by Janáček's acquaintance Bjarnat Krawc-Schneider (1861–1948). He had written to Janáček on 12 March telling him about the performance and offering him accommodation. Janáček didn't go to Dresden, but after the concert, Krawc-Schneider sent a press cutting (possibly the one quoted above) and his own reactions.

---

[64] Karl Schönenwolf: 'Janáček's Sinfonietta im Opernkonzert', *Dresdner neueste Nachrichten*, 18 March 1928, pp. 3–4.

I am sending you the review from our main newspaper. The *Sinfonietta* made a deep impression. I would like to hear it three times in a row to fully understand the piece: it is something quite extraordinary! I bought the score and am studying it diligently. The audience at the concert really didn't know what to make of the piece. They wondered if there was a touch of Honegger with his realism (locomotive![65]), perhaps also some nationalism! ... Busch was excellent. I send you a tumultuous 'Bravo!'[66]

However, news reached Janáček that the reception of the Dresden performance was much more mixed than these reports suggest – something that evidently rather pleased the composer: on 28 March, he wrote to Kamila saying, 'There was a row during the performance of my *Sinfonietta* in Dresden. Some clapped, others whistled. But the first group won. It makes me feel good that people fight over the value of my work. It's good I wasn't there – I'd have probably got involved.'[67]

27 May 1928
Brno, Municipal Theatre, as part of the Exhibition of Contemporary Culture. Brno National Theatre Orchestra, conducted by František Neumann. Janáček present.
Broadcast live on Czech Radio.

Ostrčil: *Summer*
Novák: *Toman and the Wood Nymph*[68]
Bella: *Fate and the Ideal*
Janáček: *Sinfonietta*

The last performance Janáček heard of the *Sinfonietta* was in Brno on 27 May 1928, at a concert given as part of the musical programme of the city's Exhibition of Contemporary Culture, which ran from May to September. The opening ceremony had taken place the previous day, on 26 May, when Ferdinand Vach's Moravian Teachers' Choir performed music by Josef Bohuslav Foerster, and there were 'ceremonial fanfares' by Janáček – presumably the Fanfares of the *Sinfonietta*. The whole event was broadcast on

---

[65] A reference to Honegger's *Pacific 231*, which depicts a steam locomotive.
[66] Letter to Janáček dated 21 March 1928, BmJA B00874.
[67] HŽ/IL, no. 619.
[68] The programme listing in *Radio-Journal* (26 May 1928, p. 5) begins with Novák, followed by Ostrčil.

the radio. The next morning, at 10:00 a.m., František Neumann conducted a concert including the *Sinfonietta*. Whereas the previous day's events had been very well attended, this poorly advertised concert – though broadcast – drew only a pitifully small audience, as noted by an understandably disappointed composer in his diary: 'A gala concert of the *Sinfonietta*. 56 audience members in the theatre! No one from the Exhibition Committee, no one from the theatre management.'

Writing in *Lidové noviny*, Gracian Černušák praised Neumann's conducting and expressed outrage at the apathy of the Brno public:

> The Exhibition of Contemporary Culture is a state undertaking, but it is taking place in Brno, the capital of Moravia. It was therefore only right that the great creative phenomenon of Leoš Janáček – in opera and symphonic music – was emphasised above all. The national character of the exhibition was clearly underlined in the programme... . Next to Ostrčil's *Summer*, Novák's symphonic poem *Toman and the Wood Nymph* and Janáček's *Sinfonietta*, [Jan Levoslav] Bella's symphonic poem *Fate and the Ideal* was included as the greatest artistic expression of a Slovak composer in the symphonic field, although in terms of its date of composition [1874], this work certainly seemed – despite its indisputable value – out of character with the present day... . The noble language and delicate poetics of Ostrčil's composition, Bella's neo-romantic pathos, Novák's concentrated vigour and Janáček's folk-like combativeness found vivid expression in the conductor's conception and in the orchestra's performance, although the orchestra did not play well.
>
> Why? It is downright shameful that all these efforts, carefully prepared and undertaken with the best of intentions, met with pitiful inattention from the audience, who apparently do not realise that an exhibition of contemporary culture is not just an occasion for folk festivities in an amusement park, but is primarily intended to demonstrate a lively interest in the fruits of Czech creativity. It has become clear that while serious musical undertakings draw support primarily from foreign visitors to the exhibition, they cannot rely on a permanent Brno audience. However, there is a danger that visitors, primarily interested in the exhibitions, will also overlook one of the most valuable components of contemporary Czech culture... . We must fight for it with all our might.[69]

---

[69] Gracian Černušák ['–k']: 'Kulturní kronika: Hudba o jubilejní výstavě', *Lidové noviny*, 29 May 1928.

The Sinfonietta *in Janáček's Lifetime: A Chronicle* 107

10 June 1928
Cologne, Grossen Halle im Rheinpark. Gürzenich Orchestra, conducted by Hermann Abendroth.

Bach: Opening chorus of Cantata No. 43, *Gott fähret auf mit Jauchzen*
Weber: 'Ocean, thou mighty monster' from *Oberon* (Dussolina Giannini)
Verdi: 'Ave Maria' from *Otello* (Dussolina Giannini)
Tchaikovsky: Joan's aria from *The Maid of Orleans* (Dussolina Giannini)
Bruckner: Symphony No. 5
Janáček: *Sinfonietta*

The opening concert of the Ninety-Seventh Lower Rhine Music Festival, this very substantial programme included what was described in announcements as the *Westdeutsche Erstaufführung* of the *Sinfonietta*. The same announcement also gave details of the dress rehearsal (at 8:00 p.m. on 9 June). The critic for the *Aachener Anzeiger* (identified only as 'H.S.') praised Dussolina Giannini's singing of the three operatic arias and then turned to the orchestral works on the programme. This review was an unwelcome reminder that Cologne had a tradition of hostility to Janáček's music: a few years earlier, critics had savaged *Jenůfa* and *Káťa Kabanová* when Klemperer introduced them at Cologne Opera.

> Janáček and Bruckner! One cannot imagine greater contrasts. In the former, whose *Sinfonietta* for large orchestra is being heard here in the West of Germany for the first time, dissonances with unclear motifs and noisy fanfares, and in Bruckner everything focused on beauty of sound, heavenly harmony, truth, chastity and purity. Janáček is the composer of *Jenůfa*, which was performed in Cologne years ago and then disappeared into obscurity. It is clear that Cologne, as an important musical city, must perform new works in the orchestral literature, otherwise it would appear backward. But, hand on heart, where have we come in modern orchestral music? Is this the music of the future? Can the works of musical newcomers raise the heart to heavenly heights? Is it not an illusion to say that this music speaks to the heart? It is not worth discussing the *Sinfonietta* any further here. Suffice it to say that there are only a few passages in the whole work that satisfy the ear and heart, to a limited extent. In the third movement – Moderato – the composer makes a fine start, but it is over after just a few bars. The orchestra under Abendroth is to be admired; it played the very difficult work with superb control. Needless to say, there was sporadic applause from a small group of enthusiasts. The

majority of the audience stayed to the end, but some openly expressed their dissatisfaction.[70]

There was a more positive view in the *Düsseldorfer Stadt-Anzeiger*, though the critic questioned Janáček's unorthodoxy:

> Only one contemporary composer was on the programme: Leoš Janáček, who hails from beyond the Bohemian Forests. In his *Sinfonietta* for orchestra, down-to-earth folk music bubbles up, unpurified, and lit by the iridescent colours of modern orchestral writing. There is no doubt that a true musician's blood flows in Janáček's veins – one thinks of his *Jenůfa* – but the symphonic design here is not so convincing. The love of colour is stronger than the handling of form. But the significantly enlarged orchestra – especially the brass – sounds so noble in tone, so delicate in colour and so clear in the sonority of the ensemble, that there is still plenty of good material for festive enjoyment. Abendroth was greatly acclaimed.[71]

With at least twenty performances between the premiere in June 1926 and Janáček's death on 12 August 1928, the *Sinfonietta* was well on the way to becoming Janáček's most frequently performed orchestral work, enjoying success in Germany and the United States as well as in Prague and Brno. The next chapter examines how it subsequently became established in the international concert repertory in the years that followed.

---

[70] 'H.S.': '97. Niederrheinisches Musikfest. Köln, 10 Juni 1928', *Aachener Anzeiger*, 12 June 1928, p. 5.
[71] '–ter': 'Das Niederrhenische Musikfest in Köln. Erster Tag', *Düsseldorfer Stadt-Anzeiger*, 12 June 1928, p. 9.

3
The *Sinfonietta* Makes its Way into the Repertory, 1928–45

Czechoslovakia: Prague and Brno

Although Václav Talich conducted the world premiere of the *Sinfonietta*, that occasion was almost certainly his first and last performance of it. In spite of his advocacy of Janáček's operas and of *Taras Bulba* (which he later recorded), Talich never gave another concert performance of the *Sinfonietta*. However, there is a tantalising listing in *Radio-Journal*[1] previewing a broadcast on 2 July 1938 as part of the Czech Radio programmes to celebrate the Tenth Sokol Rally. The programme for this 'gala concert for the rally' is given complete: Martinů's *Rally Overture*,[2] Suk's Fantasia for violin and orchestra, Janáček's *Sinfonietta* and Dvořák's Eighth Symphony, with the Czech Philharmonic conducted by Talich. But this concert is not listed in the Czech Philharmonic's archives, nor in Milan Kuna's exhaustive list of Talich's performances, and it is very likely that Talich was listed in error.

Despite Talich not conducting it again, the *Sinfonietta* was regularly performed in Prague in the decade after Janáček's death and, later, during the years of Nazi occupation. On 20 October 1928, it was given by the Czech Philharmonic conducted by Franz Schalk (alongside Weber's *Freischütz* Overture and Bruckner's Eighth Symphony); and on 10 February 1937, the Czech Philharmonic played it with another distinguished visitor, Erich Kleiber, whose conducting of *Jenůfa* in Berlin had so delighted Janáček in 1924.

Karel Boleslav Jirák (1891–1972) performed the *Sinfonietta* with the Czech Philharmonic on 14 October 1931 and again on 23 September 1938 in

---

[1] *Radio-Journal*, 12 June 1938, p. 4.
[2] Martinů's *Slavnostní ouvertura k všesokolskému sletu 1932* [*Overture for the Sokol rally 1932*] H211 was composed in 1931 and first performed by the Czech Philharmonic conducted by František Stupka on 3 July 1932. It remains unpublished.

a broadcast billed as the 'First Concert of the Janáček Festival' which also included *Taras Bulba*. A few months after that, Jirák conducted the work with the Prague Radio Symphony Orchestra (broadcast on 1 December 1938). Jirák had been head of the Music Department at Prague Radio since 1930. His colleague – and apparently his bitter rival – was Otakar Jeremiáš (1892–1962), principal conductor of the Prague Radio Symphony Orchestra from 1929, who expanded the orchestra to seventy permanent players by 1936.[3] Jeremiáš seems to have made a speciality of the *Sinfonietta*. He performed it with the Prague Radio Symphony Orchestra in a concert on 25 October 1935 to mark the start of a 'Week of Czech Music', and on 3 March 1936, the same forces performed it as part of the Czech contribution to a 'European Concert', organised by the International Radio Union and relayed live by radio stations throughout Europe, including the BBC; in the *Radio Times* listing, the work was called 'Sinfonietta militaire'. A performance by Jeremiáš and the Prague Radio Symphony Orchestra was broadcast on New Year's Day 1938, and he conducted it with the Czech Philharmonic in the Smetana Hall on 14 December 1938. Jeremiáš and the Prague Radio Symphony Orchestra performed it again on 28 November 1939; on 10 April 1940, he performed it with the Czech Philharmonic in the Smetana Hall. A radio listing for 26 March 1943 includes another performance by Jeremiáš and Prague Radio forces.

Rafael Kubelík (1914–96) first conducted the *Sinfonietta* on 14 January 1942, in one of his earliest concerts as chief conductor of the Czech Philharmonic. During the Nazi occupation of Prague, this was a courageous undertaking, given the work's fiercely patriotic inspiration. A few months later, on 28 May 1942 during a visit by the Czech Philharmonic to Brno, Kubelík conducted the *Sinfonietta* at the Stadion. He performed it again in 1944 as the closing item in three all-Janáček concerts at the Smetana Hall in Prague on 25, 26 and 27 October 1944 (the programme on all three occasions was the Overture to *From the House of the Dead*, *Taras Bulba* and the *Sinfonietta*). For the benefit of the Nazi censor, these concerts were announced as marking the ninetieth anniversary of Janáček's birth; but for the occupied Czechs, the dates had much deeper significance: 28 October – the day after the last of the three concerts – was when Czechoslovak independence had been declared in 1918, and it became the Czech National Day. At a time when the Nazis were becoming increasingly repressive (in the knowledge that they were losing the war), this was brave programming. Czech critics were very positive about the concerts, and

---

[3] See Patrick Lambert: 'In the shadow of Talich', *International Classical Record Collector*, vol. 2, no. 5 (Summer 1996), pp. 7–26, especially p. 12.

audiences would have been acutely aware of the significance of playing the *Sinfonietta* – a work at least partly inspired by Czech independence in 1918 – at such a perilous time.[4]

A few months earlier, on 31 July 1944, Prague Radio broadcast an all-Janáček programme (*Jealousy, Ballad of Blaník, Sinfonietta*) given by the Czech Philharmonic conducted by Alois Klíma. The *Sinfonietta* was subsequently rebroadcast on 6 October 1944, then in December 1944 and three times in 1945. Another live performance in Prague was given on 9 March 1942 by Josef Keilberth with the Orchestra of the Prague German Theatre (the core of the orchestra that became the Bamberg Symphony in 1946).

František Neumann had introduced the work to Brno audiences with performances in 1927 and 1928, but he died in February 1929. Břetislav Bakala – a pupil of both Janáček and Neumann – became conductor of the Brno Radio Symphony Orchestra in 1937. On 27 March 1941, Brno Radio broadcast a concert from the Stadion billed in *Náš rozhlas* (23 March 1941) as a 'Symphony concert of Czech Radio and the union of Czech musicians', conducted by Bakala, which ended with the *Sinfonietta* – a performance that was retransmitted a few weeks later (on 21 April 1941). A photograph shows conductor and orchestra – with the trumpets and bass trumpets of the *banda* arrayed in front of the double basses – which appears to have been taken on this occasion (plate 17).

Bakala later played the *Sinfonietta* in a broadcast with the Brno Radio Symphony Orchestra on 25 April 1946 and went on to give many more performances with orchestras from Brno and Prague, including a visit to the Warsaw Autumn Festival with the Brno State Philharmonic Orchestra on 17 October 1956.

Austria

After Jascha Horenstein's Viennese premiere in 1928, the *Sinfonietta* was given in Vienna on several occasions. Clemens Krauss had already introduced the work in Frankfurt (October 1927), and he gave the first performance in South America in one of a series of concerts given in Buenos Aires, Argentina, with the Asociación del Profesorado Orquestal in 1928.[5]

---

[4] We are extremely grateful to Patrick Lambert for drawing attention to the significance of these concerts and supplying newspaper cuttings about them.

[5] Wilhelm Lütge: 'Musikbrief aus Buenos Aires', *NZfM*, vol. 96, no. 4 (April 1929), p. 236. It has been impossible to establish a precise date for this performance. Lütge wrote, 'From June 23rd to September 9th, the Philharmonic Orchestra of the Asociación del Profesorado Orquestal under the direction of the Frankfurt master

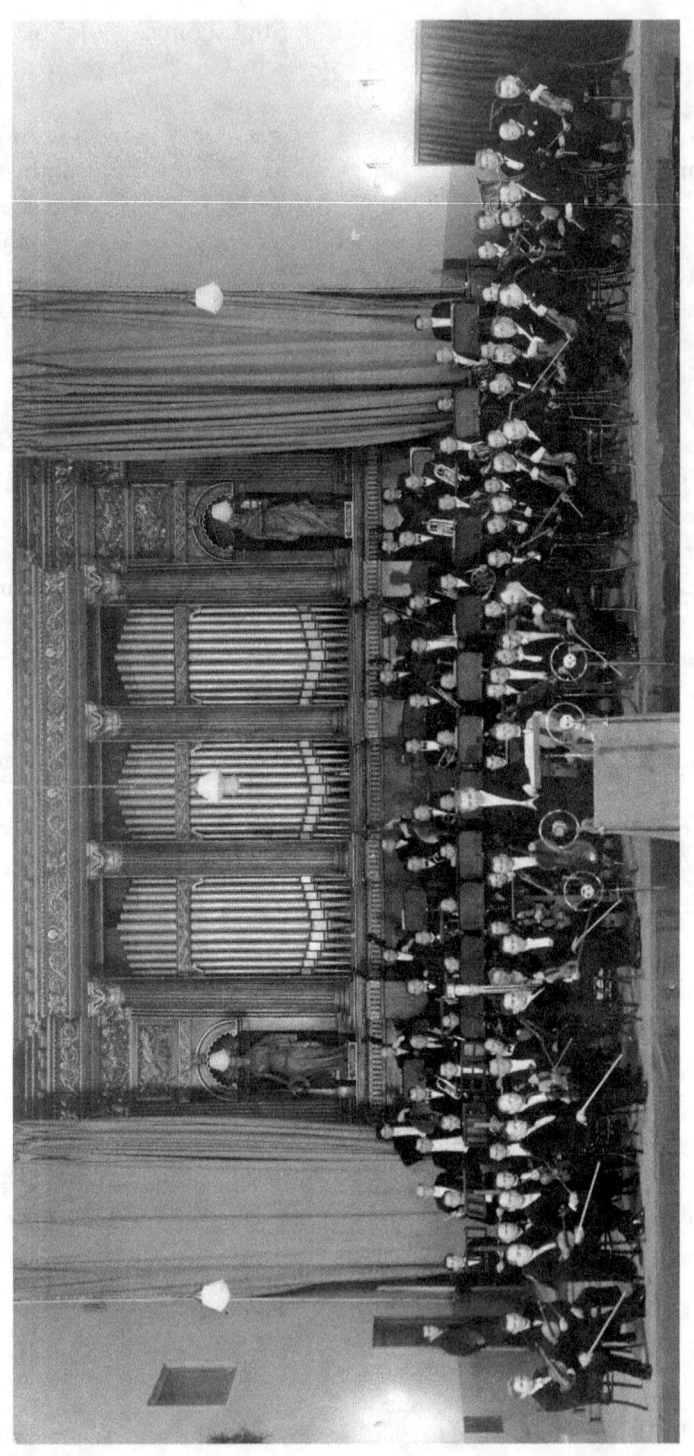

Plate 17. Břetislav Bakala and the Brno Radio Symphony Orchestra in the Stadion, Brno, on 27 March 1941 at a broadcast performance of the *Sinfonietta*. The trumpets and bass trumpets of the *banda* are clearly visible in front of the double basses (Janáček Archive, Brno).

On 18 and 19 March 1933 Krauss conducted it with the Vienna Philharmonic in the Musikverein. Hedwig Kanner in *Der Morgen* wrote that the *Sinfonietta* was 'a colourful kaleidoscope drawing from the depth and breadth of [Moravian] Slovak folk music, stylising it into something primitive but always captivating and convincing, thanks to its authenticity and truthfulness. Blazing trumpets, bright tubas in fifths, stomping ostinatos – *Petrushka* in Slovácko, but also with lovely flute tendrils, brief pastoral idylls, and a trill-filled finale which nods slightly to Smetana.'[6] Max Graf in *Der Wiener Tag* took a similar line, sharing the view that Janáček was creating a kind of musical folk art; it is particularly interesting to find him comparing Janáček's music to the artist Joža Uprka – a fellow member of the Brno Friends of Art Club with Janáček. Graf even referred to painted chests, such as the one that had been decorated for Janáček by Uprka's wife in which he kept his manuscripts:[7]

> The creator of *Jenůfa* was a man who stood alone. He was the same in [the *Sinfonietta*] which has its own form, its own sonority and its own landscape. The landscapes are the fertile plains of Moravia … where Janáček overheard folk songs, and the intonation of peasants speaking. His music grew out of this soil. It differs from Smetana's in its rhythms and colours…. . It is harder, more realistic and more concise. The first movement begins with a trumpet intrada from Moravian Slovakia, blaring like processional fanfares. Then movements follow with whirling dance themes, as colourful as a painted chest, glittering like the

---

Clemens Krauss gave a series of concerts (two concerts a week) that were very popular with the audience…. . The local audience did not know what to make of Janáček's *Sinfonietta* or Bruckner's Third Symphony, and they failed to make a deep impression, particularly as neither the orchestra nor the conductor were able to do justice to these works.'

[6] Hedwig Kanner: 'VII. Philharmonisches Konzert', *Der Morgen*, 20 March 1933, p. 4.

[7] Joža Uprka (1861–1940) studied in Prague, Munich and Paris where he established friendships with Alfons Mucha and František Ondrúšek. In 1895, he was in contact with Janáček to make arrangements for bringing musicians from villages in South Moravia to the Czecho-Slavonic Ethnographic Exhibition in Prague. In 1897, Uprka settled in Hroznová Lhota where he built a house and studio, and he married Anežka Králiková on 15 May 1899. In 1904, the house was remodelled as a handsome villa by Dušan Jurkovič (a friend of both Janáček and Uprka, and another leading member of the Brno Friends of Art Club) who blended elements of art nouveau and folk art in a way that mirrored Uprka's paintings. Janáček, Jurkovič and Vítězslav Novák all visited Uprka at the house in Hroznová Lhota as did Auguste Rodin. In 1922, Uprka moved to Klobušice in Slovakia. The painter Lhotský in Janáček's *Fate* may be based on Uprka; the character's name is thought to be a reference to Uprka's home in Hroznová Lhota. Uprka's wife, Anežka, was also an artist, and for Janáček she decorated (in 1904–5) the wooden chest in which he stored his manuscripts.

wedding adornments of peasant women, crudely carved like wooden toys. And at the end, the trumpets blaze again.... Here everything is bright daylight, the colours are all brilliant, even garish, like Uprka's paintings. What Janáček has created is folk art: artistic and primitive at the same time.[8]

Later that same year, on 18 October 1933, the *Sinfonietta* was given by the recently founded Vienna Concert Orchestra (Wiener Konzertorchester), an ensemble made up of younger players, conducted by Kurt Adler. Writing in the *Neues Wiener Journal*, Paul Stefan welcomed this new enterprise: 'These young artists are players of high quality. The equally young conductor, Kurt Adler, a Viennese, proved to be a talented musician with a subtle ear for balance and rhythmic energy.... [He] was particularly successful with his interpretation of a masterpiece like Janáček's *Sinfonietta*: the folk-like melodies found the right open-air orchestral sound, almost reminiscent of a village fair in Slovácko (with twelve trumpets and two bass trumpets as well as horns and tubas).... A large audience applauded enthusiastically.'[9]

During World War II, performances of the *Sinfonietta* were given by the Vienna Symphony Orchestra under Hans Weisbach (11 and 12 November 1941 in the Konzerthaus), and at a concert on 21 March 1945 with the Prague German Theatre orchestra, conducted by Joseph Keilberth (in the Musikverein); nine years later, in 1954, Keilberth conducted the Vienna Symphony Orchestra in four performances at the Musikverein (4, 5, 6 and 7 May).

Germany

Performances in Germany included a Janáček memorial concert broadcast by Leipzig Radio on 2 September 1928. No conductor is identified in the listings, but the music director of the Leipzig Radio Orchestra[10] in 1928 was Alfred Szendrei and it is likely that he conducted. The evening began with a talk on Janáček's life and work by Ernst Latzko, head of Leipzig Radio,

---

[8] Max Graf: 'Oper und Konzertsaal', *Der Wiener Tag*, 21 March 1933, p. 9.
[9] Paul Stefan ['P. Stf']: 'Konzert-Orchester beginnt', *Die Stunde*, 20 October 1933, p. 6. Kurt Adler (1907–77) studied with Guido Adler and Erich Kleiber (among others) and later worked for thirty years as a conductor at the Metropolitan Opera in New York.
[10] Known at the time as the Leipzig Symphony Orchestra.

followed by a reading of Janáček's article 'Without drums', the *Concertino* and finally the *Sinfonietta*.[11]

The Hamburg premiere was given on 22 October 1928, conducted by Karl Muck at a Philharmonic Concert in the Musikhalle. The critic for the *Hamburger Fremdenblatt* wrote a long review from which the following extracts are taken:

> The local premiere of the *Sinfonietta* by Leoš Janáček, was intended as a tribute to the elderly composer when the programme for our Philharmonic concerts was drawn up, and it has now become a memorial event for Janáček, who died in August this year. It was only very late in life that Janáček's achieved widespread recognition as a powerful and highly individual composer, with close ties to folk music. The rise of modern music may have paved the way for Janáček's recognition ... but he had already worked out the fundamentals of his musical language long before the battle for modernity began. His late works, including the *Sinfonietta* written in 1926, do not differ significantly in their essentials from those of his early creative period, including his masterpiece, the opera *Jenůfa*, written in 1902 [*recte* 1895–1904] and well known in Hamburg. Everything that is characteristic in the *Sinfonietta* – the strangely abrupt subject matter, the wildness of expression and occasional freedom, certain peculiarities of compositional technique and architectural design – we also find reflected in the opera: there is no more radical modernism in the *Sinfonietta* than in *Jenůfa*, both in its general form and in the details of its organisation.
>
> The main source of nourishment for the music of the *Sinfonietta* is once again folk music, which ... runs through the language of all five movements. This leaves us in no doubt about Janáček's distinctively Slavic character, but at the same time, his direct and sharply etched style stands out from impersonal and matter-of-fact international modernity. In that context, he stands alongside Smetana and Mussorgsky. The special charms that make such a decisive and positive impression in the *Sinfonietta* lie not least in its acoustical aspects: in the coloristic variety of the individual movements, in some very witty combinations of sounds and, more widely, in the truly musical verve – from the carillon-like first movement, entrusted exclusively to the brass and timpani, to the end, when this first theme returns. The evening brought honour on all those involved ... but above all to the conductor, Dr Karl Muck, who – by happy chance – conducted this

---

[11] See radio listings in *Der Grafschafter*, 1 September 1928, p. 15 and *Der Sächsischer Erzähler*, 2 September 1928, p. 10.

concert with astonishing freshness and elasticity on the evening of his 69th birthday.[12]

On the same day, 22 October 1928, the first performance in Hannover was given by the opera orchestra, conducted by Rudolf Krasselt.[13] The *Sinfonietta* was performed in Gera by the Reussiche Kapelle conducted by Heinrich Laber on 7 January 1929,[14] and in Kiel by the Verein der Musikfreunde on 1 February 1929, conducted by Fritz Stein (in a programme that also included Horowitz playing Rachmaninoff's Third Piano Concerto).[15] The Stuttgart premiere followed on 8 April 1929 at the Eighth Symphony Concert of the Stuttgart Landestheater Orchestra conducted by Carl Leonhardt. A brief unsigned review appeared in the *Schwäbischer Merkur*: Janáček's 'obstinate repetitions – rhythmic and melodic – have something compelling about them in their primitiveness. The first of the five short movements of this *Sinfonietta* features a whole array of brass instruments accompanied by high-pitched timpani. That is really original. The orchestral groups alternate with one another … with a very individual colouring and moods which captivate from start to finish, and which also astonish, despite some strange elements. This is music you want to hear again. The performance under Leonhardt's direction was also very impressive.'[16]

Later that month, on 19 April 1929, the *Sinfonietta* was performed in Münster at the Musikvereinskonzert conducted by Richard von Alpenburg.[17] The Pfalz Orchestra in Ludwigshafen announced a performance of the *Sinfonietta* on 13 November 1929, to be conducted by Ernst Boehe, but this was cancelled (the critic in the *Neue Mannheimer Zeitung* blamed the publisher for this). A week later, 20 November 1929, the work was performed for the first time in Bremen, conducted by Ernst Wendel. A review in the *Hamburger Fremdenblatt* noted the work's current popularity in

---

[12] H. Ch.: 'II. Philharmonisches Konzert', *Hamburger Fremdeblatt*, Abendausgabe, 23 October 1928, pp. 2–3.
[13] Announcement in *Signale für die musikalische Welt*, vol. 86, no. 43 (24 October 1928), p. 1276.
[14] Announcement in *NZfM*, vol. 95, no. 11 (November 1928), p. 660.
[15] Announcement in *NZfM*, vol. 95, no. 10 (October 1928), p. 603. According to a note in UE's records, this performance in Kiel was 'for small orchestra'. In October 1927, UE had published a 'Beilage für kleines Orchester' – a supplement comprising the first movement and relevant pages of the fifth movement – with a reduced orchestra version by Erwin Stein, approved by Janáček (see Chapter 1). Presumably this was the version used at this performance.
[16] 'Stuttgarter Konzerte', *Schwäbischer Merkur*, 9 April 1929, p. 9.
[17] Announcement in *Signale für die musikalische Welt*, vol. 86, no. 40 (3 October 1928), p. 1163.

Germany and suggested reasons for this: 'The main orchestral work on the programme was the *Sinfonietta* by Leoš Janáček, which has been played a lot in recent years. It is original, down to earth and captivating due to its tonal contrasts. Under Professor Wendel's lively, spirited and fresh direction ... the municipal orchestra played this work with dazzling bravura.'[18]

On 12 January 1933, Otto Klemperer returned to Berlin to conduct the *Sinfonietta* with the Staatskapelle (having previously conducted it there, in Janáček's presence, in September 1927). By all accounts, the 1933 concert was a success, as briefly reported by Josef Rufer in the *Berliner Morgenpost*: 'Janáček's *Sinfonietta*, first performed by Klemperer a few years ago, concluded this enjoyable evening, which was received with great enthusiasm.'[19] Writing in the *Hallische Nachrichten*, Oskar Bie described the *Sinfonietta* as a 'wonderful, folk-inspired work with which [Klemperer] had started his famous evenings at the Kroll Opera.'[20]

Janáček's music was never banned by the Nazis (there was even a celebrated Berlin production of *Jenůfa* in 1942), but there were many fewer performances of the *Sinfonietta* in Germany after 1933. It was performed in Hamburg on 17 February 1936 under Eugen Jochum; and the August 1942 issue of the *Neue Zeitschrift für Musik* has a report of a performance in Mainz during the 1941–2 season, conducted by Karl Maria Zwissler (described as its first performance in the city).[21]

The Netherlands

The *Sinfonietta* was performed in Amsterdam by the Concertgebouw Orchestra on 25 and 28 October 1928, conducted by Pierre Monteux, and he gave further performances with the orchestra on their visits to Utrecht on 12 December 1928 and Rotterdam on 19 December.[22] A review of the 25 October performance appeared in *De Maasbode* the next day:

> The *Sinfonietta* by Leoš Janáček ... is full of joy, and orchestrated with astonishing skill. That skill becomes cerebral here and there, but in

---

[18] H. Ch.: 'Musik in Bremen', *Hamburger Fremdenblatt*, Abendausgabe, 21 November 1929, p. 3.
[19] Josef Rufer: 'Krenek's Orchester-Variationen im dritten Sinfonie-Konzert der Staatsoper', *Berliner Morgenpost*, 14 January 1933, p. 7.
[20] Oskar Bie: 'Musik in Berlin', *Hallische Nachrichten*, 18 January 1933, p. 3.
[21] *NZfM*, vol. 109, no. 8 (August 1942), p. 376.
[22] The Rotterdam performance was reviewed in *De Maasbode* (20 December 1928) but is not listed in the Concertgebouw's online concert archive.

many places the work captivates thanks to its colour: the wonderful rhythms seem to shine and glow. The first movement (short, like all five movements) has a melodically simple motif which never becomes monotonous in spite of the frequent repetitions. There are few examples in modern music where the brass and percussion instruments are so transparently scored. The instrumentation of the second movement, in which the strings and woodwinds are used more, and which is richer and more sensitive in melody, forms an echoic relationship with that of the first. The other parts contain a wealth of contrasting thematic material. After the performance of Janáček's *Sinfonietta*, the conductor was presented with a bouquet of flowers on behalf of the Czech consulate.[23]

A long article by N. H. Wolf in *De Kunst* introduced Janáček to Dutch readers who were probably unfamiliar with his name, let alone with any of his music. Wolf quoted part of a short biographical sketch by the distinguished Dutch composer, Willem Pijper, printed in the programme for the Concertgebouw performance:

> When Janáček reached the age of seventy, one could hardly tell from his appearance ... and the music that he wrote around the age of seventy was more like that of a young man in his thirties. In the *Sinfonietta* one can hear that the work was written by an author with an unerring imagination, but certainly not that its composer was an old man of seventy-two.
>
> Janáček was a wonderful figure ... but few in Western Europe realised his significance for new music. When he was finally proclaimed one of the leaders of the modern Czech school, hardly anyone knew that this revolutionary was already over seventy. Independent of current trends, exemplified by Schoenberg, Bartók and Stravinsky, Janáček arrived at his own radical way of expressing himself. Schoenberg's leap out of tonality was around 1910, Stravinsky's revolutionary achievements were not conceived before 1911. But Janáček's *Jenůfa* was already finished in 1902 [*recte* 1904] and in this work he had already fully realised his principles.
>
> Janáček's art grew out of vocal music. Not only did his harmony have its roots in Middle and Eastern European folk song (as with Bartók), but his themes even came from the melody of spoken language. A spoken sentence, heard anywhere, in company, or from passers-by, acquired for him the value of a musical motif; Janáček was the first

---

[23] 'Concertgebouw-Orkest: Haydn–Janáček–Zimmermann', *De Maasbode*, 26 October 1928.

to consciously use the melody of spoken language as the germ cell for a musical composition. Attempts in that direction had been made long ago ... but with Janáček it became a fully developed and usable system.[24]

Wolf went on to review the *Sinfonietta* and Monteux's performance, which clearly left a deep impression:

> The *Sinfonietta* consists of five movements, the last of which is a reprise of the first, but richer in colour and more complicated thematically. All this music is very characteristic, very personal and highly original ... orchestrated in a very individual way, modern in style, but never exaggerated, full of character and really captivating. This music can be listened to with pleasure more than once in a season. We would even suggest that Mr Monteux should repeat it ... he will certainly achieve as great a success with it as on this occasion, when he and his orchestra were given a great ovation. There was also an enormous flower basket from the Czechoslovak ambassador ... as a tribute to the Dutch musicians who had honoured and commemorated the ambassador's great countryman with this sublime performance.[25]

The Concertgebouw Orchestra next performed the work with Eduard van Beinum on 12 and 14 January 1939, and again on 12 February.

United Kingdom

Following Henry Wood's premiere in 1928, the next London performance was given at the Courtauld-Sargent Concerts in Queen's Hall on 16 October 1933, with the London Philharmonic Orchestra conducted by Robert Heger. Richard Capell reviewed it for the *Daily Telegraph*.

> The good borough of Brno must be a great place for trumpeters. The score of the *Sinfonietta* contains parts for no fewer than twelve – which taxes even the wealth of London – not to speak of a couple of euphoniums. Janáček's music is the sort that Dvořák, to judge from his portraits, should have written. But Dvořák's music was tamer than his wild-man-of-the-woods looks. Dvořák, the child of nature, humbly went to school. Janáček, breaking away from school, went back to

---

[24] Pijper's biographical sketch quoted from the Concertgebouw concert programme in N. H. Wolf: 'Concertgebouw-Kroniek', *De Kunst*, 27 October 1928, pp. 1–3.
[25] Wolf, op. cit.

the land. The *Sinfonietta* – uncouth and spasmodic music, though abounding in character and in racy traits – represents his wanderings in Bohemian [!] woods and fields. Such informality has its charm, but there is something preposterous in the gap between the gigantic apparatus it calls for and the music's own vagrant nature. The trumpets made a noble noise, the LPO woodwind was exquisite and Dr Heger proved his sterling worth.[26]

Neville Cardus, writing in the *Guardian* was dismissive, calling the work 'a rather naïve essay in national idioms'[27], while Edwin Evans in the *Liverpool Daily Post* was more positive, describing it as 'a remarkable piece of orchestral virtuosity … effective and even exhilarating music'. However, Evans had doubts about the performance: it was 'well done, but even in the Janáček work, which provides ample opportunity for them, there were no thrills.'[28]

On 10 November 1936, the BBC Symphony Orchestra (Section D) gave an hour-long broadcast concert of Czech music conducted by George Szell: Suk's *Fairy Tale* and Janáček's *Sinfonietta*.[29] Another BBC Symphony Orchestra performance from a few years later was given on the Czech National Day (28 October) in 1943. To celebrate this important date in the calendar of an allied country, the orchestra gave a concert of Czech music, conducted by Sir Adrian Boult. The listing in *Radio Times* gives the Janáček work as *Taras Bulba*, but Patrick Lambert has established that Boult conducted the *Sinfonietta* in its place – his only known performance of it.[30]

Some other European performances

The *Sinfonietta* was first performed in Poland on 2 November 1928 at a Warsaw Philharmonic concert conducted by Jerzy Bojanowski (broadcast live on Polish Radio). A few days earlier, from 27 to 31 October 1928, there had been a Festival of Czech Music which included the Polish premiere of Janáček's *Intimate Letters* Quartet (27 October) played by the Czech

---

[26] Richard Capell ['R.C.']: 'Music from Brno: Twelve Trumpets in a Sinfonietta', *Daily Telegraph*, 17 October 1933, p. 8.
[27] Neville Cardus ['N.C.']: 'Music in London', *Guardian*, 17 October 1933, p. 18.
[28] Edwin Evans ['E.E.']: 'Courtauld-Sargent Concert', *Liverpool Daily Post*, 17 October 1933, p. 6.
[29] *Radio Times*, 6 November 1936, p. 42.
[30] Patrick Lambert, personal communication, 12 January 2025.

Quartet (Hoffmann, Suk, Herold and Zelenka). A review of the *Sinfonietta* appeared in *Polska Zbrojna*:

> The last item on the programme was the *Sinfonietta* by Janáček, which was a kind of complement to the festival of Czech music. This piece by the venerable Czech composer, who died two months ago, is distinguished by its excellent, compact form and the imaginative conception of its instrumentation. With his juxtaposition of strongly contrasted groups of instruments, Janáček reminds us of Stravinsky.[31]

A few weeks later, on 18 December 1928, the *Sinfonietta* was first performed in Breslau (now Wrocław) by the Silesian Philharmonic conducted by Edmund Nick as the final item in a concert broadcast on Silesian Radio (Schlesische Funkstunde).[32]

The Danish premiere took place on 14 January 1929 at the Odd-Fellow Palaeets in Copenhagen at a concert by the Danish Philharmonic Society conducted by Anders Rachlew. It was broadcast throughout Europe from Denmark's Kalundborg station.

Fritz Münch (brother of Charles Münch) conducted the Strasbourg premiere with the Strasbourg Municipal Orchestra on 18 November 1931, at one of the concerts of the 1931 Strasbourg Festival.

The first performance in Switzerland was given in Geneva on 29 October 1932 at a concert (also broadcast) of the Orchestre de la Suisse Romande, conducted by Ernest Ansermet. The work seems to have made little impact on the critic for *Der Bund* (2 November 1932):

> The premiere of the *Sinfonietta* ... was the main attraction of the concert... . The array of twelve trumpets and eight tubas and trombones alongside the orchestra made one expect something strange: but in the end it was quite straightforward, and nothing new. The work is predominantly lyrical in nature and the five short movements are based on Czech folk song motifs. The army of brass comes into action at the beginning and end of the *Sinfonietta* with a cheerful fanfare which is repeated countless times and is not recommended for sensitive ears. The conducting (Ansermet) and playing were excellent.[33]

---

[31] W.F.: 'Z Filharmonji: Piątkowy koncert symfoniczny', *Polska Zbrojna*, 4 November 1928, p. 10.
[32] 'Der Rundfunk', supplement in *Volkswacht für Schlesien*, 15 December 1928.
[33] 'Musik in Genf', *Der Bund*, 2 November 1932, p. 3.

Russia and the United States

Otto Klemperer gave more performances of the *Sinfonietta* than anyone else during Janáček's lifetime. He had previously led the German premieres of *Jenůfa* (16 November 1918) and *Káťa Kabanová* (8 December 1922), and on both occasions, local critics were hostile; as Klemperer's biographer Peter Heyworth put it, they 'demonstrated their inability to assess foreign works by standards other than those they applied to German music'.[34] Klemperer, undeterred, continued to take a lively interest in Janáček's music, and as discussed in Chapter 2, the *Sinfonietta* quickly became a speciality. He continued to champion the work after Janáček's death. In March and April 1929, he conducted a series of concerts in Moscow and Leningrad (now St Petersburg). News of these was reported internationally. The Viennese newspaper *Der Tag* noted that 'in his Moscow concerts, Otto Klemperer has had a particularly big success with the *Sinfonietta* by Janáček and a concert performance of Stravinsky's *Apollon musagète*.[35] Janáček's work may have been enjoyed by the Moscow public, but the Soviet press was unconvinced, as Peter Heyworth noted:

> Paradoxically, Janáček's *Sinfonietta*, whose folk-song material might have been expected to appeal to the organ of the RAPM [Russian Association of Proletarian Musicians], was rejected by *Proletarskij musikant* on the grounds that the composer's use of it was 'coarse' and 'mechanical'. *Muzika I revolyutsiya* concurred: 'The music is fresh and sincere ... but what poverty of development, what slightness of form, what an absence of symphonic thinking in the true sense of the word.'[36]

These reactions shed an intriguing light on how Janáček was viewed by proponents of socialist realism in Stalin's Russia – and as a proud Slav, the composer himself would have been shocked by the incomprehension of these Soviet critics. In spite of the critical strictures, the *Sinfonietta* was

---

[34] Peter Heyworth: *Otto Klemperer: His Life and Times*, vol. 1: 1885–1933 (Cambridge: Cambridge University Press, 1983), p. 166.

[35] 'Klemperer in Russland', *Der Tag*, 9 April 1929, p. 8. The concert referred to in the article was probably given on 4 April 1929, though Klemperer may have conducted another performance on 31 March, perhaps with the Leningrad Philharmonic. UE's performance records include two separate entries for the Central Concert Bureau in Moscow and the Leningrad Philharmonic hiring orchestral sets on 7 March 1929, and both are annotated 'Klemperer'.

[36] Heyworth, op. cit., p. 315.

played again in the Soviet Union during the 1934–5 season of the Leningrad Philharmonic when it was conducted by Fritz Stiedry.[37] Klemperer took the *Sinfonietta* back to New York in 1934. His 1927 concerts there had been with the New York Symphony Orchestra. In 1928, this merged with the Philharmonic Society to form the Philharmonic-Symphony Society of New York (later the New York Philharmonic). He gave four performances on 25, 26, 27 and 28 October 1934, the last of which was broadcast nationwide. Olin Downes wrote an enthusiastic review in the *New York Times*:

> We knew Janáček in his seventieth year.... . A hale and hearty soul, he had an impetuous temperament, with a gift of humour all his own, and a prodigious love of life. His music proves it... . [The *Sinfonietta*] is perhaps a hundred measures too long, but it is replete with invention and impulse. The method of using the orchestra is triumphantly effective and of fresh, frequently primitive colours. Mr Klemperer performed this *Sinfonietta* seven years ago, March 4, 1927, when he conducted concerts of the New York Symphony Orchestra. If memory over the gap of years is at all reliable, the performance last night was considerably superior to the earlier one, if only because of the superb orchestra and the full brass choir.[38]

Artur Rodziński conducted the piece with the same orchestra (New York Philharmonic) on 7 and 8 February 1946. A few months later, on 31 October 1946, George Szell performed the *Sinfonietta* with the Cleveland Orchestra for the first time. As well as repeating it there on several occasions, Szell also conducted it with the New York Philharmonic on 9, 10 and 11 December 1954 to mark the centenary of Janáček's birth. The *Sinfonietta* took much longer to find a permanent home in the repertory of other major American orchestras. For instance, the first performance by the San Francisco Symphony was in March 1960 (conducted by Werner Torkanowsky), the Boston Symphony first played it in October 1968 (conducted by Erich Leinsdorf) and the Los Angeles Philharmonic gave its local premiere in 1974 (conducted by Charles Mackerras).

In the Southern hemisphere, the Australian premiere was given in Melbourne on 23 March 1957, conducted by Kurt Woess and broadcast by the Australian Broadcasting Commission (ABC). Over a year later (14

---

[37] See Pauline Fairclough: *Classics for the Masses: Shaping Soviet Musical Identity* (New Haven: Yale University Press, 2016), p. 112.

[38] Olin Downes: 'Klemperer gives work by Janáček', *New York Times*, 26 October 1934, p. 24.

July 1958), Woess performed it with the Sydney Symphony, and this was also broadcast by the ABC. The South African premiere was given in Cape Town on 29 January 1959, conducted by Charles Mackerras – his own first performance of the work.

4
The *Sinfonietta* Recorded: 1946 Onwards

From 1946 onwards, the *Sinfonietta* made its way around the world, particularly through recordings. This chapter considers the work's recorded legacy by examining the approaches of different conductors, ranging from specialists like Kubelík, Bakala, Ančerl, Mackerras and Jílek to others who were less regular performers of Janáček's music.

Otto Klemperer

Following his early advocacy of the work, Klemperer conducted further performances of the *Sinfonietta* in the 1950s, starting with the Concertgebouw Orchestra in Amsterdam on 10 and 11 January 1951. These were warmly received, and the 11 January concert was broadcast and later issued on CD. So, too, was the performance Klemperer gave with the Cologne Radio Symphony Orchestra on 27 February 1956 – apparently the last time he conducted the work.

Klemperer's reputation in the 1960s was for granite-like readings that were often powerfully effective but became increasingly slow in his final years. However, apart from his unduly stately tempo for the Fanfares, his surviving accounts of the *Sinfonietta* show him more animated: Klemperer's conducting has a trenchant, rugged muscularity which reveals a persuasive grasp of Janáček's score. Moreover, these performances get us as close as possible to one that Janáček himself heard and apparently admired (he described Klemperer's Berlin performance in 1927 as 'unmatched'). In short, Klemperer's recorded versions constitute an important link with the composer. The two performances are similar, with the Cologne one in slightly better sound.

Rafael Kubelík

After the war ended, Rafael Kubelík (1914–96) performed the *Sinfonietta* on many occasions. Plans for him to conduct it at a BBC Symphony Orchestra concert on 27 January 1946 were abandoned at the last minute. The performance was listed in *Radio Times* and publicity had been circulated (and programmes printed), but as the *Western Morning Post* reported, 'The BBC's concert at the People's Palace was marred by the last-moment withdrawal of Janáček's *Sinfonietta*, which many must have made the journey eastward especially to hear.'[1] The reason for the late change emerged many years later. In his obituary of Kubelík, Robert Ponsonby wrote, 'Janáček's *Sinfonietta* had to be replaced ... because the BBC had not budgeted for the extra trumpets.'[2] But Kubelík did conduct it in Prague two months later at the Smetana Hall on 23 March 1946, the first of several performances that year with the Czech Philharmonic. They performed it again at the closing concert of the first Prague Spring Festival on 4 June 1946 (on a programme with Novák's *De profundis* and Dvořák's Piano Concerto), and a few months later, they made the first recording of the *Sinfonietta* on 4–5 October 1946. This took place in Prague's Slovanský Hall at sessions produced by Walter Legge for the London-based HMV record company. It was a landmark in the reception history of the work, played by the orchestra that had given its premiere twenty years earlier. Further performances quickly followed during a European tour: at the Théâtre des Champs-Élysées in Paris on 29 and 30 October 1946 (to celebrate the foundation of UNESCO), at Victoria Hall, Geneva on 2 November, and at the Zurich Tonhalle on 3 November.[3] Ten days later on 13 November 1946, Kubelík included the *Sinfonietta* in his programme with the BBC Symphony Orchestra at the Royal Albert Hall (this time the BBC had presumably sorted out its budget for the extra trumpets). The concert was broadcast, and an unnamed reviewer in the *Western Morning News* wrote, 'A vigorous conductor, Mr Kubelík managed to stir the sometimes rather phlegmatic BBC Orchestra into considerable vitality.'[4]

Kubelík's HMV recording was issued in May 1947 and received mixed reviews in the British press (and little coverage elsewhere). The critic in *The Scotsman* was excited to have discovered this music for the first time:

[1] 'Our London Letter: Recent Concerts', *Western Morning News*, 29 January 1946, p. 2.
[2] Robert Ponsonby: 'Rafael Kubelík' [obituary], *Independent*, 13 August 1996, p. 12.
[3] Information from Nikol Kraftová: *Dramaturgie koncertů Rafaela Kubelíka v České filharmonii*, bachelor's thesis (Janáčkova akademie, Brno, 2015), pp. 39, 40, 43–4.
[4] 'Our London Letter: BBC Symphony Concert', *Western Morning News*, 15 November 1946, p. 2.

Those in search of something out of the ordinary ... will find it in the records made by the Czech Philharmonic Orchestra under Rafael Kubelík of Janáček's *Sinfonietta*. This is music which one feels one should have got to know long ago, and yet much of it is so contemporary in idiom that one has constantly to remind oneself that Janáček died in 1928... . The discs (HMV) of one of his comparatively few instrumental works – he is best known in Czechoslovakia for his operas – make one eager to hear more of the music of a composer so obviously original and lively.[5]

That warm welcome did not, unfortunately, set the tone for other British critics. There was a particularly curmudgeonly review by W. R. Anderson in *Gramophone* who found 'something both oddly pathetic and irritating about [Janáček's] life and his writing... . There seems something undisciplined about him that need be no repelling quality; but I think he tends to wind away in rhodomontade, rather than to build convincingly... . I can't help feeling this composer is trying to storm heaven in a Model T Ford.'[6] Fortunately, the *Gramophone* panel soon acquired critics who were much more sympathetic towards Janáček's music: Anderson's review can perhaps be considered a postwar low point in the British critical response to Janáček, but it is a sign of how much remained to be done to win over musical hearts and minds for the composer.

Kubelík's years as conductor of the Chicago Symphony Orchestra (1950–3) were bedevilled by the hostility of Claudia Cassidy, music critic for the *Chicago Tribune*. Her reaction to the performance of the *Sinfonietta* on 2 November 1950 was more positive than many of her notices during Kubelík's tenure, though she was sceptical about the lasting value of the music.

> The Janáček was brilliantly played, and it holds attention on first hearing, though I suspect its five movements lack the variety to wear well in the repertory. It is an extremely agitated, almost an angry, piece of music, with feverish, chattering string given the cooling benison of lyrical winds and brass. A dozen trumpeters high on the stage demanded attention for what it had to say, and assisted in a finale almost as roof shaking as that of Janáček's *Taras Bulba* which Kubelík played last season. But the *Sinfonietta* is a far more interesting work, with an acute sense of the vocal sound of instruments... . It was in the Janáček that Mr Kubelík won, and earned, his major success of the evening.[7]

---

[5] S.D.: 'Gramophone Notes: Janáček's Sinfonietta', *The Scotsman*, 29 May 1947, p. 7.
[6] *Gramophone*, May 1947, p. 178.
[7] Claudia Cassidy: 'On the Aisle', *Chicago Tribune*, 3 November 1950, p. 31.

During his time in Chicago, Kubelík continued to work extensively in Europe and performances of the *Sinfonietta* in the early 1950s included an appearance with the Orchestra dell'Accademia nazionale di Santa Cecilia in Rome (26 April 1950) and two with the Concertgebouw Orchestra in Amsterdam (21 and 22 January 1953).

Kubelík included the *Sinfonietta* in his concerts with the Vienna Philharmonic on 5 and 6 March 1955 which were given immediately before their Decca recording sessions (8 and 9 March) – all in the Musikverein. That record itself is something of a disappointment: the playing sounds tentative in places, lacking in real commitment; unsurprisingly, Kubelík drew a far more idiomatic response from the Czech Philharmonic in his earlier version and found much more drama in his later recordings.

It was during his time as music director of the Bavarian Radio Symphony Orchestra (1961–79) that Kubelík became established as a conductor of incontestable stature. Finding a congenial working environment after his brief and often unhappy appointments in Chicago and at Covent Garden in London, the years in Munich were when he did much of his finest work, and after relinquishing the post of music director, he maintained close links with the orchestra. He performed Janáček regularly in Munich and the *Sinfonietta* appeared several times in the orchestra's subscription concerts at the Herkulessaal, including 31 May and 1 June 1962, 21 and 22 November 1968, 19 and 20 February 1976 and 15 and 16 October 1981. Kubelík's 1970 Deutsche Grammophon recording with the Bavarian Radio Symphony Orchestra had a warm welcome on its first release and has maintained its place as one of the most enduringly successful versions. A later live performance (from 16 October 1981) has also been released. It is not quite as crisply played, and the timpani in the Fanfares sound a little tame, but it is interesting to compare with the studio recording. On both versions, the orchestra plays with the confidence and rhythmic flexibility that comes from close familiarity with the music.

Of all Kubelík's recordings, it is the 1970 version with Bavarian Radio Symphony Orchestra that most effectively combines rhythmic energy, transparent textures, and lightness of touch to produce a performance of great individuality, particularly in the inner movements.

Břetislav Bakala

Bakala (1897–1958) studied composition with Janáček and conducting with František Neumann. In 1920 he became a pianist and staff conductor at the Brno Opera, and Janáček asked him to make the piano-vocal scores of *Káťa*

Plate 18. Rafael Kubelík and Břetislav Bakala in Salzburg, 1957 (Janáček Archive, Brno).

Kabanová and *The Cunning Little Vixen*. In February 1925 Janáček heard Bakala – an inexperienced conductor at the time – rehearsing the *Lachian Dances* at the Brno Opera. He wrote to Kamila Stösslová, 'I'm in such a depressed mood today. I was present at a rehearsal in the theatre and saw how the conductor there was burrowing like a gimlet into the score – and didn't look at the players. That's bad! It sends everyone to sleep.'

But a few months later, on 20 August 1925, Janáček wrote in much more enthusiastic terms to UE: 'The young conductor Břetislav Bakala works at the local National Theatre – he's the one who did the vocal scores [of *Káťa* and *Vixen*] for me. Everything that's been given here is really his work. Conductor Neumann simply goes to the desk and conducts. Working with the soloists, chorus etc. is Bakala's job. He's worked for six years at the local theatre but has done little conducting. He understands my operatic matters – tempos – outstandingly.' This letter suggests that Janáček regarded Bakala as a musician with an exceptional grasp of the essential details of his most complex scores, even if he lacked practical conducting experience at the time.

Bakala became principal conductor of the Brno Radio Symphony Orchestra in 1937, and Janáček's music was at the core of his repertoire for the next two decades. In October 1958, a few months after Bakala's death, Rudolf Pečman outlined his significance as a Janáček interpreter:

> Following in the tradition of ... František Neumann ... [Bakala] deepened his own interpretative relationship with Janáček's symphonic works, especially as the conductor of Radiojournal (1926–8 and 1929), later as the permanent conductor and director of the Brno Radio Symphony Orchestra (1932–55), and then as artistic director of the Brno State Philharmonic.... . We can say that through his work at the Brno Radio and the State Philharmonic Orchestra, Břetislav Bakala created an authentic performing style for Janáček, relying not only on the full cooperation and artistry of both orchestras but also on his painstaking study of Janáček's scores and manuscripts.[8]

As well as championing Janáček's orchestral and choral works, Bakala conducted at least eight broadcast performances of his operas for Brno Radio between 1946 and 1957, a series that Charles Mackerras described as 'a great milestone – real treasure.'[9]

[8] Rudolf Pečman: 'Symfonické dílo Leoše Janáčka v pojetí Břetislava Bakaly', in *Leoš Janáček a soudobá hudba: mezinárodní hudebně vědecký kongres, Brno 1958* (Prague: Hudební rozhlédy, 1963), p. 250.

[9] Charles Mackerras in Jan Králík: 'Sir Charles Mackerras Interviewed', *Czech Music*, vol. 6, no. 3, October 1980, pp. 11–12. Bakala's surviving Brno radio performances include *Šárka* (1953), *Jenůfa* (1953), *Fate* (1948 and 1954), *Káťa Kabanová* (1953), *The*

According to Janáček's notebook, Bakala was present at the dress rehearsal for Talich's world premiere of the *Sinfonietta* in June 1926, and there are four published recordings of the work conducted by him, made between 1950 and 1956, each with a different orchestra. The earliest is a studio recording from October 1950 with the Czech Philharmonic. Spongy timpani in the Fanfares are a drawback, but otherwise this is notable for its propulsive energy as well as Bakala's evident delight in the originality of Janáček's orchestration. In his performances with the Brno Radio Symphony Orchestra and Prague Radio Symphony Orchestra from 1953 and 1955, respectively, Bakala is a little swifter in the Fanfares (though the timpani are still anaemic) and the fourth movement is particularly lively in both. In all Bakala's accounts, there's a kind of unfussy brusqueness that suits the work well.

Bakala's best recording of the *Sinfonietta* is one that has so far only been released on LP. It was made with the Brno State Philharmonic during a visit to the Warsaw Autumn Festival in October 1956 and issued on the Polish Muza label (reissued in East Germany by Eterna). This shares many of the virtues of Bakala's earlier versions, but it has the advantage over them of crisper timpani and an orchestra that had prepared the work very thoroughly prior to taking it on tour. This exciting record is the version of the *Sinfonietta* that perhaps best embodies what Pečman called Bakala's 'authentic Janáček performing style'. It deserves to be better known.

Karel Ančerl

A pupil of Hermann Scherchen and Václav Talich, Karel Ančerl (1908–73) first conducted the *Sinfonietta* on 14 May 1948 with the Prague Radio Symphony Orchestra in a broadcast concert from the Smetana Hall to celebrate the twenty-fifth anniversary of Czechoslovak Radio. Further Czech Radio performances followed on 17 November 1948 and 6 October 1949. Ančerl performed the work abroad for the first time on 7 November 1951 in a broadcast with the Berlin Radio Symphony Orchestra. In 1950 he had been appointed artistic director of the Czech Philharmonic, and the *Sinfonietta* was included in their gala concert, given in the Rudolfinum on 1 March 1954 to celebrate the Year of Czech Music. A year later, Ančerl and the Czech Philharmonic gave three performances (10, 11 and 12 November 1955) and on 20 April 1956 played the *Sinfonietta* on a visit to Budapest (a

---

Cunning Little Vixen (1953) and *The Makropulos Affair* (1955). These have all been published by CRQ editions (CRQ DVD10).

few months before the Hungarian Uprising). Ančerl conducted the work with the Leipzig Gewandhaus Orchestra on 15 January 1958 and, back with the Czech Philharmonic, included it in a concert at the Prague Spring Festival (12 May 1958), before conductor and orchestra travelled to Brussels for the Exposition Universelle and a concert there on 23 July 1958 in which members of the Czechoslovak Army Central Band joined the orchestra for the *Sinfonietta*.

Ančerl's next performance was his celebrated and widely circulated Supraphon recording, made with the Czech Philharmonic on 9–11 January 1961 in the Rudolfinum. By this time, conductor and orchestra knew the piece extremely well and that deep understanding shines through in a performance of real authority. The splendid and characterful sound of the Czech wind and brass is another notable feature of this recording, but the most important factors in its success are Ančerl's handling of pace and his ear for orchestral balance. If there is a drawback, it is Ančerl's occasional tendency to be unyielding, almost obstinately rhythmical. This could be regarded as an asset in Janáček, but Kubelík (among others) maintained the same kind of energy and momentum with greater flexibility. It ultimately comes down to matters of taste, and by any reckoning, Ančerl's is one of the outstanding versions.

Ančerl and his orchestra performed the work five times in 1964, all in the Rudolfinum: on 20 August at a gala concert for the Fourth European Congress of Cardiology (with more than 1,500 delegates from all over Europe), then on 21, 22, 23 and 24 October – the last of these marking United Nations Day. Two further Czech Philharmonic performances followed in 1966: on 13 May and 13 June. In December 1966, Ančerl conducted five performances with the Vienna Symphony Orchestra in the Musikverein (14, 15, 16, 17 and 19 December). Two months later (23 February 1967), he appeared as a guest conductor with the London Philharmonic Orchestra at the Royal Festival Hall, though if Peter Stadlen's review in the *Daily Telegraph* is to be believed, Ančerl was not at his best (Stadlen wrote about 'uninspiring readings of Janáček's *Sinfonietta* and Dvořák's Symphony No. 7').[10] On 5 June 1968, the work was chosen for the Czech Philharmonic's gala concert to celebrate Ančerl's sixtieth birthday. Any elation was short-lived: in August 1968, Ančerl left Prague in protest at the Soviet invasion and only returned to his old orchestra for one last visit in May 1969 when he conducted Suk's *Asrael* Symphony. For the rest of his career, he worked in the United States, Canada and Western Europe. Later performances of the *Sinfonietta* began

---

[10] Peter Stadlen: 'Ančerl's Reading of Dvořák Uninspiring', *Daily Telegraph*, 24 February 1967, p. 19.

with an appearance with the Cleveland Orchestra at its outdoor summer home, the Blossom Music Center, on 10 July 1969 – a concert attended by over 3,400 people. Frank Hruby reviewed it for the *Cleveland Press*:

> Without question the most colorful work of the evening was the Janáček *Sinfonietta*. Its five movements contain some of the most open music of modern times. Its general brilliance makes it perfect for open-air performances. Its qualities suggest wide-open spaces somehow, which Blossom provides handsomely. A dozen years ago the name Janáček was known to only a few musicians. Today, largely through the work of Ančerl ... it has taken on that certain familiarity which makes it instantly attractive.[11]

On 20 February 1970, Ančerl conducted a broadcast concert with the Cologne Radio Symphony Orchestra, later privately issued on CD and another fine performance to set alongside his Supraphon recording. In 1971, Ančerl conducted eight performances of the *Sinfonietta*: with the Hamburg Philharmonic (31 January and 1 February 1971), the Toronto Symphony Orchestra (11 and 12 May), at the Lucerne Festival (21 August 1971) and a series of three with the Cleveland Orchestra (23, 24 and 25 September). These were the opening concerts of the orchestra's 1971–2 season, and once again, Frank Hruby reported for the *Cleveland Press*:

> Janáček's *Sinfonietta*, is fast becoming a 20th century favorite, and unquestionably it was the high point of the evening. Under Ančerl's hands the work took off in the opening measures and flew, bounced and ricocheted around Severance Hall with extraordinary aplomb, its heady contrasts and splendidly original combinations of instruments a constant delight.[12]

John Von Rhein in the *Akron Beacon Journal* had some specific comments on Ančerl's conducting of the work: 'Ančerl kept the angular rhythms taut, driving, but never hectic; the expressive scheme grand and impassioned. Every juicy effect came across with proper impact.'[13] These were the last performances Ančerl conducted of the *Sinfonietta*, and his final years

---

[11] Frank Hruby: 'Orchestra Scores in Blossom Opener', *Cleveland Press*, 11 July 1969, p. 8.
[12] Frank Hruby: 'Orchestra Opens with Bright Program', *Cleveland Press*, 24 September 1971.
[13] John Von Rhein: 'Audience Down, but Cleveland Orchestra Glows', *Akron Beacon Journal*, 24 September 1971, p. A26.

were dogged by ill health.[14] His studio recording of the *Sinfonietta* with the Czech Philharmonic remains a memorably impressive version, notable for its determined conviction and playing of the highest quality.

Charles Mackerras

Charles Mackerras (1925–2010) was another Talich pupil. He gave numerous performances of the *Sinfonietta* and made several recordings. He conducted the work for the first time at a concert with the Cape Town Orchestra where he spent three months as guest conductor from November 1958 until February 1959. It was played on 29 January 1959 in a programme that also included Mahler's First Symphony and orchestral songs by Hugo Wolf.[15] The extra brass players for the *banda* were brought in from the band at Simonstown Naval Base,[16] and the critic in the *Cape Argus* described the concert as 'exhilarating'. Soon after returning to London, Mackerras was able to make his first Janáček recording for Pye, a programme comprising the *Sinfonietta* and four opera preludes. Made at Walthamstow Assembly Hall on 19–24 July 1959, it was given a warm welcome on its first (mono) release in January 1960. Andrew Porter wrote in *Gramophone*,

> At Sadler's Wells, where he introduced *Katya Kabanova* in 1951, and where he has just been in charge of a triumphant revival of the opera, Charles Mackerras has shown himself to be one of the finest Janáček conductors. He studied in Czechoslovakia. His readings convey a sense of burning belief in and love of Janáček's music; they are well prepared, yet on each occasion it is as if the strangeness and beauty of the music were being revealed for the first time.[17]

Comparing Mackerras's Pye record of the *Sinfonietta* with Kubelík's 1955 Vienna Philharmonic version, Porter noted that,

> This new one has more bite and brilliance... . The timbres are thrown together more boldly. The muted trombones which cluck through the opening and close of the second movement, for example, are kept well in the foreground (unlike the Vienna performance), and impart a

[14] For full details of Karel Ančerl's concerts, see www.karel-ancerl.com.
[15] Sjoerd Alkema: *Conductors of the Cape Town Municipal Orchestra, 1914–1965: A Historical Perspective*, PhD thesis (University of Cape Town, 2012), p. 207.
[16] Nancy Phelan: *Charles Mackerras: A Musician's Musician* (London: Gollancz, 1987), p. 113.
[17] *Gramophone*, January 1960, p. 354.

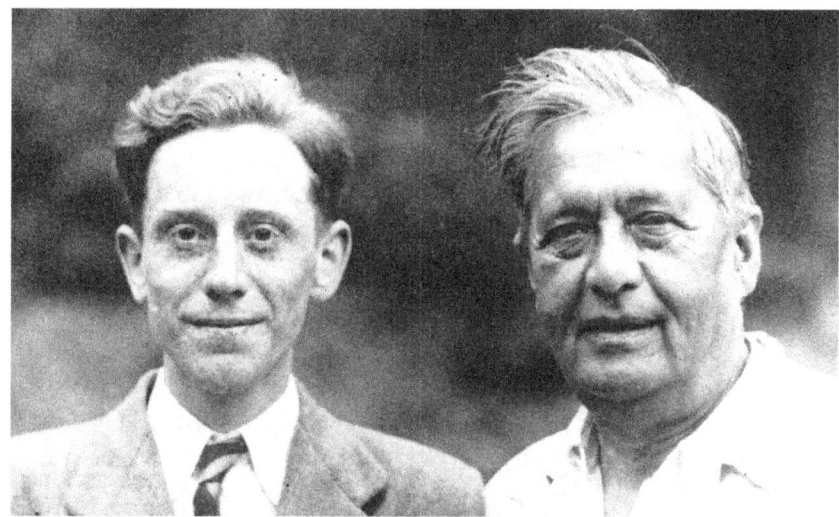

Plate 19. Charles Mackerras and Václav Talich in 1948. A faded inscription at the foot of the photograph reads, 'To dear Mr Mackerras in remembrance, Václav Talich, 8–7–48.' (Charles Mackerras archive).

kind of dry rattle to the oboe, then string melody. There is much languorous beauty in Mackerras's handling of the third movement; and a springy lilt to the opposed trumpet and string lines in the opening of the fourth... . Mackerras shapes the movements so well that the progress of each is convincing, and at the close one feels on top of the world, elated and happy, in tune with the positive and affirmative quality of Janáček's music.[18]

In his 'Quarterly Retrospect' the following month, John Warrack was equally enthusiastic: 'The *Sinfonietta*, with its flaring fanfares, comes off brilliantly and is something of a triumph for Pye. And Mackerras, a Talich pupil ... knows the Czech idiom thoroughly.'[19] It was not until 1964 that this record appeared in stereo, and Andrew Porter was very taken by the superior sound of the stereo version: 'An exciting reissue. Charles Mackerras conducts the music with passion and vigour, and in the third movement of the *Sinfonietta*, with beauty. The recording, especially in the new stereo edition, is so vivid as to be "larger than life", which makes it all the more

---

[18] Ibid.
[19] *Gramophone*, February 1960, p. 402.

exciting, since Janáček's scoring often implies a kind of boldness, strength and purity of colour hardly obtainable in concert halls.'[20]

In spite of this record's success, Mackerras had few opportunities to conduct live performances of the *Sinfonietta* in the 1960s, largely on account of the work's unusual requirements and its technical demands which needed thorough rehearsal. On 27 January 1973, he conducted it in a concert with the Royal Liverpool Philharmonic Orchestra, and an enthusiastic review appeared in the local press:

> Charles Mackerras conducted Janáček's *Sinfonietta* with splendid passion and energy at the Philharmonic Hall on Saturday. The work bears the imprint of the composer's neurotic disposition ... yet the result is thrilling.... . The performance by the Royal Liverpool Philharmonic had qualities of geniality and extroversion characteristic of the conductor's highly individual approach.... . In the middle movement the playing had an affecting tonal beauty.... . The brass section showed slight strain under Janáček's virtuoso demands, but kept the rhythmic layout of the various ostinatos scrupulously intact. There can be few more exciting moments in music than the passage in the finale where the 12 trumpets ring out across the orchestra and this majestic fanfare came across superbly.[21]

The next year, Mackerras made his debut with the Los Angeles Philharmonic at the Hollywood Bowl on 23 July 1974, opening this concert with the local premiere of the *Sinfonietta*. He conducted it at the London Proms with the BBC Symphony Orchestra on 2 September 1977 in the spacious acoustics of the Royal Albert Hall, and Andrew Porter wrote in the *Daily Telegraph* that this account created 'such a feeling of exhilaration.... . This is music, of course, which Mr Mackerras has made absolutely his own, and this fine performance was first and foremost one of complete authenticity in matters of tempo and phrase, but one also in which the BBC players produced a splendidly earthy and sonorous response.'[22] A performance with the Royal Philharmonic Orchestra at the recently opened Barbican Hall on 10 December 1982 brought a similar response from Alan Blyth:

> A superbly controlled account of Janáček's *Sinfonietta*. This was undoubtedly the most original and forward-looking work on display with its quirky but always intriguing rhythms and accents, its

---

[20] *Gramophone*, April 1964, p. 503.
[21] 'M.M.E.': 'Passion and Energy', *Runcorn Weekly News*, 1 February 1973, p. 7.
[22] Andrew Porter: 'Mackerras Prevails over Routine', *Daily Telegraph*, 3 September 1977, p. 9.

The Sinfonietta Recorded: 1946 Onwards 137

raw strokes of colour, its evocation of strange moods. All these are familiar from the operas, but in a sense their abstract form in this purely orchestral work allows us to study them more inquiringly and admire the composer's amazing instrumentation. They do not fail to be inspired and inspiring, particularly when conducted and played with such acuteness and vigour.[23]

On 29 August 1983, Mackerras conducted the *Sinfonietta* with the Sydney Symphony Orchestra at the Concert Hall of Sydney Opera House. Fred Blanks, writing in the *Sydney Morning Herald*, noted that 'Sir Charles Mackerras performed the Janáček work in a version based on the composer's autograph, quite different in significant respects from the normally used edition. The result has additional weight, especially in the majestic fanfare. The conductor set a spanking pace whenever the music encouraged this.'[24] The critic gives no details of what the differences were in this performance, but some of them were enumerated by Mackerras himself in the booklet for his 2002 Supraphon recording (see p. 140), and they are a feature of all his recordings from the 1980 Vienna Philharmonic version onwards.

That Vienna recording was made at the Sofiensaal in March 1980. In December 1976, conductor and orchestra had started a project to record Janáček's operas, beginning with *Káťa Kabanová* (of which Mackerras had conducted the British premiere in 1951). On 24 and 25 November 1979, Mackerras conducted two performances of the *Sinfonietta* with the Vienna Philharmonic in the Musikverein (with Dvořák's Fifth Symphony and songs by Mahler sung by Christa Ludwig) which served as valuable preparation for the sessions a few months later. Recorded in brilliant digital sound, this version first appeared in 1981. The recording was given enthusiastic reviews in Europe and the United States, and in Australia one critic, Roger Covell, praised not only the performance but also the scholarship behind it:

> Another superlative recording of Janáček, conducted by Mackerras and recorded by the excellent Decca team of Mallinson and Lock in the Sofiensaal in Vienna, brings together the composer's major orchestral works [the *Sinfonietta* and *Taras Bulba*]. The *Sinfonietta* grew out of a fanfare Janáček wrote for a gymnastic festival in 1926. The bucking rhythms of its brass and timpani phrases are exhilarating: and so is

---

[23] Alan Blyth ['A.B.']: 'Concerts: RPO, Mackerrras', *Daily Telegraph*, 11 December 1982, p. 11.
[24] Fred Blanks: 'Physiological Audience and a Concert of Curiosities', *Sydney Morning Herald*, 31 August 1983, p. 10.

their return at the end of the work... . A taut performance and vivid recording seem to bind this attractive piece together as never before.

Mackerras the restorer is at work here too, by the way. That rare instrument, the viola d'amore, is correctly assigned a solo intended for it (but rarely so performed) in the third movement. Piccolo arabesques, usually played an octave lower to make them practicable, are restored to their original altitude with striking effect.[25]

Fine though the Decca version is, Mackerras himself wanted to record the *Sinfonietta* with a Czech orchestra. There were provisional plans for him to make a recording with the Brno State Philharmonic during his visit to the 1990 Brno Festival when he conducted the work in the festival's closing concert on 7 October 1990. It was a magnificent performance (broadcast live on Czech TV), but the precarious state of the Czech economy in the months after the Velvet Revolution meant that the sessions had to be cancelled. This memorable Brno account of the *Sinfonietta* was, in fact, the first time Mackerras had conducted it with a Czech orchestra. Fortunately, he was able to record it with the Czech Philharmonic in 2002.

In 1995, the year of Mackerras's seventieth birthday, there were performances of the *Sinfonietta* by the Royal Philharmonic in Nottingham (Royal Concert Hall, 12 March) and London (Barbican, 17 March) which drew a great deal of praise. Reviewing the London concert, Edward Seckerson wrote,

> A dozen trumpets cleaving the sound barrier; timpani skins tightened to their topmost register; woodwind and string trills throwing a dazzling glaze over it all. On Friday at the Barbican, Sir Charles Mackerras rode the final crescendo of Janáček's *Sinfonietta* like he was making one last bid for the freedom of the Czech nation. Such advocacy ... is rare in Prague now, let alone in London... . What a performance this was, a whirlwind tour through the Czech heartlands, all the grit and husk and primitivism of the piece back in the musical mix. And such trumpetings as would have saved Gabriel.[26]

In 1997, Mackerras became principal guest conductor of the Czech Philharmonic and on 10 and 11 April 1997, he gave two performances of the

---

[25] Roger Covell: 'Classical', *Sydney Morning Herald*, 5 March 1984, p. 39. For further details of Mackerras's restoration of the text, see his interview with John Tyrrell on p. 140.
[26] Edward Seckerson: 'Whirlwind Tour: RPO/Mackerras', *Independent*, 20 March 1995, p. 20.

Sinfonietta with the orchestra at the Rudolfinum in Prague. Their appearances at the Edinburgh Festival in 2000 began with Suk's *Asrael* Symphony (28 August), followed on 30 and 31 August by two performances of the *Sinfonietta* at the Edinburgh Playhouse, accompanying Jiří Kylián's ballet version with the Netherlands Dance Theatre; finally, on 1 September, the *Sinfonietta* was performed in a concert at the Usher Hall. Kenneth Walton reviewed this in *The Scotsman*: 'Put together Sir Charles Mackerras, the Czech Philharmonic Orchestra and Janáček's jubilant *Sinfonietta* and you cannot go wrong... . There was fire in their belly, evident in the bombastic opening trumpet fanfares – the massed Czech trumpeters standing to deliver their thrilling and inspiring chorus – and the mystical, opaque textures of those passive and reflective moments where Janáček vividly captures the haunting spirit of his homeland.'[27]

The ballet performances also attracted plenty of press attention. In a preview of the 2000 festival, Christoper Brown interviewed Mackerras for *Scotland on Sunday* about the prospect of conducting the *Sinfonietta* as a ballet. His comments were characteristic:

> 'I haven't seen Kylián's *Sinfonietta* but I do know his work and I don't think one can possibly say he would do it at the wrong tempo. I know the Ančerl recording he based it on. If I disagreed violently with that interpretation, I wouldn't have agreed to do the ballet performances.' So Kylián can relax? 'Oh sure. And even if we have to do it at the wrong tempo for the ballet, people can always come to hear it at the concert.' Mackerras can't suppress the chuckle bubbling under his last remark.[28]

The ballet performance at the Edinburgh Playhouse was reviewed by Ismene Brown in the *Daily Telegraph*: 'This was dance with the musicians as part of the show... . The Czech PO [Philharmonic Orchestra] provided a second spectacle, packed into the pit, trumpets and drums overflowing into the theatre's boxes, and Sir Charles Mackerras conducting it all like God creating the world.'[29] This remarkable combination of music and dance produced a memorable evening, as Don Morris reported in *The Scotsman*, 'If ever a festival performance invited hyperbole this year, the alliance of

---

[27] Kenneth Walton: 'Czech Philharmonic Orchestra', *The Scotsman*, 4 September 2000, p. 58.
[28] Christopher Bowen: 'Tempo Is Everything', *Scotland on Sunday*, 2 April 2000, pp. 136–7.
[29] Ismene Brown: 'Edinburgh Dance', *Daily Telegraph*, 4 September 2000, p. 19.

the great Dutch dance company, the great Czech orchestra and the great conductor Sir Charles Mackerras was the one which richly deserved it.'[30]

A few weeks after these Edinburgh performances, Mackerras conducted the work in London on 26 September, with the BBC Symphony Orchestra at the Barbican. Tom Service reviewed it in the *Guardian*:

> [Mackerras's] interpretation of the *Sinfonietta* underlines his understanding of one of the composer's most demanding scores. Mackerras allowed the phalanx of extra trumpets required by Janáček to generate a suitable sonic superabundance. Yet this spectacular fanfare was only one dimension of his performance. He delineated the sometimes bizarre juxtapositions of mood, texture and melody with unerring conviction. The result was a riotous musical pageant, which encompassed everything from heraldic splendour to bawdy abandon.[31]

Mackerras returned to the *Sinfonietta* with the Czech Philharmonic in two concerts at the Rudolfinum on 17 and 18 October 2002, and a live recording (drawn from both performances) was issued by Supraphon. The booklet for this release includes a discussion between Mackerras and John Tyrrell in which the conductor mentioned some of the issues revealed by his study of the sources:

> Janáček recommended the use of non-standard wooden sticks for the timpani which are so important because they create a very hard, outdoor sound… . Another interesting thing about the percussion is that in the last movement of Janáček's own manuscript the clash of the cymbal introduced the trumpets a bar earlier than later printed. The copyist wrote it in the wrong bar and Janáček did not notice! I always do it as in the autograph, in fact I have persuaded the Czech Philharmonic's percussionists that this is the right way. In the *Sinfonietta* manuscript there are also various other interesting passages. For example, a place where the cellos and basses were transcribed the wrong way round in the second movement. This passage should be for the basses playing the melody alone (at Fig. 3). Janáček simplified some passages such as the rushing *prestissimo* … on the flutes and piccolos in the third movement. This was originally written so high for the piccolos that in 1926 it would have been unplayable on the instrument. I have now restored Janáček's original as today the players have no real difficulties with it. It was this passage that was

---

[30] Don Morris: 'Anguished and Miraculous', *The Scotsman*, 31 August 2000, p. 5.
[31] Tom Service: 'BBC Symphony Orchestra/Mackerras', *Guardian*, 28 September 2000, p. 20.

Plate 20. Charles Mackerras conducting the Czech Philharmonic in 2002 (Charles Mackerras archive).

proclaimed by the famous Czech Philharmonic flautist [Gustav] Nesporý as unplayable during the rehearsal for the premiere. It is said that Janáček irritably answered: 'Playable, unplayable – it has got to be like the wind. I heard it.'[32]

This 2002 version is a majestic account, with Mackerras and the orchestra captured in warm, natural sound. It has less digital 'glamour' than the Decca recording in Vienna, but while Mackerras's interpretation had mellowed over the decades, it had not lost any of its energy or colour.

That was by no means Mackerras's last word on the *Sinfonietta*. He made his belated debut with the Berlin Philharmonic in January 2004, when he was seventy-eight years old. Their first concerts (on 22 and 24 January) were a great success, ending with a thrilling performance of the *Sinfonietta*. It was broadcast and subsequently issued on a privately circulated recording. A few months later, on 22 May 2004, Mackerras conducted the *Sinfonietta* with the Czech Philharmonic on a visit to the Vienna Musikverein (a rare disappointment judging from an in-house recording of the concert). At the

---

[32] 'My Life with Janáček's Music. Sir Charles Mackerras in Conversation with the Janáček Specialist John Tyrrell', booklet note for Supraphon SU-3739-2 032.

Vienna Konzerthaus on 14 and 15 October 2006, he conducted two further performances with the Vienna Philharmonic.

Mackerras returned to the *Sinfonietta* in 2007: at the Royal Festival Hall in London with the Philharmonia Orchestra on 24 June; at the Proms with the BBC Philharmonic on 28 July; and with the Sydney Symphony Orchestra for three concerts on 11–13 October during his last visit to Australia. Of these, the performance at the Proms – the culminating event of a 'Brass Day' – was issued as a cover disc for the *BBC Music Magazine* and is among Mackerras's most exhilarating performances of the *Sinfonietta* – one of his last and emphatically one of his best.

František Jílek

František Jílek (1913–93) was born in Brno and attended the conservatory there, studying piano and composition with Jaroslav Kvapil and conducting with Antonín Balatka and Zdeněk Chalabala. In the 1930s he worked as repetiteur at the Brno National Theatre before his appointment in 1939 as second conductor at the Ostrava National Theatre under Jaroslav Vogel. Jílek returned to the Brno National Theatre in 1948, becoming principal conductor in 1952 when Chalabala left for the Prague National Theatre. Jílek remained in this post until 1978, overseeing the move into the Janáček Theatre and conducting a very large repertoire. He left the opera house in 1978 to become principal conductor of the Brno State Philharmonic, retiring in 1991.

There are two notable Jílek recordings of the *Sinfonietta*: a live performance from 1978 and a studio version from 1986, both with the Brno State Philharmonic Orchestra. The live performance in October 1978[33] was given at the closing concert of the 1978 Brno Festival which celebrated the fiftieth anniversary of Janáček's death. It has exciting timpani (hard sticks) and eloquent brass playing in the Fanfares, and the phrasing at the start of the third movement – which flows in a most natural way – is captivating. Like Bakala, Jílek takes a very sprightly approach to the fourth movement. He also brings a lightness and delicacy to it that has a capricious quality, slightly different from Bakala's gruffness. It's easy to see why many of those

---

[33] This performance was given in the Janáček Theatre, Brno. Though the applause has been edited out, occasional audience sounds indicate that it is live. According to *Rozhlas* (2 October 1978, p. 9) the *Sinfonietta* was the final item in a broadcast on 13 October 1978, from the closing concert of the 1978 Brno International Festival. It has been issued twice on CD by the Czech Radio label RadioServis, both times with different dates. See Discography for further details.

Plate 21. František Jílek at the Brno National Theatre (Brno National Theatre).

who attended Jílek's performances of Janáček in Brno remember them as special occasions: here the *Sinfonietta* is gripping and resplendent, though with a few moments of untidiness that are inevitable in a live performance. The 1986 studio recording for Supraphon (made in the Brno Stadion) benefits from more careful preparation, and the finale in particular is magnificent. Everything here is well judged, and the jagged edges of Janáček's orchestration are heard to their fullest effect, thanks to Jílek's acute ear for detail and the intense conviction of his conducting.

More Czech conductors

Václav Neumann first conducted the *Sinfonietta* with the Czech Philharmonic at a concert on 20 November 1949 and performed it with them on many occasions between 1970 and 1992. Few conductors gave more performances of the work, but none of Neumann's recordings really stands out. His earliest, with the Leipzig Radio Orchestra in 1951, sounds underpowered beside the pioneering versions by Kubelík and Bakala. Neumann's best-known recording was with the Czech Philharmonic in

1982, but it does not show the conductor at his best – there's a lack of vigour and drive. The recordings by Otakar Trhlík, Zdeněk Mácal and Zdeněk Košler are all competent but lack real fire or interpretative imagination. Ondrej Lenárd and the Slovak Radio Symphony Orchestra start badly – the timpanist gets lost six bars after Fig. 2 in the Fanfares – and the whole performance feels tentative.

Libor Pešek (with the Philharmonia Orchestra in London) is much more interesting. His is a well-played and atmospheric account with moments of great lyrical beauty. But the work's exultant, visceral qualities seem to be kept at bay. Pešek conducts an eminently civilised account, but the music's contours are smoothed out. There's a similar quality in an attractive version conducted by Radomil Eliška with the Sapporo Symphony Orchestra, taken from concerts in 2010. As with Pešek, there's no doubt about Eliška's sensitive musicianship, but in general the performance sounds too tame.

Vladimír Válek made a recording with the Czech Philharmonic for the Japanese label Exton in the Rudolfinum in May 1997, a couple of weeks after he had conducted the military band arrangement (see Curiosities below). This performance is captured in magnificent sound and is strongly characterised. It deserves wider circulation; apart from some unduly restrained timpani playing, it is often very persuasive.

Jiří Bělohlávek recorded the *Sinfonietta* three times. His first, with the Brno State Philharmonic, was made in 1977 by Panton (later reissued on Supraphon). Orchestra and conductor sound at their freshest, though the bass trumpets in the Fanfares are perhaps a little too raw. The bright, open-air quality of the woodwind at the start of the second movement is very attractive, and the last movement has impressive cumulative power. Bělohlávek first conducted it with the Czech Philharmonic on 2 June 1990, and his second recording was made immediately after this concert. It has far less impact than his earlier Brno version: the edges seem dulled and the performance lacks momentum. Bělohlávek's third recording, with the Czech Philharmonic on Decca, is much more successful. Recorded at concert performances which were the first to use the new critical edition by Jiří Zahrádka, it's an affectionate and purposeful reading – similar in some ways to the bucolic spirit of Kubelík – as well as being admirably attentive to the details of the score.

Several Czech conductors of the present day have taken up Janáček's music with enthusiasm, but at the time of writing only one has recorded the *Sinfonietta*. Tomáš Netopil, a Bělohlávek pupil, has given admirable performances of Janáček's music, but his *Sinfonietta* is disappointing. Recorded with the Prague Radio Symphony Orchestra in 2012, it's a slightly cautious reading, not helped by a slightly murky recording.

Jakub Hrůša was born in Brno and studied with Jiří Bělohlávek and Radomil Eliška. At the time of writing, he has not made a commercial recording of the *Sinfonietta*, but he conducted televised performances with the NHK Symphony Orchestra in 2019 and with the Czech Philharmonic on 31 December 2019 and again on New Year's Day 2020 (with the *banda* provided by the Band of the Prague Castle Guards and the Police, resplendent in uniform). Hrůša's televised Prague performance is extremely impressive, and he conducted four further performances with the Czech Philharmonic in December 2022. It is to be hoped that conductor and orchestra record the work one day.

Other conductors

Apart from Klemperer (discussed above), Jascha Horenstein was the only other conductor who not only performed the *Sinfonietta* during Janáček's lifetime but also made a recording of it. His 1955 version with the Vienna Symphony Orchestra (with which he had given the Viennese premiere in 1928) begins with the Fanfares at an impossibly slow speed. The other movements fare slightly better, but the overall feeling is sluggish. As with the Fanfares, the finale is drawn out to unfeasible lengths. A French radio recording from 1952 has all the same drawbacks, compounded by unidiomatic playing. Neither performance can be recommended.

Born in Croatia, Lovro von Matačić had a long association with Janáček's music. In October 1922, he conducted the Ljubljana premiere of *Jenůfa* – only its fourth staging outside Czechoslovakia. During his long career, Matačić conducted *Jenůfa* in Zagreb (1927), Belgrade (1928 and 1939), Berlin (1955), Chicago (1959), Frankfurt (1961) and Rome (1976). He came to the *Sinfonietta* later, but it quickly became a regular feature of his programmes. The earliest performance documented in Eva Sedak's *Matačić* (Zagreb, 1996) was with the Berlin Philharmonic in March 1971; he performed it in Essen (1972), then with the Orchestre de la Suisse Romande in Geneva (March 1973), at the Museum Concerts in Frankfurt (18 and 19 November 1973) and with the NHK Symphony Orchestra (14 December 1973, published on CD). The *Sinfonietta* was in his concerts with the Cleveland Orchestra on 2, 4 and 5 May 1974, and a review in the *Cleveland Plain Dealer* was full of admiration for Matačić's conducting: 'The Janáček work ended the evening in a hearty blaze of brass sound. Yet even here von Matačić was careful to emphasise the extroverted work's solidly musical values rather than its decibel level. The Cleveland Orchestra played splendidly. It had been clear all evening long that the musicians respected and admired von Matačić.'[34] In July 1974, Matačić conducted the *Sinfonietta* with the Zagreb Philharmonic in Dubrovnik and gave four performances with the Vienna Symphony Orchestra in the Musikverein on 20, 21, 22 and 23 November 1974. In September 1975, he performed it with the Berlin Radio Symphony Orchestra and further performances followed in Monte Carlo and Paris (1977), then in 1979 with the Zagreb Philharmonic (published on CD). His final performance of the *Sinfonietta* was with the Berlin Philharmonic in 1982.

This is an impressive tally, and Matačić's published live performances demonstrate a conductor with a fine grasp of the score. His 1979 Zagreb account starts with a fast and fluid account of the Fanfares while the 1973 version with NHK forces in Tokyo is rather steadier, but the playing is far superior. The Zagreb performance has a number of serious technical imperfections, including very inaccurate timpani, while the Tokyo version sounds much better prepared and the orchestra is in excellent form. Although the conductor's approach is less intense in the Fanfares, the Tokyo performance as a whole is one that builds in an exciting way and is full of rugged character.

Another Croatian conductor, Milan Horvat, recorded the *Sinfonietta* in the Musikverein with the ORF Symphony Orchestra a few days before they gave two concert performances in February 1971. This is a thoughtful and considered reading, marked by Horvat's careful orchestral balance and his natural feeling for pace. It's played with more conviction than several better-known versions, but there's some shaky trombone intonation in the third movement.

Moving forwards three decades, a performance from April 2002 posted on the WDR Klassik YouTube channel, with the WDR Symphony Orchestra conducted by Semyon Bychkov, is muscular but unforced, eloquently phrased and unfailingly well-paced. The exultant aspects of the score are relished to the full, with an excellent *banda*. Like Matačić before him, Bychkov demonstrates how to combine discipline and excitement to create a performance with a strong dramatic arc.

Klaus Tennstedt and the London Philharmonic Orchestra were in outstanding form at the Royal Festival Hall in April 1991. At his best, Tennstedt was an inspirational conductor, and his grasp of the emotional trajectory of the *Sinfonietta* is compelling. The LPO brass and timpani in the outer movements are splendid, and there is great character and rhythmic control in the inner movements. An earlier Tennstedt performance, with the NDR Symphony Orchestra in 1980, is more forceful but less polished, with

---

[34] Robert Finn: 'Maturity Satisfies at Severance', *Cleveland Plain Dealer*, 4 May 1974.

raucous brass in the Fanfares, and Tennstedt's conducting feels a shade unyielding compared to the spontaneous flow of his LPO version.

Rudolf Kempe is best remembered as a great Strauss and Wagner conductor, but he performed Janáček regularly in his later years. Two live performances of the *Sinfonietta* have been published, from 1974 and 1975, both with the BBC Symphony Orchestra. Though not as dramatic as some readings, both are very winning. The brass and timpani are slightly crisper in the 1975 concert, but the 1974 Prom is especially poetic in the third movement, buoyant in the fourth, and builds to a warm-hearted ending that is perhaps more radiant than triumphant.

Among other conductors of international renown to have tackled the *Sinfonietta*, Georg Solti gave a stirring performance with the Vienna Philharmonic in June 1964 and this concert was televised (and later issued on DVD). Solti conducted very little Janáček even though he was crucial in persuading Decca to undertake the Mackerras recordings of the operas. His *Sinfonietta* is red-blooded and clear-sighted, with plenty of propulsive energy and some imposing climaxes. It's a little short on subtlety and nuance, but Solti and his players certainly generate plenty of excitement.

George Szell and the Cleveland Orchestra recorded the *Sinfonietta* in October 1965 at the same time as a series of concert performances. Szell knew the piece very well: he had conducted it with the BBC Symphony Orchestra at a broadcast concert in 1936 (see Chapter 3); he introduced it to Cleveland on 31 October 1946 during his first season as music director and played it again in 1954 and 1961. In his review for the *Cleveland Plain Dealer* of Szell's 1946 performance, Herbert Elwell (erroneously describing the Hungarian Szell as 'returning to the land of his birth' for a Czech programme) gave his first impressions of Janáček's work:

> Terse folk speech rhythms, the burly fanfare of an augmented brass section, and an unwillingness to dilute his expression with sophisticated procedures made of his Suite [i.e. *Sinfonietta*] something adventurously close to the soil and compensated in a large degree for its episodic character. It was a stimulating experience to make the acquaintance of so sincere and original a composer, and this work, completed in 1926 ... certainly confirms Janáček's position as one of Czechoslovakia's most important creative personalities. Incidentally, to the amazement of most of us, Szell continues to conduct everything from memory.[35]

---

[35] Herbert Elwell: 'Szell Draws on Homeland for Warm Czech Program', *Cleveland Plain Dealer*, 1 November 1946, p. 16.

From an interpretative point of view, Szell's 1965 recording is slightly perplexing. In the Fanfares, Szell adds strong (unmarked) accents on each of the tuba's parallel fifths and the result is over-emphatic and choppy, impeding the flow of the music. That tendency to inflexibility is evident throughout, and in spite of excellent playing, this reading comes across as somewhat unyielding – and unsmiling.

Even so, Szell brings plenty of character to the music, which is more than can be said for the mostly disappointing versions by Seiji Ozawa with the Chicago Symphony Orchestra, Claudio Abbado with the LSO and Berlin Philharmonic Orchestra, André Previn and the Los Angeles Philharmonic Orchestra, Charles Dutoit and the Montreal Symphony Orchestra, David Zinman and the Rotterdam Philharmonic Orchestra, Heinz Rögner and the Berlin Radio Symphony Orchestra, and Neeme Järvi with the Bamberg Symphony Orchestra. One of the strangest performances of the *Sinfonietta* was given at the 2008 London Proms by Pierre Boulez. In general, he came late to Janáček's music, though he had conducted the *Sinfonietta* with the New York Philharmonic at three concerts on 12, 13 and 17 December 1974. In 2009, he spoke about Janáček as 'a kind of meteorite with fascinating strangeness and oddity,'[36] but his 2008 *Sinfonietta* with the BBC Symphony Orchestra was a lukewarm reading that gave no hint of the 'fascinating strangeness' or the 'oddity' of the music. The concert was televised, but plans for a recording were quietly dropped.

There's a better feeling for idiom in Eliahu Inbal's recording with the Berlin Radio Symphony Orchestra, in a live performance by Christoph von Dohnányi and the Cleveland Orchestra, and from Herbert Kegel with the Leipzig Radio Symphony Orchestra (a serious and imposing reading, very well played and paced). Sylvain Cambreling's 2005 version made in Baden-Baden is another success, while Antoni Wit and the Warsaw Philharmonic Orchestra are tidy but lacking in drama and impact. The right kind of musical tension is more apparent in the recording by Jonathan Nott and the Bamberg Symphony: an intelligent reading, with plenty of sinew in the orchestral textures and a stirring finale.

José Serebrier and the 'Czech State Philharmonic, Brno' (the Brno State Philharmonic Orchestra) recorded a gritty performance, though particularly in the last movement, Serebrier seems to prefer sheer volume to transparent orchestral textures, so detail is sacrificed. Leon Botstein and the American Symphony Orchestra give an engaging account, but in passages

---

[36] At the ceremony where Boulez was awarded an honorary doctorate by the Janáček Academy of Performing Arts; see https://en.jamu.cz/artistic-and-research-activities/honorary-doctors-of-jamu/pierre-boulez.

with frequent tempo changes (for instance in the fourth movement), Botstein's approach sounds too careful.

The recording by Michael Tilson Thomas and the London Symphony Orchestra feels unduly cosmopolitan: for all the virtuosity of the players and the intelligence of the conducting, the Slavic character of the music is lost. That certainly can't be said of Gennadi Rozhdestvensky and the USSR Radio Symphony Orchestra: their 1965 recording opens with the unmistakable sound of Russian brass, and Rozhdestvensky conducts the whole performance with real verve and a clear sense of musical trajectory; the playing – particularly by the woodwind – is full of individuality. There's also plenty to enjoy in Rozhdestvensky's second recording, a vigorous concert performance with the BBC Symphony Orchestra from 1981, in good broadcast sound.

Several British conductors in the generation after Charles Mackerras have taken up the *Sinfonietta*. Simon Rattle has made two recordings. The first, from 1982 with the Philharmonia Orchestra, is never less than efficient, but the recorded sound is recessed and Rattle keeps the music on too tight a leash. His live performance from 2018 with the LSO is far more successful: there's much greater freedom and spontaneity, and a keener sense of drama. Other British conductors who have tackled the *Sinfonietta* include Edward Gardner (a very good recording with the Bergen Philharmonic) and Andrew Davis (a tidy reading with the Royal Stockholm Orchestra). Mark Elder has not recorded it but has given some fine live performances, including a London Prom with the Hallé in 2011 (televised) and a broadcast with the Boston Symphony in March 2024.

A period instrument version was made by Jos van Immerseel with his Bruges-based Anima Eterna. The timbre of the woodwind and brass instruments from a century ago is not very different from that of the historic recordings by Kubelík (1946), Bakala (1950) or Klemperer (1951), though this recording allows us to hear them captured in modern sound. Immerseel conducts a straightforward but rather cautious performance, and the pacing in the last movement is distinctly laboured. The main interest of this record is its attempt to recreate the orchestral sonorities of Janáček's own time.

Curiosities

It is intriguing to hear the *Sinfonietta* in an arrangement for military band by Karel Bělohoubek, particularly in a fine performance by the Czech Army Central Band, conducted by Vladimír Válek. This is predictably impressive in the Fanfares, but the playing is exciting throughout and the arrangement is ingenious. Parts of the *Sinfonietta* have received contemporary treatments: the jazz track 'Sinfonietta' by the Emil Viklický Trio (on the album *Sinfonietta: Janáček in Jazz*) is based on the third movement; 'Knife Edge', from the 1970 debut album by the British progressive rock group Emerson, Lake & Palmer, was loosely based on the Fanfares. A short 1998 animated film by Emma Calder (produced by Pearly Oyster Productions and BBC Bristol) entitled *The Queen's Monastery* was inspired by the third movement and uses a recording of it as the soundtrack. Older British readers will recall that an extract from the fourth movement was used as the opening theme music for the daytime Granada TV series *Crown Court* (1972–84).

Performing an authentic text?

There are a number of issues – audible to any attentive listener – concerning details in the *Sinfonietta*. Some were clarified in the editions by Füssl (UE) and Barvík and Zimmermann (Peters) in 1980, but the most important points of detail emerged for the first time in the critical edition by Jiří Zahrádka in 2017 (UE).

The following is a summary of some conspicuous examples:

1. Movements I and V: 'Wooden sticks' (*dřevěné paličky*). These are prescribed by Janáček for the timpani in I and V, but this instruction was not printed in scores until the editions by Füssl (UE) and Barvík and Zimmermann (Peters) in 1980. Conductors before that date couldn't be expected to know about this important marking, though some earlier recordings do at least use hard sticks, including Mackerras in 1959, Ančerl in 1961, Kubelík in 1970 and Jílek in 1978. But Kubelík's earlier recordings (1946 and 1955) use soft sticks. Most recordings since 1980, including Mackerras (1980 and 2002), Rattle (1982 and 2018), Jílek (1986), Järvi (1989), Neumann (1990), Pešek (1990), Tennstedt (1991), Cambreling (2005), Gardner (2014), Van Immerseel (2015), Bělohlávek (2017) and Letonja (2022), use hard sticks. However, there are versions made since 1980 that use softer sticks in spite of Janáček's instructions. These include Abbado (1997), Neumann (1982 and 1992), Lenárd (1990), Masur (1993), Wit (2009), Eliška (2010) and Netopil (2012), all of which lose impact as a result.

2. Movement II: The cellos and basses at Fig. 3 (bars 61–4): the 1980 UE and Peters scores corrected an error that was in all previous editions, switching around the cello and bass parts. The melody for these four bars should be in the basses. This is correct in most recordings made since 1980 and is incorrect (with the melody in the cellos) on the recordings made before then.

3. Movement III: Viola d'amore or orchestral violas? Janáček's autograph and the authorised copy are both clear that the viola part for the whole of this movement should be played on a viola d'amore. However, when Janáček wrote to Talich before the first performance, he recommended using the orchestral violas instead – so he appears not to have been particularly concerned either way. Recordings with a viola d'amore are very rare. Mackerras used one in his 1980 Vienna Philharmonic version, a worthwhile experiment only possible in studio conditions. His other recordings use orchestral violas.

4. Movement III: The piccolo at bars 75–85: Janáček's original version did not appear in any printed score until Jiří Zahrádka's 2017 edition, though Mackerras included it in his recordings from 1980 onwards. The piccolo part was simplified and partly transposed down an octave on the authorised copy. This was made by Janáček's most reliable copyist, Václav Sedláček, whose other job was as the piccolo player in the Brno Opera orchestra: he may have advised Janáček that what he had written was unplayable. According to Mackerras, the piccolo player of the Czech Philharmonic, Gustav Nesporý, made the same suggestion, provoking Janáček's comment that it needed to sound 'like the wind.' Modern piccolo players can play the original: as well as Mackerras's recordings, it can also be heard on the most recent recordings by Bělohlávek (2017) and Rattle (2018).

5. Movements III and IV: What sort of bells did Janáček want? This remains a vexed question. There are parts for 'campanelli' in both the third and fourth movements. In the third, they are notated as unpitched in all sources, whereas in the fourth movement they are notated as A flats. Janáček specifies 'zvonky' – small bells – in both movements, but Vogel (1981, pp. 388–9) suggested that in the third movement, the unpitched part could have been intended for a triangle. That argument would carry more weight had Janáček not specified a triangle when he wanted one in earlier pieces (*The Fiddler's Child* and *Taras Bulba* as well as most of his operas). The solution that has most often been used for the unpitched 'campanelli' in the third movement is for them to play E flats, doubling the clarinets. For that, the usual choice is a glockenspiel. Vogel (1981, p. 389) also wrote – a little optimistically – that the notated A flats in the fourth movement present 'no problem – Janáček's manuscript clearly states "little bells" and gives the pitch.' But even if it's not of Janáček's making, there is enough ambiguity for conductors to have differing opinions on what these 'little bells' should be. To give a few examples: Bělohlávek in 2017 uses quite a delicate glockenspiel, as does Mackerras in 2002. Mackerras in 1980 has a much louder glockenspiel, played with a heavier mallet, and Hrůša followed that example in his 2020 televised performance. Other conductors have tried

different solutions: Kubelík (1970) and Ančerl (1961) both used a tubular bell, a very different sound that reflected the designation of this part for 'campane' – larger bells – in the 1927 and 1937 editions of the score. Janáček heard Klemperer conduct the work in Berlin and attended a rehearsal. He would surely have objected if he'd disapproved of Klemperer's choice of instrument and it was almost certainly a tubular bell, as used in his recorded performances from Amsterdam (1951) and Cologne (1956). Even so, 'zvonky' indicates *small* bells, so it's hard to imagine that a tubular bell is what Janáček intended. Moreover, the fourth movement is a street scene (according to Janáček's programme), while a tubular bell is more redolent of a church. Though it's pure speculation, Janáček may have had in mind an evocation of the warning bells on Brno trams of the time, which would play four rapidly repeated notes (as in bars 115–16) to alert pedestrians. That may be a fanciful notion, but a piercing glockenspiel certainly helps to evoke a bustling Brno street scene in the 1920s.

6. Movement V: Where should the cymbal clash come after Fig. 8? The answer depends on which source is consulted. The autograph is absolutely clear: the cymbal clash is one bar after Fig. 8 (bar 151), the bar *before* the fanfare trumpets enter (see plate 4). In Sedláček's authorised copy it appears two bars after Fig. 8 (bar 152) – in other words in the *same* bar as the trumpets enter (see plate 5). Before the 2017 revised score, all published editions followed the authorised copy. However, Mackerras and others had long been convinced that this was a slip by Sedláček that Janáček did not notice when he was correcting the authorised copy (an easy mistake to miss as it occurs on a page turn), and the evidence from the autograph is unambiguous. From his 1980 recording onwards, Mackerras restored the cymbal clash to its place in the autograph, a bar before the entry of the fanfare trumpets. Bělohlávek does the same in 2017 (but not in 1977 and 1990), as do Rattle in 2018 (but not in 1982), Válek in his 1997 Czech Philharmonic recording, and Hrůša in his televised performances (2019 and 2020). However, not all recent recordings follow this example: Letonja (2022) opts for the incorrect reading (cymbals and trumpets together), as does Immerseel in his 2015 period instrument version.

7. Movement V: The last chord (bars 283–5). In the 1927 printings of the full score and pocket score, there is no part for the fanfare trumpets, but in reprints from 1937 onwards, an extra stave was added for trumpets 1–9 to play a D flat major chord. In the Füssl edition (UE 1980) these parts are printed in square brackets, and in Barvík and Zimmermann (Peters 1980) they are given in small notes, with an explanation in the critical report. Zahrádka (UE 2017) prints them as a footnote. How the *banda* chord got there in the first place seems to be due to František Neumann. He wrote the

additional chord on the corrected copy of the score that he sent to UE in 1928 (see the Appendix and plate 23). Given that Neumann's score is only concerned with corrections (it was not his conducting score), it is certainly possible that this addition was an afterthought by Janáček himself.

This change has also been attributed to Otto Klemperer, but his revision was more far-reaching. In his letter to Janáček of 19 September 1927, Klemperer asked, 'Would you allow the last bars to be played by all *12* trumpets?' Though no reply from Janáček survives, Klemperer added *banda* parts in his score for all of the last seven bars (see the Appendix and plate 25). Janáček attended the concert in Berlin where these extra parts were presumably played and declared after the final rehearsal that Klemperer's performance was 'unmatched'. However, Klemperer's revision concerned all seven bars of the coda, and in the 1937 score, the *banda* only plays in the last three bars, as indicated by Neumann. Whatever Janáček's original intentions, leaving out the *banda* for the last chord in a live performance would be virtually unthinkable, and the same holds true with recordings.

Timings for selected recordings

Alongside contemporary reviews and the authors' assessments, it is worth presenting some objective data provided by the movement timings for selected recordings of the *Sinfonietta*. Table 4.1 shows this information for 26 versions, ranging chronologically from the very first recording in 1946 to a performance from 2018.

This data needs to be treated with caution. It must be emphasised that timings are only one way of 'measuring' a performance. They tell us little about musical characterisation, and two very different performances – in terms of phrasing, articulation, orchestral balance, timbre, tempo flexibility and so on – can have almost identical timings.

However, timings can give a broad indication of pace, particularly in a movement like the opening Fanfares where the pulse is constant throughout. It is perhaps unsurprising that this is a movement that shows a particularly wide variation of tempo choices: two conductors (Horenstein and Klemperer) are markedly slower than any of the others, as shown in Table 4.1. Horenstein's 3:26 for the Fanfares is at the furthest extreme, with Klemperer's performances coming in only a little quicker at 3:02 and 3:03. Most other versions take between 2:05 and 2:15, a marked difference.

In the second movement, timings range from Rozhdestvensky (5:17) and Klemperer in Amsterdam (5:28) to Mackerras's first recording and Tennstedt (both 6:15). In striking contrast to his stately first movement,

Klemperer's is among the quickest performances of the second movement, but Horenstein remains an outlier, taking almost seven minutes.

For the fourth movement, Bakala, Jílek, Kempe, Kubelík and Rozhdestvensky are a notch quicker (between 2:30 and 2:35) than their rivals, with Mackerras's performances consistently at around 3:00, and the others lying somewhere in between.

In the finale, raw timings might appear to suggest consistency between almost all the recordings, with most taking between 6:30 and 7:00, but this is very misleading as the movement has multiple tempo changes that conductors handle quite differently. For example, Klemperer's Amsterdam performance has a virtually identical overall timing to versions by Jílek (1986), Bělohlávek (1978) and Rattle (2018). But Klemperer's opening (up to the *Meno mosso* at bar 48) takes just 57 seconds, while Jílek and Bělohlávek and Rattle all take around 1:15. This situation is reversed at the close of the movement: from Fig. 9 (the start of the reprise of the Fanfares) to the end, Rattle takes 2:40 and Bělohlávek and Jílek are very similar at 2:37. But Klemperer – returning to his broad speed for the opening Fanfares – clocks in at 3:25.

The third movement also needs a more fine-grained level of detail to demonstrate the similarities and differences between recordings. Table 4.2 shows the timings for eight versions, with the movement divided into four sections: the opening *Moderato* up to bar 42; from the *Con moto* at bar 42 to the *Più mosso* at bar 86; from the *Più mosso* to the *Tempo I* at bar 199; and from bar 199 to the end of the movement. This reveals two distinctive interpretative approaches to the slower outer sections: one takes Janáček's *Moderato* indication at face value, while the other treats the same music more like a 'slow' movement. In the case of Rafael Kubelík, he does both: broader in 1946 and more flowing in 1970. Jílek (1986), Ančerl (1961) and Bělohlávek (2017) range from 1:40 to 1:50 in this passage, while Bakala (1950), Kubelík (1946) and Mackerras (1960 and 1980) range from 2:00 to 2:20. But turning to the next section, the *Con moto*, there's almost complete unanimity: all but two of the performance are between 55 and 57 seconds. The exceptions are Kubelík (1970) at 51 seconds, and Mackerras's first recording (1959) at 1:07. From the *Più mosso* in bar 86 to the *Tempo I* at bar 199, there's relatively little variation, with the recordings ranging from 1:20 to 1:28. But from the *Tempo I* to the end, there's again more variety, ranging from Jílek's sprightly 36 seconds to Mackerras's 1959 recording, which takes 55 seconds for the same passage.

Table 4.1: Timings for 26 selected recordings.

Conductor, orchestra, date	I.	II.	III.	IV.	V.	Total time
Ančerl, Czech Philharmonic Orchestra, 1961	2:11	5:25	4:41	2:41	6:38	21:55
Bakala, Czech Philharmonic Orchestra, 1950	2:16	5:40	5:02	2:35	7:00	22:50
Bakala, Brno State Philharmonic Orchestra, 1956	2:10	5:40	5:02	2:32	6:40	22:20
Bělohlávek, Brno State Philharmonic Orchestra, 1978	2:11	5:40	5:00	2:44	6:45	22:40
Bělohlávek, Czech Philharmonic Orchestra, 2017	2:11	5:45	5:00	2:45	6:51	22:50
Gardner, Bergen Philharmonic Orchestra, 2014	2:05	6:05	5:12	2:55	6:32	23:20
Jílek, Brno State Philharmonic Orchestra, 1978 L	2:14	5:43	4:41	2:34	6:35	22:10
Jílek, Brno State Philharmonic Orchestra, 1986	2:12	5:35	4:36	2:40	6:48	22:15
Horenstein, Vienna Symphony Orchestra, 1955	3:26	6:52	6:22	3:00	8:32	28:30
Kempe, BBC Symphony Orchestra, 1974 L	2:20	5:53	5:10	2:32	7:04	23:35
Klemperer, COA, 1951 L	3:03	5:28	5:11	2:41	6:45	23:30
Klemperer, Cologne RSO, 1955	3:02	5:38	4:47	2:42	7:00	23:35
Kubelík, Czech Philharmonic Orchestra, 1946	2:16	5:30	5:12	2:35	6:37	22:10
Kubelík, Bavarian RSO, 1970	2:13	5:16	4:50	2:31	6:33	22:00
Kubelík, Bavarian RSO, 1981 L	2:17	5:40	5:20	2:38	7:02	23:10
Mackerras, Pro Arte O, 1959	2:20	6:15	5:50	3:00	7:24	25:15
Mackerras, Vienna Philharmonic Orchestra, 1980	2:15	6:05	5:18	3:00	7:10	24:10
Mackerras, Czech Philharmonic Orchestra, 2002 L	2:10	5:47	5:20	2:56	6:55	23:20
Mackerras, BBC Philharmonic Orchestra, 2007 L	2:12	6:05	5:25	3:03	7:10	24:00
Matačić, NHK Symphony Orchestra, 1973 L	2:22	5:35	5:18	2:47	6:51	23:10
Rattle, Philharmonia, 1982	2:15	5:35	5:17	2:45	6:40	23:00
Rattle, LSO, 2018 L	2:13	5:45	5:20	2:50	6:45	23:20

Conductor, orchestra, date	I.	II.	III.	IV.	V.	Total time
Rozhdestvensky, USSR Symphony Orchestra, 1965	2:08	5:17	4:32	2:33	6:45	21:50
Szell, Cleveland, 1965	2:30	5:58	5:22	2:48	6:50	23:45
Tennstedt, LPO, 1991 L	2:15	6:15	5:30	2:38	7:11	24:10
Válek, Czech Philharmonic Orchestra, 1997	2:20	5:55	5:00	2:55	6:55	23:25

Note: Timings for individual movements are from the start to the finish of each movement, ignoring silences at the beginning or end of tracks, or any applause at the end of live versions. The total time column includes movement breaks, but not any applause. L = live performance.

Table 4.2: Timings in the third movement. Bar numbers refer to the UE 2017 score; cumulative timings are given in square brackets.

Bars (UE 2017)	Ančerl 1961	Bakala 1950	Bělohlávek 2017	Jílek 1986	Kubelík 1946	Kubelík 1970	Mackerras 1959	Mackerras 1980
1–41	1:45	2:00	1:50	1:40	2:07	1:51	2:20	2:05
42–85	0:57 [2:42]	0:55 [2:55]	0:56 [2:46]	0:56 [2:37]	0:51 [2:58]	0:58 [2:49]	1:07 [3:27]	0:55 [3:01]
86–198	1:20 [4:02]	1:25 [4:20]	1:28 [4:14]	1:23 [4:00]	1:22 [4:20]	1:20 [4:09]	1:28 [4:55]	1:24 [4:25]
199–end	0:39 [4:41]	0:42 [5:02]	0:46 [5:00]	0:36 [4:36]	0:52 [5:12]	0:41 [4:50]	0:55 [5:50]	0:53 [5:18]

These tables reveal some differences in matters of tempo, but there are other important criteria by which any recorded performance of the *Sinfonietta* should be judged. One, discussed above, is the matter of an authentic text. Other factors – whether it's orchestral balance, timbre or rhythmic momentum – are far less tangible. And while it would be wrong-headed to suggest that there is an 'ideal' recording of this work, there are several that perhaps stand above the others. The earliest versions by Kubelík (1946) and Bakala (1950 and 1956) have a pioneering spirit that is hard to resist, while later versions by the likes of Ančerl (1961), Kubelík (1970), Jílek (1986) and Mackerras (1980, 2002 and 2007) bring exceptional energy and interpretative insights, and their recordings continue to shine brightly. There's also cause for optimism in the future, with a younger generation of Janáček conductors likely to further enhance this impressive legacy.

5
A Conductor's Perspective: Jakub Hrůša in Conversation

In a wide-ranging conversation with Nigel Simeone on 22 March 2025, Jakub Hrůša discussed the history of the *Sinfonietta* on record, the challenges of rehearsing and performing the work, and broader issues of Janáček interpretation. He offers some particularly valuable insights into the practicalities of preparing the *Sinfonietta*, especially the problems of orchestral balance. We began with a discussion of recordings and Hrůša was particularly eloquent on the great Janáček specialist František Jílek, whose work was revered in Brno, and a conductor who deserves to be known more widely.

NS: My first encounters with the *Sinfonietta* were on record: Karel Ančerl's famous recording, Charles Mackerras's passionate first version, and the more subtle (and very effective) Rafael Kubelík version with the Bavarian Radio Symphony Orchestra. How did you first get to hear the piece?

JH: František Jílek, with the Brno Philharmonic. It was not even on an LP but on a cassette tape which had the *Sinfonietta* on one side and *Taras Bulba* on the other. The 'advantage' of those tapes was it was not so easy to jump around, so it made you really listen to the music! But let me tell you what I think about Jílek – and what an important figure he was. It's very interesting because he conducted almost *everything* by Janáček, much more, I think, than other famous Janáček interpreters like Karel Ančerl or Rafael Kubelík. Jílek conducted the whole œuvre. He did all the mature operas from *Jenůfa* onwards and even *The Beginning of a Romance*. But I had a more personal kind of indoctrination into Jílek's Janáček because the person who taught me when I was taking my very first steps in conducting was Evžen Holiš, who was Jílek's assistant for many years at the Brno National Theatre. He was born in 1930 and he's still alive and still on wonderful form, in his nineties. He worked with Jílek for his whole career and though he occasionally criticised physical aspects of Jílek's technique – he was quite undemonstrative and didn't have the kind of 'look' that today would have given him worldwide success – what Jílek did have was tremendous *authority*. As Mr Holiš told me, that was something you couldn't escape. Then there was his deep knowledge, his conception of the music and his extraordinary ear. Musicians who still remember him talk about his ability to hear detail in the way we might talk about Pierre Boulez. He would stand there with quite dry gestures, and he would hear everything, no matter how complex or difficult the work – and of course this also meant that he had a wonderful ear for balance. When he was conducting, the orchestra always felt the music had a sense of structural coherence. In huge pieces – above all operas – everything appeared to be seamless, clear and logical, very much serving the composer. So his first aim was to deliver a conception of the whole work which was convincing. Maybe the wild, romantic side of Janáček was something that didn't come so naturally to him – but I should qualify that, because his interpretations sometimes do have a certain wildness, particularly in terms of their momentum and energy, and the *marcato* rhythms. With his huge experience of conducting Janáček's operas in the theatre, he knew exactly how to bring off an utterly convincing performance: every corner would be negotiated without difficulty, and the results could be marvellous. There's a nice story about his years at the Brno Opera. He really knew Janáček inside out – and so did the company – so if a production ever had to be cancelled or changed, it was always *The Cunning Little Vixen* that was put in it its place, because it was so well studied that they could basically play the whole thing by heart and with anyone – obviously in Jílek's interpretation – no matter who stood there to conduct it.

NS: That's very interesting – particularly what you say about his overall conception of a piece. Adrian Boult used to say that the great Hans Richter was an 'architectural' conductor who had the uncanny ability to present a whole work as if it were a single span. It sounds as if Jílek conceived things in a similar way.

JH: Yes. And the living composers he collaborated with couldn't stop praising him because he always made everything 'work'. Now, to be a little bit critical – though the results were admirable – he did sometimes smooth out awkward corners. In order to achieve the kind of sweep he wanted – this sense of inevitable musical direction – he sometimes simply ignored a *ritardando* or a *meno mosso* – he just wouldn't do it. In symphonic repertoire, he also had an idea (similar to the view of Karajan and others on Beethoven, for example) that a whole work needed some sort of underlying, unifying tempo. And in a piece like the second movement ('The Death of Ostap') of *Taras Bulba* he was pretty well right. All those tempo changes are underpinned by a unified pulse. For some conductors this is a problem – they want to generate more excitement with constant changes – but Jílek, with his classically minded approach, used it to his advantage: as the movement progresses, you feel it like one completely coherent musical statement. He would even say, 'I always try to discover the underlying symphonic logic in Janáček's operas and concert pieces – I believe it's always there.' Whatever the discrepancies in notation and other pitfalls, he would do it in a way that made perfect musical sense. That's why the musicians playing Janáček with him adored it – because he made them feel as if there were no problems and everything worked logically. If there was one aspect of Janáček's language where he was less persuasive, it was the elements of conflict and struggle, of pain – the Romantic characteristics which are there alongside the modernism.

Turning specifically to the *Sinfonietta*, for me Jílek is probably better than anyone in the Fanfares. The balancing of the voices – of the nine trumpets, and the other brass with the timpani – is so well done. He always wanted the motivically important things to be audible, and the way he did that in the Fanfares is meticulous.

NS: Another thing is the way the trumpets shape their phrases in that recording. And the fact that the timpani and bass trumpets don't just bang out the rhythms but impart a real sense of musical trajectory.

JH: And there's one more point: I watched him conducting and he always used small gestures which were constantly giving a little motivational impulse – to tease out the kinetic energy that's so essential to Janáček. In general, he tended to do everything on the quicker side. If you take the third movement of the *Sinfonietta*, he maybe comes closest to Janáček's intentions. Just look at the metronome mark [minim = 66]. Everyone tends to beat it in crotchets rather than *alla breve*, but Jílek did it – and felt it – in minims, which is what Janáček asked for.

NS: I agree. It really seems to move in song-like phrases and to breathe so naturally. You can tell there's an opera conductor at work in that performance.

Going back to the Fanfares for a minute, you've done them played by a military band,[1] which is a wonderful thing to do, as we know from Janáček's

---

[1] For example, Jakub Hrůša conducted the *Sinfonietta* with the Czech Philharmonic and the Prague Castle Guard and Police Band at the Rudolfinum in Prague on 31 December 2019 and 1 January 2020.

letters to Universal Edition that it's what he hoped for and always had in mind. Does it make a real difference?

JH: Yes, I think it does. In Jílek's case, even though they weren't military players, his *banda* was made up of passionate musicians from local bands and the like – so they had the same kind of straightforward, bright, slightly 'rough' sound which was then refined by Jílek in rehearsals – but without losing the edge. It's rather like having a slightly wild animal which is then tamed to serve the purpose of the piece …

NS: … whereas a superb ensemble of nine orchestral trumpet players – unless they are from a brass band background – might be tempted to make everything sound a little too polished and glamorous: they can lose that 'edge' you talked about. But what about another detail in the Fanfares, which really only became widely known with the corrected 1980 edition of the UE score by Karl Heinz Füssl, which was Janáček's instruction for the timpani to use wooden sticks?

JH: I don't think Jílek used wooden sticks (though they are certainly hard). But I do think it is one of his greatest recordings.

NS: Someone who definitely did use wooden sticks was your teacher, Jiří Bělohlávek, in his last recording of the piece – the first time Jiří Zahrádka's new edition was used. One of the things I find so attractive about that performance is that even though the sound has the bite and crispness of wooden sticks, they are played quite delicately rather than thumped. In that 2017 performance, there's a lightness and buoyancy to the Fanfares which is really quite unusual, and, like Jílek, Bělohlávek's also on the fast side.

JH: How does that compare with Kubelík in the Fanfares? I remember him being quite bold and brave – but subtle too.

NS: Yes. I like it for quite similar reasons to Bělohlávek: it's very rhythmical, but it's transparent and feels flexible too. If I can be a little controversial for a moment, there's much more sense of ebb and flow from Kubelík than there is in Karel Ančerl's famous version. Now I know that is still many people's favourite recording of the work – and it's unquestionably very fine. But there are places where to me he feels a little stiff and unyielding.

JH: He could sometimes be a little bit four-square – very precise but also slightly stiff. Like Jílek, he was quite dry, but Jílek had all that experience

A Conductor's Perspective: Jakub Hrůša in Conversation 161

of working daily with singers – and of the flexibility you need as an opera conductor. It's interesting that in Jílek's diary there's a comment about Ančerl conducting a live performance of the *Glagolitic Mass* where Jílek wrote – alongside positive comments – that he was irritated by Ančerl's stop-and-go approach at *caesuras*. Jílek said that was definitely not what Janáček wanted – and somewhere there's a comment from Janáček himself about a performance which had too much stopping and starting, losing the flow of the music. You can find a similar distinction – albeit in the operas – between Jílek's Brno readings and Bohumil Gregor's contemporaneous ones at the National Theatre in Prague. Jílek's focus was on the musical essence of the whole work, while Gregor was fascinated by elements of the text and the drama, and on particular details. I only mention all this because it relates to how we react to different interpretations of the *Sinfonietta*. If there's any weakness in Ančerl's performance, it's that it sometimes tends to go along in blocks, rather than really flowing.

NS: Let's cast the net a bit wider. You certainly don't have to be a Czech conductor to bring off the *Sinfonietta*, but you *do* have to understand how Janáček's music works. A problem with some recordings – by Czech and non-Czech musicians – is that they don't seem to capture the amazing, energising life-forces in this music. These can be quite small things, like the way those bars and bars of demisemiquavers for the cellos in the last movement are played [bars 48–90, starting at the *meno mosso* eleven bars after Fig. 2]. They are an accompaniment, of course, but they are also the little musical engine that drives the music along at this point, so they need tension and a sense of direction.

JH: And you can also think of them as a disturbing or disruptive factor, which a conductor who doesn't quite trust Janáček might try to suppress or smooth over. It's an interesting question with that passage because you must not subdue the cello line and make it so inaudible that it doesn't disturb the texture, but at the same time you can't bring it to the foreground because that's not what it's meant to be. You need it to have just the right level of audibility so that those cello demisemiquavers are somehow provocative – and the element which gives the music its impetus and sense of direction.

NS: That's such an interesting way of putting it. There are so many other disruptive – or provocative – elements in that same passage which can easily go for nothing. For instance, those wonderful double bass pizzicatos, marked *sf* [in bars 55, 63 and 70] – they're another disruptive colour. And the trombone chords, which growl away in thick four-part harmony, but Janáček was very careful to put hairpins for crescendos and decrescendos – and we want to hear all that too.

JH: And don't forget that hilarious trombone descent! [the upbeat to Fig. 4]

NS: Quite so. And all the while, the cellos rumble along like some kind of musical outboard motor. I think the other thing you want to hear in those cello ostinatos is a sense of struggle.

JH: Absolutely. An engine, but also one that's struggling, not too smooth.

NS: When you're rehearsing the *Sinfonietta* how do you work at bringing out these layers of colour – because you don't want them all to sound as if they belong too comfortably together, do you?

JH: That's right: you want clarity without any self-indulgent smoothness. And something else I think you always need to remember with Janáček is that he was used to hearing an orchestra in the dry acoustic of an opera house. So in a more reverberant hall like the Musikverein or the Concertgebouw or the Rudolfinum, you have to work at getting a drier, clearer sound. With a piece like the *Sinfonietta*, I find it helps to rehearse quite analytically, so that players get a chance to really listen to what's going on elsewhere in the orchestra: to understand what the other details are and how their parts contribute to the bigger picture. Going back to that passage in the last movement [bars 48–90], the clarinets and trombones need to know what the motoric character of the cello writing is – and the cellos need to know what's going on in the trombones. Now it's not always easy for players to hear that – to do one thing while listening to another – so in rehearsal you need to create a space where everyone can listen carefully to all the different components. And it's also great for the players – it helps them realise how important their part is in the scheme of things. After you've separated those individual components, then you can bring them all together in a much more purposeful and intelligent way. There needs to be quite a lot of this analytical work because, as we've said, Janáček is a composer who combines modernity with Romantic elements and neither of them must be missing: if it's too Romantic it's wrong; and if it's purely modernist and the Romantic charisma is missing, it's also wrong. But by carefully anatomising things and then putting them back together, it usually works! The musicians playing lyrical melodies must notice and respect the fervent ostinato, and vice versa. A bit of flexibility is needed on both sides – but you want a bit of tension between them too!

NS: We've already talked about several of the great conductors of the *Sinfonietta* but not yet about Charles Mackerras.

JH: I observed Sir Charles rehearsing the Czech Philharmonic when he was quite an old man. Like Jílek he had huge experience with Janáček, and he also had this incredibly fresh and charismatic intuition for it. He believed in this music so passionately and always went for interpretations that were dynamic and full of impulse (that inner conflict was never missing in his performance) – what I'd call an approach to the music with the gloves off! He was never afraid of extreme contrasts – in fact he loved them – and liked very sharp attacks. And of course, he was always fascinated by the manuscript sources and in trying to reflect exactly what Janáček had written – bringing out the originality of the music like very few others. Though the details obviously mattered, Sir Charles was someone who was maybe more interested in the rhetoric – the bold gestures and contours of the music – rather than worrying unduly over how to manage this or that transition. On the other hand, Sir Charles's interpretative opinions dominated some of the editorial decision-making at Universal Edition – his personal solutions for certain problematic passages are printed as if they are the solutions for everyone – and I don't always agree with those.

NS: He often had a kind of inspired pragmatism – which isn't surprising for someone who spent a large part of his career in opera houses, making sure things worked.

JH: I think you've nailed it there. And just think of everything he achieved in all those incredible recordings of the operas with the Vienna Philharmonic, for instance – where he had to teach them these works from scratch back then. One of his missions was to make orchestras who didn't really have any tradition of playing Janáček really understand it – and to go for it. And the Vienna Philharmonic has a real flair for it which is easy to understand when you think about it: I know we love the exotic qualities of Janáček's music, but he did spend his whole working life an hour and a half away from Vienna. He was above all an operatic composer, and the Vienna Philharmonic is, for much of the time, an opera orchestra – though when I conduct Janáček with them, it always amuses me that I hear so much Richard Strauss in their sound too!

NS: Sir Charles's recording of the *Sinfonietta* with the Vienna Philharmonic has one very unusual feature, using a viola d'amore in the third movement. That was Janáček's original intention, which he scrapped before the premiere, though when you look at the copied score that Talich used, there is 'viola d'amore', but it's been scratched out. It's a nice experiment – and you can do it on a recording even though it's completely impractical in a live performance.

I watched Sir Charles rehearsing the *Sinfonietta* with the Brno Philharmonic in 1990 and that was fascinating. It was almost the opposite process to what you were talking about with the Vienna Philharmonic: persuading them to change some old habits: cajoling the cymbal player to come in a bar earlier than he was used to in the finale, and persuading František Vlk, the excellent timpanist, to use wooden sticks. It's just as well that Charles was such a respected figure by then as that orchestra could legitimately claim to know the piece as well as any, except perhaps the Czech Philharmonic – but he charmed them, all in Czech of course, and the performance they gave at the concert that night was still one of the best I've ever heard. It was electrifying.

JH: That illustrates the one slight disadvantage of Jílek's Janáček legacy in Brno. He played the *Sinfonietta* so many times, in festival concerts or on tour, and – as someone who was used to the way European repertoire opera houses worked – it was crucial that the interpretation was something that would mostly hold good for a decade. So every time they came back to that piece, very little changed except for delving deeper into the work from Jílek's particular interpretative viewpoint. Now, when Sir Charles came along a few years later and wanted to do things a little differently, the orchestra will have found it difficult to adjust. Jílek was still alive then, by the way, so they would constantly refer to his authority. They were so used to one very effective way of doing it that a new approach was quite disconcerting, at least until they got used to it. Even I experienced something like that many years later in Brno – and it was a similar situation with Bohumil Gregor's *Vixen* at the National Theatre in Prague: his was effectively the only interpretative approach there between World War II and the 2000s!

NS Yes, and there are also things about Sir Charles's approach to the piece which are quite distinctive, particularly the third movement which he liked to do very broadly – it sounded lovely but was noticeably more spacious (in the slower passages) than Jílek's very fluid view, which we've already talked about. Both conductors make it work extremely well but in very different ways. It's quite interesting that Sir Charles is also relatively steady in the fourth movement – Jílek and, going back further, Břetislav Bakala are significantly quicker. Bakala in particular keeps it very light on its feet and that works really well. There's a wonderful lineage of Janáček conductors in Brno, isn't there? – from Neumann, to Bakala, and then Jílek, who was a pupil of Zdeněk Chalabala, another Neumann pupil. They didn't just play this music, but they played it extremely well.

JH: In his diary, Jílek remembers Bakala being rather neglected or overlooked by some in Brno who thought his conducting lacked the operatic qualities which František Neumann definitely had – as did Milan Sachs, an exciting conductor from Croatia. Those who remembered Neumann's and Sachs's performances always talked about their very Romantic approach. Jílek always wanted to combine elements of both, though ultimately his natural tendency was towards a more architectural and classical approach.

NS: Bakala at his best gave some magnificent Janáček performances – and with his pedigree, as a pupil of both František Neumann and Janáček himself, we *have* to take him seriously, even if his surviving recordings are a little inconsistent. But he cared deeply about the music and knew it intimately. It's amazing that back in 1941 he gave a broadcast of extracts from *Jenůfa* using Janáček's original orchestration – and he said at the time that conductors should go back to it instead of using Kovařovic's version. It took everyone else another fifty years to come round to that view.

JH: Two of my conducting teachers – Evžen Holiš and Radomil Eliška – were pupils of Bakala at the Janáček Academy in Brno. They were both very proud of being his students, and they adored him. They admired his excellent ear and also his very precise and thorough preparation of everything he did – he was a real role model for them.

NS: Well, that puts you in a direct line of musical descent from Holiš and Eliška to Bakala and to his teachers, Neumann and Janáček. Talking of Bakala – and his careful preparation – brings us to the question of editions. Obviously Jiří Zahrádka's 2017 edition of the *Sinfonietta* is a huge improvement from a purely practical point of view: a score with bar numbers, a very well printed set of parts that match the score – these are all obvious practical advantages, but what about musical ones?

JH: I'm always delighted when a new edition comes along: I've so much respect for musicologists and I'm genuinely fascinated by their discoveries. So I love having new editions available – and I love debates about them (some of my colleagues feel differently – they hate to be bothered). But I must also say that if you bring a new edition to an orchestra who have been playing a certain piece for decades from the same set of parts, even the most open-minded musicians have to make a serious effort to get used to the different layout on the page, never mind any changes to the actual notes. Now, with the very good recent editions from UE – such as Jiří's *Sinfonietta* – that's not so much of a problem, but with the experimental notation used in some of Jarmil Burghauser's complete edition volumes, it can be really difficult – unless an orchestra is new to a piece and they aren't used to playing it from something notated differently – they have to learn it afresh.

But look, it's terribly important that these new editions are done – and that we learn from all the research that goes with them. Even so, one big issue with them concerns orchestral balance. In a scholarly edition, if Janáček wrote *forte* for a particular instrument in his manuscript, then the editor must, of course, print it that way, as *forte*. But with dynamics and orchestral balance, *everything* is relative: it depends on where you are playing, with whom you are playing, the power of particular instruments or players. And the conductor has to modify dynamics to get a particular balance, sometimes radically: it's absolutely crucial. And it's also the fun part because every conductor has different preferences, wanting to prioritise one thing over another and so on. But you really have to work on it, and that's maybe the one thing where a new edition can't help much. Having it, you risk losing some of the wisdom of previous generations – though of course you gain the knowledge of modern research.

NS Talking about balance reminds me of a particular bugbear that I have in the fifth movement of the *Sinfonietta*: being able to hear clearly the new line Janáček added for the orchestral trumpets in the reprise of the Fanfares [starting at the *Maestoso* in bar 237, Fig. 12]. It's a really exciting new layer added into the tremendous mixture of the original Fanfares for the *banda* and the frenetic trills above and below – but it's sometimes inaudible.

JH: Yes, you're right. And while it's relatively easy to ask the trumpets to play louder, there's more to it because, at the same time, you also want to hear all the string and woodwind colour on the trills, you want to hear the crescendo in the *banda* [at Fig. 12] and so on.

This takes us back to the issue of playing from new editions – and here I'm talking about the orchestral material – the parts – rather than the conductor's score. Older, heavily used sets of part often contain markings from players that reveal a lot about the interpretative tradition.

NS I know exactly what you mean. I've looked at the old set of material used by the players in the Czech Philharmonic since at least the 1940s – and they are full of interesting markings, often with notes about the preferences of particular conductors, their names jotted down in the parts too.

JH: A new set of material can make for a lot of extra work for the players. Getting used to a different physical layout of the notes on the page is one thing, but you also need to be aware of the musical judgements of our predecessors. As you said, clues to that are often found in the old parts – and you certainly don't want to miss any of that. Still, it's worth the effort as new editions are a very *good* thing: an active and well-informed revisiting of a familiar work for a new generation of performers and listeners is a thoroughly positive step, though of course you don't always have enough time to work at it in as much detail as you'd like.

NS: Could we have a look at some of the places in the *Sinfonietta* which are particularly problematic in terms of balance?

JH: Let's start with the Fanfares at Fig. 4 [bar 95]. Everything is marked *ff*, but it's very difficult to get the main thematic line on trumpets 1–3 to really come through if you don't ask them to play even more strongly than marked, and ask the fourth and fifth trumpets to play their higher-lying music at something more like *mf*. If you don't do that, you'll never hear the melody on the first trumpets. There's another interesting case at the fifth bar of Fig. 5 [bar 113]: you have trumpets 4–6, à 3, playing the main idea [A flat, D flat], but in the next bar [114] trumpets 1–3 don't play à 3 because they have three-part chords [A flat, F, E flat, then D flat, A flat, F]. So you are faced with a choice. Did Janáček really want the top line of the chordal version to be weaker? Because that's inevitably what happens if you play it as written, without adjusting the dynamics. I'm not sure if an audience will notice that kind of detail in the overall sweep of a performance – they might just think that the first trumpet sounds weaker than the fourth – but working on this kind of balance is so essential. The other issue throughout the first movement is the relatively thick sound of the tenor tubas obscuring the trumpet textures.

In the second movement, there's a tricky moment at Fig. 3. This is where the double basses and bass clarinet have the tune, with sustained notes on cellos and bassoons, and rapid figuration in the violins [this passage was printed incorrectly in earlier editions, where the cello and bass parts were switched round, but it's been correct in editions since 1980]. Here you simply *must* be able to hear the double basses, but all the instruments are marked *mf*. You have to adjust the dynamics, with the basses playing *forte* –

their colour has to come first – and the other instruments playing down as necessary. This is why I keep on saying the dynamics are so important. If the basses play *forte* and the violins play *mf* or even *p* it can work. And the bassoons have to play much more quietly than the bass clarinet.

NS: The bass clarinet writing in this piece is really extraordinary, isn't it? Quite often it's the most important bass instrument in the wind section.

JH: Yes. The bass line is not typically cellos and double basses, but instead it's often bass clarinet and low horn and just occasionally (more conventionally) the bassoons – although in this piece the bassoon writing is a ridiculous situation – it's really hilarious. In the second movement they have some spiky staccato music and a couple of long bass notes, then they don't play until four bars in the fourth movement. And then, in the last movement, the whole orchestra is blasting away, red in the face with effort, while the bassoons sit there with nothing to play.

NS: I've an amusing aside about that. When he first did the piece in 1959, Charles Mackerras wrote bassoon parts for the last movement to give them something to do – his part set is in the Royal Academy of Music. Of course, Charles soon abandoned this bit of retouching, but it's fun to see them – particularly as they have players' markings on them – so we know they were used at least once.

But to get back to the bass clarinet, it's so crucial in this piece. And when Janáček sent Universal Edition his first batch of corrections – a couple of months after publication of the score – many of them concerned the bass clarinet part, transposing it up an octave in several places so that it was more audible.

JH: That's right. It's such a distinctive colour, and works very well so long as you've got a strong bass clarinet player. A little further into the second movement, you have the question of where the trumpets should be – and how many of them should play. I really like the idea of revisiting the sound of the *banda* from the first movement, but I also understand people who think it should just be the orchestral trumpets here.

NS: And of course there are no timpani playing with them in this movement, which feels like an anomaly.

JH: Exactly. I've tried it every possible way – and I mention all this now because we're talking about balance. If you unleash the nine *banda* trumpets from the gallery at the *Maestoso* in the second movement [the fifth bar after Fig. 8, bar 163] it's just too loud. I usually end up with three of the *banda* playing as well as the three orchestral trumpets, which are – confusingly – written in C here – just like the *banda*, whereas everywhere else the orchestral trumpets are in F. Having some of the *banda* playing from the balcony certainly makes for an impressive moment, but you could argue that it diminishes the effect of having the extra trumpets playing just at the beginning and the end of the work. It's even more of a problem near the end of the movement [one bar before Fig. 12, bar 218] where they come back as a kind of echo, marked *pianissimo*, and muted. That's nine *banda* trumpets *and* the three orchestral trumpets, against which the harp and violins – with tricky figurations – have to fight to be heard. Honestly, in my experience, even with the most wonderful players, it's basically impossible to bring it off when all the *banda* play at this point, so I came round to thinking that perhaps it works best with just the orchestral trumpets. But this is a personal choice: there's no doubt that Janáček intended to have all twelve trumpets here.

NS: You're in very good company. In the copied manuscript that Talich used for the premiere, Janáček originally specified '3 orchestral trumpets and 9 fanfare trumpets' – so it was definitely his idea – but Talich crossed out the '9 fanfare trumpets', leaving just the three in the orchestra. It can certainly work either way, although Janáček's instructions are quite clear.

JH: In the third movement, I suppose the first question is the viola d'amore, but it's not really practicable in a concert performance – it's a very different situation from the viola d'amore parts in the operas (*Fate, Káťa Kabanová, Makropulos*). But the viola writing is difficult and exposed in this movement, particularly at Fig. 3 [bar 35]. I know some conductors add violins here to lend a bit of support, but I've never done that – partly because I always want to be faithful to the score, but also because if you have a really good viola section who are well prepared, then of course it's manageable the way it is, and it keeps the viola colour. By the way, something else about this passage – a practical matter – it's impossible to make it work unless the violas and the harp (which doubles the viola line) are close together on the platform.

Then there's the *con moto* [bar 42, four bars before Fig. 4] which raises the question of how the trombone and tuba rhythm should be articulated: it's notated as quaver–dotted crotchet, each with a staccato dot but also with a slur over each pair of notes. The interpretation differs quite a lot among conductors, some of them preferring a slightly gentler articulation, others preferring something more jagged. I suspect the slurs are probably just a way of grouping the notes.

But this movement throws up all sorts of challenges. The famous passage for the flutes is crazy ...

NS The great first flute of the Czech Philharmonic, Gustav Nesporý, told Janáček at a rehearsal for the premiere that it was unplayable – and even before that, Janáček's copyist, Václav Sedláček, who was the piccolo player in the Brno opera orchestra, made a few modifications. Anyway, Janáček seems to have wanted something more like a sound-effect ...

JH: Ah, yes – when he said, 'It's got to be like the wind – I heard it!' I've been able to get some exciting results in that passage – but it takes a bit of diplomacy because you have to encourage very fine players not to be too precise but instead to aim for the overall effect. At the *Prestissimo*, Fig. 11, if you go for the tempo that's written – crotchet = 152 – it's absolutely impossible for the flutes to play their music [starting at bar 172]. So you can't stay strictly in tempo for the flute phrases – I mean it's unimaginable. But what I try to do is make the flute bars as fast as possible to create one big, dramatic gesture.

NS: We know from Janáček's letters that he thought this *Prestissimo* passage was never fast enough in the performances he heard! I like your solution – it keeps the wild spirit of the music.

JH: I definitely don't subscribe to the view of many conductors – including my teacher Jiří [Bělohlávek] who would halve the speed there – so that the one-in-a-bar 2/4 of the *Prestissimo* became a crotchet beat for the flute passages. That used to be the usual solution, but it sacrifices the wildness and energy of this music.

NS: So the trick is to create the illusion that it's all in one tempo even if it needs to be stretched slightly to accommodate the flutes?

JH: Exactly. Let's turn to the fourth movement and the eternal debate about Janáček's 'zvonky'.

NS: You always use a glockenspiel here, don't you?

JH: Certainly in more recent years, yes. After all, it's the sound of the street – not a church.

NS: Yes – actually, it reminds me of the warning bells on old Brno trams! Jaroslav Vogel, who was at the premiere, said it was played by a glockenspiel then, and there's no reason to disbelieve him. I think it's the most effective solution, though I did hear a performance by Simon Rattle and the LSO a few years ago which used a particularly tinny sounding tubular bell, and actually, that worked fine – but I'd always go for a glockenspiel – above all because I think it's what Janáček wanted.

JH: And we should remember that linguistically, 'zvonky' cannot be big bells – it's a diminutive, so it's completely clear to me that he meant something small.

NS: Things were confused by the first edition of the score, where the orchestra list at the front specified 'campane' rather than 'campanelli'. And on the original printed part, it also says 'Campane'. The 'Campane' part in the Czech Philharmonic's set of the old printed parts is covered in the alternatives chosen by generations of different conductors – they've tried everything over the years: a glockenspiel, a keyed glockenspiel, a tubular bell... . But I think the consensus is now for a glockenspiel, and 'campanelli' are now specified in Jiří Zahrádka's edition, which should really settle the matter.

By the way, another thing Vogel said, in his review of Talich's premiere, was that Talich didn't play the *Sinfonietta* as if it was by Suk or Strauss, but instead he 'let Janáček be Janáček'. I like that: he trusted the composer to know what he was doing – and that this was slightly crazy music.

JH: And Janáček was very happy with that performance. There's another amazing remark by Talich which I particularly like: 'We all wanted to help Janáček, and he crushed us all.' Very touching, isn't it?

NS: It is – and we should discuss the changes Talich made at the very end of the *Sinfonietta*, the last seven bars, marked *Adagio* [bars 279–85].

JH: There's a lot to talk about there. Talich added horns, trumpets and timpani. But my friend Michael Kroutil, the timpanist of the Czech Philharmonic, makes a very good point. He says it makes no sense, in any context, to play the timpani rolls at the end with wooden sticks – and of course there's no time to change from wooden sticks to something else after the reprise of the Fanfares. Now, elsewhere in the piece, the timpani play exclusively with the *banda*. And then suddenly, there's this roll and I'm not convinced it should be there.

NS: Putting the timpani to one side for a moment, the *banda* don't have anything to play at the end in the original edition, or in the manuscript sources, but František Neumann wrote a chord for them into his corrected copy of the score – and that suggests this idea might have been an afterthought by Janáček himself – it's much simpler than the elaborate rescoring Klemperer noted in his score [see the Appendix for illustrations of both]. But have you ever done the ending as Janáček first wrote it, before any of Talich's adjustments?

JH: Yes – I tried it in a rehearsal with the Czech Philharmonic, using the original scoring so that the *Adagio* bars started without timpani, without trumpets and without horns. After all the triumph of the fanfares, I thought it would be interesting to hear a less grandiose little coda to the whole piece, with a slightly leaner sound. And it was *shocking* – [laughter] – I just had to say, 'No! No!' But a couple of players in the Czech Phil said to me, 'You're just not used to it; you should persevere!' They were actually excited about it, and Michael Kroutil, the timpanist, thought it made much more sense – with no need for the impossible change of mallets. And Janáček did this kind of thing in other pieces too – for instance, at the end of *Fate* where the timpani are missing. I suppose at the end of the *Sinfonietta*, a compromise would be to have the timpani and the *banda* only coming in for the last three bars.

NS: I totally agree – except there's no authority for it, so it would certainly be provocative – but then, so would playing the ending as Janáček first wrote it!

JH: There's a similar case at the climax of the Kostelinička's aria in Act II of *Jenůfa* [starting one bar after Fig. 71]. I had a passionate debate with Jiří [Zahrádka] about this, as those *fortissimo* horn quavers were crossed out by Janáček – he was looking for a sound which was leaner. It's a really interesting question: maybe what he wanted was something more effortful from the woodwinds at that point, rather than the easy-going splendour of the brass. If you look at Janáček's scores, while there's writing that is very edgy and brassy – full of metallic sounds – for the most part they are much more transparent. He was never a fan of the big, opulent Germanic sound. Even in his most Romantic-sounding scores, like *Taras Bulba*, it's not conventional scoring. Think about the Coda [between bars 166 and 190]. Now, Talich, Bakala and Mackerras all doubled the organ right hand with trumpets, but that's not what Janáček wrote: it is only on the organ in his original. So if you have a very powerful organ (and a very good organist who can really articulate the melodic line with those octave jumps), then that would be my ideal. If I ever get to record it in somewhere like the Rudolfinum – which has an excellent organ – with the Czech Phil, then I think I will go for it and do it as Janáček wrote it, with very bright organ registration – and get rid of those added trumpet parts. There's a similar situation a bit earlier on in the third movement of *Taras Bulba* [starting at bar 123, ten bars before Fig. 27]. For the last few years, I've left out the added trumpets there too. Having those chords just on the trombones gives a completely different – and thrilling – sound.

NS: I'm so glad you do that because it also means that the wonderful woodwind phrase over the top of everything at that point [bar 123] can actually be heard! It always frustrates me if that doesn't come through. Even though it's marked *fortissimo*, the woodwind don't stand a chance if they're swamped by trumpets.

JH: It's a piece I always love to do – and you have to work at trying to get it right. Speaking purely personally, it's more of a challenge as a conductor, and it's also Janáček at his most ambitious. Having said that, the *Sinfonietta* is undoubtedly his most effective orchestral piece. You cannot escape its charm!

NS: 'Charm' is a great word to describe it, and it's a quality that's sometimes missing from performances of the *Sinfonietta*, when people take the 'Military' of Janáček's original title a bit too seriously and forgot that it's a 'Sinfonietta' after all. Of course, the big moments need to be tremendous, but there's a capricious spirit – humour too – in the central movements, and we need to feel that. I do hope you're going to record the *Sinfonietta* yourself one day?

JH: Definitely, and with the Czech Philharmonic, when time permits. And who knows, I may be able to record those alternative endings!

6
The *Sinfonietta*:
A Musical Commentary

An examination of the musical material of the *Sinfonietta* reveals the extent to which Janáček had achieved an extraordinary level of compositional sophistication by the time he came to write the work. Hans Hollander declared that with the *Sinfonietta*, 'Janáček reached the zenith of his orchestral works.... Although he remains faithful to his characteristic idiom, his style is of a thematic density and formal conciseness as in no other work. His inspiration has freed itself from its habitual literary and extra-musical stimulus, and has created a series of five orchestral miniatures that are of absolute mastery in invention, sound and structure.'[1] The overall five-movement form of the *Sinfonietta* has been likened at various times to a 'suite' (by Helfert and others), a 'divertimento' (by Hollander), and even a 'symphony' (by Janáček himself in a letter to his wife). These attempts to redefine or explain the title demonstrate how difficult it is to pin any conventional genre description on this highly original structure. In the published score, seen through the press by the composer, the movement titles have no programmatic designations, underlining Hollander's point about the composer moving away from any specific non-musical stimulus:

I. Allegretto
II. Andante
III. Moderato
IV. Allegretto
V. Andante con moto [Allegro[2]]

The Písek, Sokol and Brno inspirations, all discussed at length in Chapter 1, were of great significance for Janáček himself, but no mention of them is to

---

[1] Hollander 1963, p. 181.
[2] Given incorrectly as 'Allegro' in the first edition (UE 1927), Burghauser 1979 and Füssl 1980.

be found in his manuscript or in the editions published in his lifetime. The 'Military' part of Janáček's original title – another extra-musical hint – was dropped before publication, apparently with the composer's acquiescence. The implication of all this has to be that by the end of 1926 when the score was printed, Janáček had decided that the piece was to be understood and listened to as abstract music, however personal its external stimuli may have been. As early as April 1927, Vladimír Helfert argued, persuasively, that the *Sinfonietta* signalled a move by Janáček towards a kind of Moravian-inflected neoclassicism: 'If it didn't sound so contradictory, I would say that Janáček is here approaching a kind of classical period in his work.'[3] The very close integration of thematic material not only within movements but across the work as a whole lends strong support to Helfert's viewpoint. This aspect of the *Sinfonietta* has been described by John K. Novak as demonstrating 'a remarkable unity', and he added that 'all five movements are closely linked through pitch class, motive and key relationships.'[4]

The broader structure can be viewed as a kind of arch form – a design more usually associated with works by Janáček's younger contemporary, Bartók. This 'arch' is not only a consequence of the return of the Fanfares at the end the work but is also due to the similar, variation-like character of the second and fourth movements, and at the heart of the work, the slow–fast–slow–fast–slow form of the rhapsodic third movement, which has within it echoes of a Dvořákian dumka. Below is a diagram of the overall design of the *Sinfonietta*.

The accounts of each movement that follow are intended as a straightforward guide to Janáček's compositional method. They include quotations from commentaries ranging from those by writers who knew Janáček (Helfert, Vogel and Hollander) to the much more recent analytical studies by Zdeněk Skoumal (2020) and John K. Novak (2016), which should be consulted by anyone seeking a greater level of forensic detail. This chapter includes a number of music examples that are intended to enable readers to read the commentary as a stand-alone document. However, it may also be helpful to have a copy of the score to hand. Note that here, as elsewhere, all bar numbers refer to the 2017 UE score edited by Jiří Zahrádka.

---

[3] Helfert 1927, p. 111.
[4] Novak 2016, p. 232. Novak's extended discussion of the *Sinfonietta* is to be found on pp. 225–47.

Sinfonietta: overall design

I. Allegretto
Fanfares
A–B–A¹

II. Andante
Developing variations

III. Moderato
'Dumka', A–B–A–B–A
Moderato
Con moto
Moderato
Più mosso – Prestissimo
Moderato

IV. Allegretto
Variations ['Scherzo']

V. Andante con moto
A–B–C–development–Fanfares–Coda

I. Allegretto

The Fanfares are played by the *banda* alone (nine trumpets in C, two bass trumpets, two tenor tubas and timpani). This tremendously arresting music is a fine illustration of what Zdeněk Skoumal has described as Janáček's gift for creating 'interest and vitality while maintaining unity';[5] for Jaroslav Vogel, the Fanfares were 'a good example of Janáček's way of gradually hatching his motifs'[6] – a process that unfolds in a most imaginative way.

---

[5] A detailed analysis of the first movement of the *Sinfonietta* can be found in Skoumal 2020, pp. 238–46. Interested readers are urged to read Skoumal's compelling account of Janáček's composing methods.
[6] Vogel 1981, p. 323.

The movement can be divided into three distinct sections: A, comprising bars 1–59; B, starting with the time-signature change at bar 60; and A¹ (since it is closely based on the opening material) from the *Maestoso* at bar 76 to the end. Underpinning the whole movement is the palindromic rhythm of two quavers–crotchet–crotchet–two quavers first heard in bars 6–7 on the timpani and bass trumpets (**ex. 6.1b**). This is the fundamental rhythmic motif that drives the movement, and Skoumal identifies 'distinct but related'[7] melodic ideas associated with it which are heard separately and in combination. First, there are the tenor tubas that start the work in parallel open fifths (bars 1–21) (**ex. 6.1a**). The pitches of the second tuba are A flat–G flat–E flat–G flat–E flat–G flat–E flat, and the tubas play three seven-bar phrases (of 3 + 4 bars each). From this grows its very close relative, the timpani/bass trumpet motif with the palindromic rhythm in bars 6–7, 13–14 and 20–21 on the notes G flat–E flat–G flat–E flat–G flat–E flat (**ex. 6.1b**). The nine trumpets enter in unison at bar 11 with an idea (**ex. 6.1c**), which is an inversion and extension of the timpani motif. While the underlying shape is of 3 x 7 bars (articulated by the tubas), the phrase structure is more subtle than that as the timpani/bass trumpets play two-bar phrases which interlock with the unison trumpets playing three-bar phrases.

What happens next (bar 22, Fig. 1) is a demonstration of composing skill of the highest order. The wheeling fifths of the tubas are doubled in speed, now in crotchets, preceded by a rest, and grouped in threes (a crotchet rest, then 3 + 3 + 3 crotchets) to underpin five-bar phrases (**ex. 6.1d**). Over the next twenty bars (5 + 5 + 5 + 5 bars), the trumpets play in three-part harmony, in four-bar phrases (each followed by a one-bar rest), their rhythm expanded by additional bars at the start of each phrase of two quavers and a crotchet) at the same time as the intervals also expand (**ex. 6.1e**). At bar 32 there's further variety, with the first bar of each phrase becoming a group of four quavers (**ex. 6.1f**).

The music continues to gain momentum from bar 42 (Fig. 2) to bar 59: the intervals of the trumpet phrases become wider, and there's a subtle change in the rhythms and the phrase lengths, which are now nine bars long (3 + 2 + 2 + 2 bars), each punctuated by two iterations of the familiar timpani and bass trumpet motif (**ex. 6.1g**). Meanwhile, the tubas play sustained notes, marking out the divisions within each phrase (3 bars, then 3 x 2 bars).

At bar 60, there's a change of time signature to 3/4, but the pulse of each bar remains the same (minim = 72 becomes dotted minim = 72). With ingenious (and exciting) metrical shifts, the palindromic timpani rhythm is

---

[7] Skoumal 2020, p. 238.

still there, but it is now woven into a more rhythmically complex texture: in trumpets 4–6, then in the timpani and bass trumpets (**ex. 6.1h**), while the tubas play repeated dotted minims, marking each bar with a *sforzando*. Phrase lengths are now varied: 3 + 3 bars, then 4 bars, then 6 bars (with the trumpet figure developing still further) until the return to 2/4 at bar 76 (marked *maestoso* but still with the underlying pulse remaining the same). Now the trumpet motif is transformed into a triumphant, rhythmically augmented variant (**ex. 6.1i**), each phrase of 2 + 2 + 2 bars starting with two minims; at the same time, the tubas underpin this with *three*-bar phrases in minims (so 3 + 3 bars) while the bass trumpets (punctuated in part by the timpani) continue to play the five-quaver idea that had emerged in the previous section. At bar 88, trumpets 7–9 in the *banda* fall silent while the upper two groups (trumpets 1–3 and 4–6) engage in a brief dialogue over fragmented pairs of quavers in the bass trumpets and timpani. After the symmetry of the preceding six-bar phrases, Janáček continues to create ambiguity and excitement with a seven-bar phrase leading to bar 95 (Fig. 4) which continues in seven-bar groups (each 2 + 2 + 3 bars) until the climax of the Fanfares at bar 109 with the change in time signature to 3/2 and the establishment of D flat major, over nine consecutive repetitions of the timpani/bass trumpet palindromic rhythm. For the first time in the movement, a kind of rhythmic stability is established here, but Janáček maintains interest by introducing a kind of hemiola effect in trumpets 1–3 and 4–6 from bar 114 to the end, their chords grouped in pairs of minims and thus crossing the bar lines (**ex. 6.1j**). The final D flat major chord deserves special mention: Janáček introduces an E flat in the trumpet 9 part, an effect that seems to add extra resonance to the sound (as well as harmonic spice) and the special kind of brilliance that comes from colouring the chord in this way (**ex. 6.1k**).

Ex. 6.1. I. Allegretto, themes.

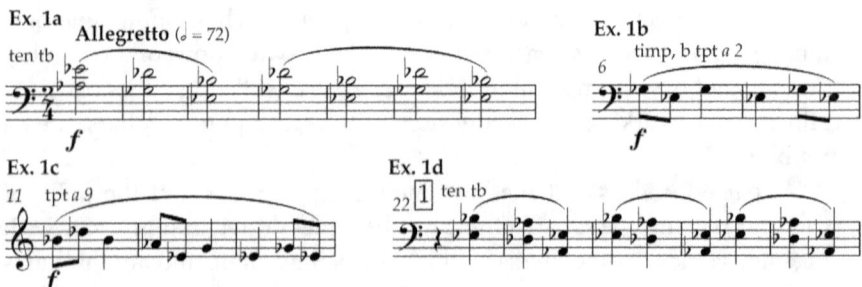

Ex. 6.1. cont.

II. Andante

This movement contains a number of themes all of which have common features and with accompaniments based on variants of the same material: the level of thematic integration is remarkable, as is the variety Janáček creates using these ideas. The structure is hard to describe and can perhaps best be thought of as a continually evolving series of free variations on interrelated motifs. Peter Brown has proposed an ingenious description: 'a variation chain, whose links are of different materials and different shapes.'[8] He goes on to say that 'for all its unusual combinations of gesture and its sense of spontaneous improvisation, the piece provides its own, perhaps not completely explainable, brand of coherence.'[9] Hollander makes a similar

---

[8] A. Peter Brown: *The Symphonic Repertoire. Vol. 4: The Second Golden Age of the Viennese Symphony* (Bloomington: Indiana University Press, 2003), p. 519.
[9] Brown 2003, p. 519.

point, noting that almost all the significant musical components are either derived from, or variants of, each other (references to bar numbers have been adjusted to match the UE 2017 edition):

> The second movement ... begins with a rotating demi-semiquaver figure on the clarinets, with which a brief syncopated motif (trombones, bassoons) is combined. Later (bar 46) a lyrical melody detaches itself from the rotating figure – an augmentation of the former motif, accompanied by its original form. In a further episode (Fig. 4, bars 80–97), the melody appears once more, in A flat minor and in rhythmic variation; lastly, its melodic inversion, blown by the trumpets, comes to the fore (*Maestoso*, bars 163–73). The main subject of the movement (bar 5) is a lively dance tune[10] which, after a broad exposition subsequently returns and rounds off the movement by way of a coda.[11]

Novak points out that as well as the variations and motivic transformations in this movement, there are two places which might suggest a more conventional concept of symphonic development. He describes these passages as 'developmental sections' – starting at Fig. 4 (bar 80), and at bar 194.[12]

Jaroslav Vogel describes the main theme (starting at bar 5) as a 'burlesque, dance-like tune ... which is introduced by a simultaneous diminution of its own material (drawn from bar 9) in the clarinets, and an augmentation in the trombones [bars 1–4]' (**ex. 6.2a**). The rising pair of notes in bar 8 and in the trombones in bars 1–4 is another of the brief gestures that will return later in the work, particularly in the fourth movement. The *più mosso* at bar 69 is an apparently new idea, but Vogel notes that it is 'a derivation from the repeated-note hammerings of the doubled Es of the introductory clarinet figure', and he adds an important observation that 'this is yet another proof that Janáček did not arrive at his motivic variants by mere speculation.' He also points out that the trumpet fanfares (starting at bar 163) are 'a festive-sounding variant of the main theme' (**ex. 6.2b**).

Vogel, Hollander and Novak emphasise that this is a movement in which the closely related musical components are continually transformed and modified. The result may be an unconventional structure, but within it there is complete coherence: Janáček finds spontaneous-sounding contrasts of tempo, texture and expressive intention while maintaining extraordinary control over the ideas themselves.

---

[10] Elsewhere (p. 97, ex. 9), Hollander demonstrates the similarity of this tune to a Moravian dance song.
[11] Hollander 1963, p. 182.
[12] Novak 2016, pp. 235–8. Bar numbers adjusted to match UE 2017.

Ex. 6.2. II. Andante, themes.

III. Moderato

The closest the *Sinfonietta* comes to a slow movement is the third, marked *Moderato*, but any sense of tranquillity and calm is relatively short-lived because of Janáček's chosen design for the movement. In 1927, Vladimír Helfert summarised it as follows:

> The third movement is an interesting structure. In it, Janáček created something that is very close in form to Dvořák's dumky, with their characteristic alternations of a freely meditative theme interrupted by passages that are sharply rhythmicised.[13]

Hollander also described the third movement as 'dumka-like', with slower sections contrasting with fast episodes. He further noted that some of the musical material of the faster music is 'formed out of the original accompanying figure of the subject'. There's an even closer integration than that since so many of the component parts of this movement are derivatives or variants of each other – a notable feature of the first two movements too, albeit with a completely different expressive end in view. The Dvořák model – marked by its sudden alternations of slow material with fast, exuberant music and back again – is one Janáček repurposes here in a highly imaginative way, and the parallels don't stop with the tempo changes. In Dvořák's well-known Slavonic Dance in E minor, Op. 46, No. 2, a classic Dvořákian dumka, another notable feature is the extreme economy of the musical material – the slower more lyrical sections and the faster ones with which they alternate are based on very closely related thematic material. The same is true of this movement which can be divided into five sections of greatly differing length, A–B–A–B–A. The opening tempo marking is *Moderato* with the metronome minim = 66 and the music notated in 2/2 time, suggesting that Janáček intended it not to feel too slow but to sway in a gentle two in a bar. The opening is over a long E flat (dominant) pedal in the bass clarinet and tuba, unchanging for the first fourteen bars. Vogel wrote that it 'seems to spread darkness over the earth', while the main theme unfurls above it: 'a sweetly yearning melody' on muted violins and cellos, accompanied by arpeggio figures in the violas and harp. As Janáček repeats the last bar of the violin and cello theme (Fig. 1, bars 12–15), the bass descends by step to a rich cadence into C flat major. While the arpeggios continue to animate the music, the melodic line is taken over first by the cor anglais, then by the first oboe, and then a more impassioned variant on

---

[13] Helfert 1927, p. 112.

unmuted violins, in octaves. At Fig. 3 (bar 35), the bass moves to a pedal A in the tuba for two bars, then an A flat, and there's a delicate and beautiful change of colour, the melodic material in chordal harmony played by four flutes and the bass clarinet (marked *pp*) while the arpeggio figure starts to assume greater prominence, with four very exposed bars for the violas and harp, marked *mf*. Janáček once again extends the end of the phrase by repeating its last bar three more times (bars 39–41), leading to a cadence into D flat minor. This coincides with the change of tempo to *Con moto* in 2/4 (crotchet = 100) at bar 42. Though harmonically quite mobile, up to this point all the musical material has evolved naturally from the violin and cello theme in the first few bars, and its accompanying arpeggios on violas and harp (**ex. 6.3a, 6.3b and 6.3c**).

With the arrival of the new tempo, three trombones and tuba take up a short–long motif which is directly related – melodically and rhythmically – to the opening theme, so much so that the third trombone has the same notes, E flat–F flat, as the violins at the start (**ex. 6.3a**), now repeated three times (**ex. 6.3d**). At bar 45 (one bar before Fig. 4) the first of the flute and piccolo semiquaver flourishes sends a kind of shiver through the texture, an idea that is derived directly from the viola and harp arpeggios (**ex. 6.3e**). These two derivatives urge the music forward, the scoring pared back to trombones, tuba, three flutes and piccolo (bars 42–78), ending in a longer cadenza-like passage for flutes and piccolo. A return to the opening tempo brings an impassioned variant of the opening melody at Fig. 6 (bar 79) – this time accompanied by sustained low flute E flats notes intercut by uneasy arpeggiated murmurings. This leads to the *Più mosso* at bar 86, led off by the first trombone with a new motif, again clearly related to the opening, though now at a significantly faster tempo of crotchet = 144 (**ex. 6.3f**) with a spiky off-beat quaver accompaniment. The answering phrase on the first clarinet is another close relative of the opening. The music that follows this is a magnificent demonstration of Janáček's gift for gradually animating a musical texture: from Fig. 9 (bar 122) onwards (a time signature change from 2/4 to 2/8, but with the underlying pulse remaining the same), the ostinato figures begin as choppy offbeats supporting brusque horn figurations. With the entry of the 'trombone' theme from bar 86 – now on the oboes – the violins begin frenetic demisemiquavers (bar 129), more woodwinds join in (bar 134), the first horn ostinatos reach ever higher, and fragments of them are passed from trombones and lower strings to the three orchestral trumpets (in unison). The variety and energy of the accompaniment figures throughout the whole of this passage, especially from Fig. 9 to Fig. 11, is an astonishing display of Janáček's compositional virtuosity, piling on tension through the cumulative use of multiple ostinatos until the dam bursts at

The Sinfonietta: A Musical Commentary 185

Fig. 11: a riotous *Prestissimo* apotheosis of the music that had first emerged on the trombones at bar 42 (four bars before Fig. 4), the flutes and piccolo swirling even more wildly now, until their last descending shrieks subside to a quiet echo of the trombone chords (at bar 199). A return to the initial *Moderato* gives way to a much-condensed reprise of the opening material, first on the oboe, followed by a last, hushed reminiscence of the trombone chords, then the cor anglais, and an exquisite cadential phrase, repeated three times, establishing a serene close in E flat major, the notes of the tonic triad picked out by violas and harp, the underlying harmony (three iterations of V–I, B flat–E flat) softly etched in by bass clarinet, cellos and basses, and the first and second violins adding delicate colour in the upper register.

Ex. 6.3. III. Moderato, themes.

Ex. 6.3. *cont.*

IV. Allegretto

For Jaroslav Vogel, this movement 'takes the place of a scherzo',[14] and its character suggests a certain playfulness, though the structure is that of a miniature theme and variations. The dance-like theme, announced *leggero* by the three orchestral trumpets in unison, has hints of a polka but also has within it (in bars 2–3 and bars 5–6) echoes of the palindromic timpani rhythm from the Fanfares; and the two rising crotchets (sounding D flat–E flat) in bar 7 also have links with music heard earlier, notably from bars 1–4 and bar 9 of the second movement (**ex. 6.4a**). Here this pair of notes is used as a springboard for a three-bar extension of the polka melody in the cellos and basses, each pair of crotchets starting a whole tone lower. What follows is a series of variations. At bar 22 (variation 1) the theme is accompanied by a string descant (**ex. 6.4b**) and at bar 30 (variation 2) by a more lyrical string theme with descending quavers that are themselves varied later in the movement (from bar 140 onwards) (**ex. 6.4c**). Bar 40 (variation 3) introduces a rising figure in the strings which intensifies the sense of urgency. All three variations are on different pedal notes (B flat at bar 23, E flat at bar 30, C flat at bar 40) which produce a tantalisingly ambiguous harmonic perspective. As Novak writes, 'the elastic ability of this motive [the trumpet theme] to function in different keys is a core feature of the movement.'[15] The key only settles on A flat minor at bar 50 (Fig. 3) for variation 4, when the tune is taken over by oboes, clarinets and horns over an A flat pedal, coloured by trills in the upper strings, followed by five bars of string tutti and horns developing the two-crotchet idea. Variation 5 (bar 63) moves into D flat major, with the addition of an ardent violin counterpoint (**ex. 6.4d**), and in variation 6 (bar 88, one after Fig. 4) the woodwind develop the falling sixths of the violin descant from the previous variation over the theme on muted horns (**ex. 6.4e**).

Hollander wrote that the trumpet theme in this movement is 'developed in the manner of an ostinato, by changes in the scoring and key', but as already noted, this theme generates two distinct ostinatos: one derived from the four quavers (in bar 1) and the other from the pairs of crotchets (in bar 7). These come together in a highly compressed form at Fig. 5 (bars 105–11) while the remaining component of the original trumpet theme – the palindromic timpani rhythm from the first movement – interjects on trombones (bars 110–1) (**ex. 6.4f**). Further developments of the polka tune (variations 7–9) lead to a cadential figure, first heard at Fig. 7 (bars 138–9). The *Presto* which follows (variation 10) has a descending chromatic

---

[14] Vogel 1981, p. 325.
[15] Novak 2016, p. 243.

idea over the whole-tone crotchet pairs. The *Meno mosso* at Fig. 8 brings a return of the theme (variation 11), this time on oboes, accompanied by a new figure made up of arpeggiated perfect fourths (E flat, A flat, D flat, A flat) in the harp and violas (**ex. 6.4g**), and this is continued (at bar 62) by the theme on the trumpet, with the quaver accompaniment moving to cellos and basses (variation 12). A slower recollection of the theme on the clarinet (variation 13) never reaches the seventh bar of the phrase (the rising crotchet pair); instead, it is brusquely interrupted by a *Presto* coda at bar 178 in which the harp/viola fourths are taken up by piccolo, flutes, oboes violins, while clarinets, horns, violas (and trombones, cellos and basses from bar 182) play a quaver–dotted crotchet variant of the two-note motif from the first statement of the theme (and, by extension, from the start of the second movement), to drive things to a frenetic close.

In this movement, Hans Hollander detected a clear folk influence, 'with its modal polka theme [that] underlines Janáček's affinity with East Moravian folk music.'[16] Elsewhere (p. 98, ex. 10 and ex. 11), Hollander also suggested parallels between the theme and the folk song 'Ach, měl jsem já milenki' from Hustopeče. Zdeněk Skoumal is more circumspect about this apparent connection, noting that 'the similarities are the repeated notes at the beginning and the descending major third at the end. Although these resemblances may be coincidental, they do point to an approach to melody that could have been influenced by Janáček's study of folk music.'[17]

[16] Hollander 1963, p. 183.
[17] Skoumal 2020, pp. 106–7.

Ex. 6.4. IV. Allegretto, themes.

Ex. 6.4. *cont.*

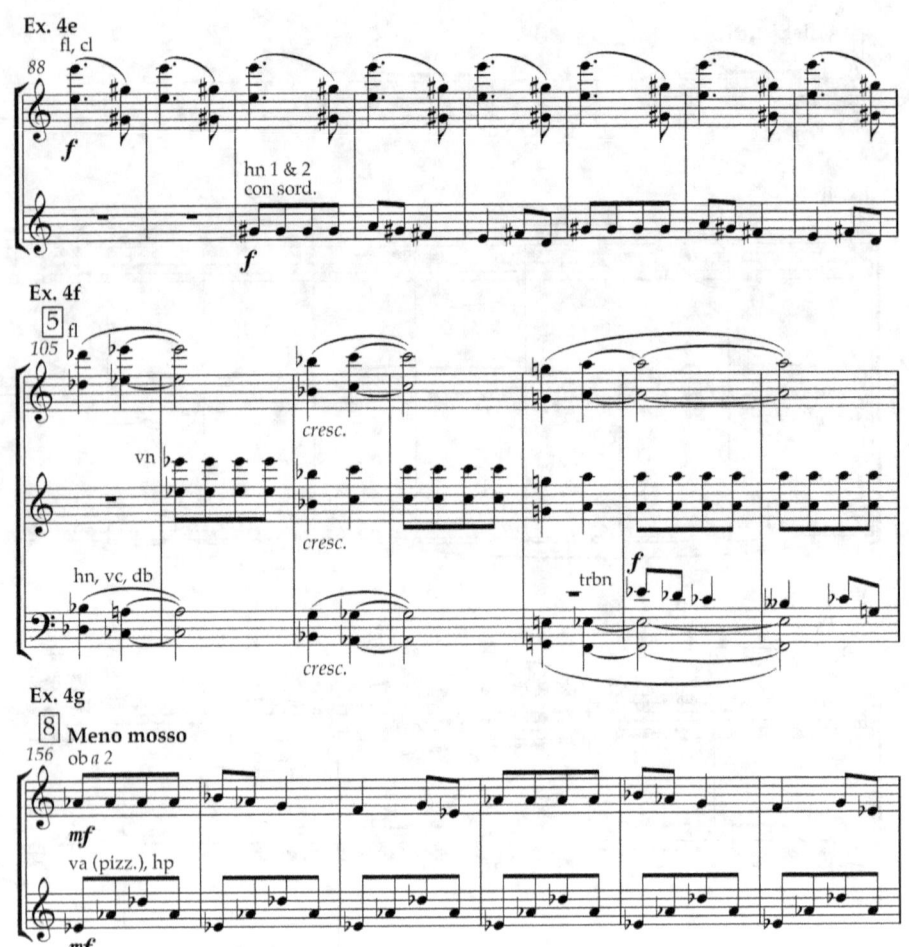

V. Andante con moto

The last movement is a more complex design. The structure can be summarised as A–B–C–development–Fanfares–Coda or, more cumbersomely, A–B–C–B¹–A¹–C¹–Fanfares–Coda.[18] The A section is dominated by the plaintive minor-key flute melody with which it begins (and multiple ideas derived from it); the B section (bars 48–90) grows out of the same rising three-note motif as the start of the movement but serves a far more dramatic purpose, creating what Novak has described as 'growing tension and excitement.' Section C (bars 91–121) is a faster contrasting passage, with a complete change of texture. Greatly varied and abbreviated developments of B and A, and an even shorter recollection of C (dominated by the return of the *banda*) lead to a complete reprise of the Fanfares from the first movement, accompanied by increasingly urgent and colourful contributions from the orchestra, transforming the character of the original version into something yet more exultant. The form of this finale may be unorthodox, but it is entirely right for Janáček's purposes.

The A section begins with a gentle phrase on the flutes, the last three notes of which (bars 3–4) are a direct echo of the first three notes played by the tubas at the start of the work, and at the same pitches (E flat, D flat, B flat) (**ex. 6.5a**). These three notes in turn generate the string ostinatos (in sextuplets) which are the other main component of the opening section (**ex. 6.5b**). It provides another striking example in the *Sinfonietta* of Janáček's ability to develop ideas by generating one from another, then fragmenting or expanding them to create tension and momentum. After repeating the opening phrase, Janáček shifts the music up a fourth (Fig. 1, bar 12). The violin sextuplets become more agitated (bars 21–4) before being fragmented (bar 25), a process that Janáček then applies to the opening theme (in bar 34), using its first bar to push towards Fig. 2 (bar 38). Now the first three notes of the sextuplets evolve into a more urgent and propulsive ostinato, split between violins and violas, while the flute theme is compressed, eventually reduced to its first three notes (bars 41–5). These now become the start of a new idea at bar 48 (*meno mosso*): a dramatic clarinet solo in the upper reaches of its register, shadowed by sustained single notes on the piccolo (**ex. 6.5c**). Some entirely new ideas rumble in the bass

---

[18] Novak, p. 244, proposes a formal outline of the movement as A–B–C–development–retransition–return of movement 1. As he points out, Burghauser's suggestion of A–B–C–B–A is an oversimplification: 'While the themes of section A and B do return in that order, their function, as revealed by harmony and texture, is not one of restatement, but one of development and retransition.'

beneath this: thick, four-part trombone chords (sometimes supported by double basses, which also punctuate the texture with *sf* pizzicato chords), while the cellos teem with activity, playing many bars of a motoric ostinato in demisemiquavers. At Fig. 3 (bar 64), the oboe (sometimes doubled an octave lower by cor anglais) takes over the clarinet line. Then there is a shift in tone colour as the main theme moves to the flute, while the trombones, basses and hyperactive cellos, continue as before. The final iteration of the clarinet theme is on violins (in octaves), leading to the tempo change (*Più mosso*, 2/8) at bar 91 (the start of section C), the textures lighter and more transparent, with a swirling flute motif (echoed by clarinets), supported by repeated upper string chords (**ex. 6.5d**). The *Maestoso* at Fig. 6 – with its shrieking E flat clarinet solo – marks the start of an unconventional development section. It leads first to a varied return of the B section at Fig. 7 (bar 128). The trombone chords and the cello demisemiquavers are back as before, but the flutes now take the main theme, along with a new countermelody on E flat clarinet, and high-lying violin tremolos. As the tension builds, this leads seamlessly to a varied (and completely reharmonised) return of music from the A section (bar 141), its character now militant and propulsive, the textures sinewy and brilliantly lit – and intercut by answering phrases on E flat clarinet echoing the B section. This is followed by a brief passage derived from section C, dramatically disrupted by the thrilling re-entry of the *banda*. With the reprise of the opening Fanfares (Fig. 9, bar 162), the additions – building tension and excitement above and below the *banda* – are both exhilarating and subtle. To begin with (bars 162–92) there are expectant trills in the upper strings; flutes are added at bar 193, and at bar 203 a change in colour sees cellos and basses enter and the upper strings drop out for five bars before returning with emphatic crotchet trills (bars 208–11) doubled by flutes, oboes, trumpets and – to emphasise the cadence in bars 211–2 – trombones. Janáček continues to build this passage with considerable patience: at the time signature change (bar 221) the long trills are shifted to upper woodwind (flutes and clarinets) and lower strings (violas, cellos, basses), while oboes and orchestral trumpets add a new four-note motif (a triumphant variant of the crotchet trills from bar 208–11) which assumes greater importance in what follows. The trombones are kept in reserve until bar 236 (one bar before Fig. 12) where they now lend their full weight, underpinning the whole texture with the modulation into G flat major. At this point, too, the orchestral trumpets play a jubilant descant drawn from the trilling woodwind and string ostinatos – an unforgettable moment that needs very careful balance for all the strands to be heard clearly (**ex. 6.5e**). At Fig. 13 (bar 256) the crotchet trills evolve into a repeating four-note figure on woodwind and violas, punctuated by single chords in the rest of the strings. In bar 278 (one bar before the *Adagio*), Janáček gives the final word on the four-note idea (F–A flat–E flat–D flat) to the three orchestral trumpets, *fortissimo*, in unison: a telling detail that crowns this whole section. The coda comprises seven bars of solemn chords – D flat major–A flat minor–E major–D flat major – played by the orchestral brass (trombones – with trumpets and horns added by Talich), decorated by the trilling four-note idea (on upper strings and clarinets – customarily, if inauthentically, doubled by piccolo, flutes and oboes), until the magnificent resolution on to D flat, where – following suggestions made to Janáček by František Neumann and Otto Klemperer – the nine trumpets from the *banda* double the orchestral trumpets for the final chord (**ex. 6.5f**). What makes this magnificent finale so effective (and so exhilarating) is the way Janáček layers the orchestration in the reprise of the Fanfares, creating ever-growing levels of intensity to lead the work towards its cathartic and exultant coda.

Ex. 6.5. V. Andante con moto.

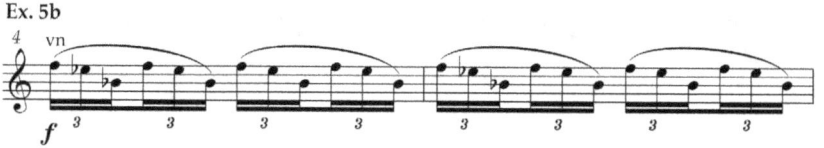

Ex. 6.5. cont.

Ex. 5d

Ex. 5e

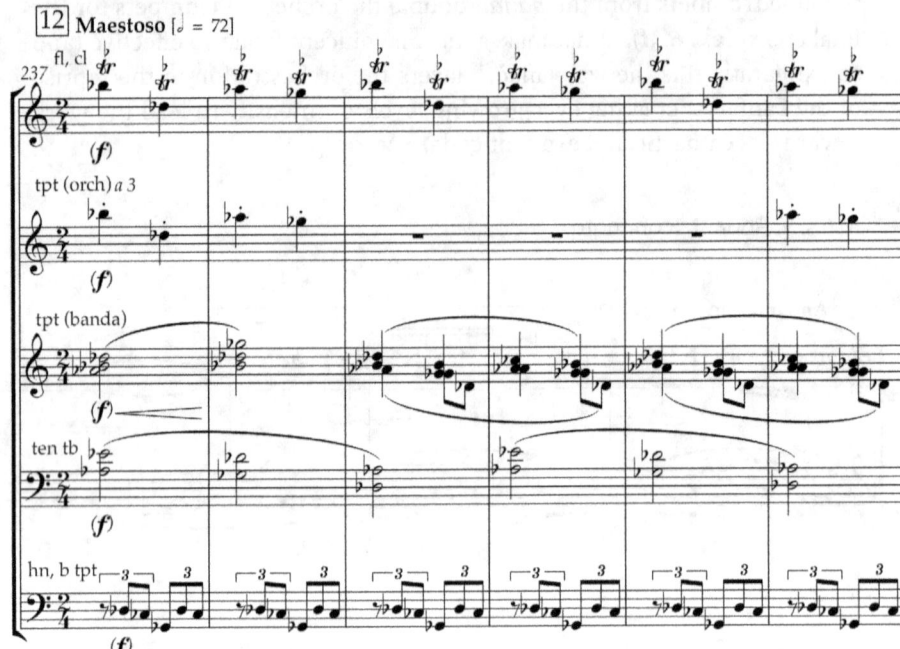

Ex. 5f

Coda
Rosa Newmarch on the *Sinfonietta*

One of the earliest English-language programme notes on the *Sinfonietta* was written by Rosa Newmarch (1857–1940), Janáček's most enthusiastic advocate in Britain and the person to whom Janáček dedicated the work – a fact Newmarch mentions in the heading of her note. She gives no hint of any extra-musical significance or inspiration, preferring instead to approach it entirely in terms of absolute music. Originally written for the work's London premiere in 1928 conducted by Henry Wood, Newmarch's note was reprinted in 1938.[1] Its historical interest lies primarily in its status as an introduction to British audiences of a composer whose music was completely unfamiliar at the time. In general, Newmarch's comments are typically concise and clearly expressed, though curiously she makes no mention of the entry of the *banda* trumpets in the second movement (she even omits trumpets from the list of instruments). She is more perceptive about the structure and thematic inter-relationships of the third movement and has useful comments on the finale. Above all, this note is fascinating in presenting the thoughts of the work's dedicatee – a dedication of which Newmarch was understandably proud. In her later book, *The Music of Czechoslovakia*, Newmarch summarised Janáček's style in this piece: 'What he has to say is said tersely, swiftly, and directly, with no time lost upon extended developments. This is strongly marked in the *Sinfonietta* for orchestra, a work in five movements, each of which is scored for a different combination of instruments.'[2] Her earlier thoughts provide a more detailed commentary:

---

[1] Rosa Newmarch: *The Concert-goer's Library of Descriptive Notes*, vol. 5 (London: Oxford University Press, 1938), pp. 58–60.
[2] Rosa Newmarch: *The Music of Czechoslovakia* (London: Oxford University Press, 1942), p. 224.

Sinfonietta for Orchestra. Leoš Janáček

(Dedicated to Mrs Rosa Newmarch)

The *Sinfonietta* dates from 1925 [*recte* 1926]. It is in five movements, each of which is scored for a different combination of instruments.

1. *Allegretto*, 2/4, for a rarely used combination of nine trumpets in C ... two tenor tubas, one bass trumpet [*recte* two bass trumpets], and a very original and interesting timpani part, for which a special military timpanum giving high B flat is used. The theme of this concise movement is heard throughout its three divisions: first in 2/4, then in a middle section, the measure altered to 3/4, and finally *maestoso* in the original time, but more fully orchestrated, over a pedal-point of fifths, held by tenor tubas.

2. *Andante*, 4/8. The orchestra employed consists of woodwind, [trumpets], trombones, and strings. After four introductory bars in which the clarinets have a continuous figure in demisemiquavers, a dance theme (in 2/4 time) enters in the oboes, accompanied by a humorous staccato figure for the four trombones, continuing for fifty bars. This is worked out in various guises. It interchanges with a second melody of a sustained character, introduced *meno mosso* by the woodwind over the clarinet figure, now given to the strings. The development of the dance theme and its rhythmic derivations is carried on till a *maestoso* is reached in which a derivative figure of accompaniment appears in the bass strings and assumes an important part. It accompanies a four-bar theme in the horns. A climax is built up, after which the dance section is recalled with variations and added figures. In this way the movement comes to a close.

3. *Moderato*. The feature of the scoring in this movement is that bassoons are replaced by a bass clarinet. It starts with muted strings and a very important quaver figure for harp. The movement continues with the working of a theme having a recurrent chord-figure of accompaniment. These chords form the thematic material of the first interlude (*con moto*, 2/4). This is succeeded by a brief return to *tempo primo*, leading to another and more lively episode (*più mosso*). Here the opening theme becomes more distinctly a dance motive, and, with new figures of accompaniment and sprightly counter-motives, it works up to a gay – even jovial – mood. Wild scale passages in the woodwind prepare the final return of the *moderato* section, the music dying away in reminiscent snatches from the opening bars of the movement.

4. *Allegretto*, 2/4. Three trumpets, unaccompanied, give out a playful polka theme on which the entire movement is constructed. Phrases of accompaniment and counter-motives are added by the strings and

horn. During a succession of trills in violins and violas, the polka tune is heard from the horns and oboes. It continues its wanderings through the clarinet, back to the muted horns, doubled by the flutes in octaves. Finally, the muted trumpets pick it up very gently. The theme and its members are then elaborated for a time with sudden transitions from quick to slow. Oboe, trumpet, and clarinet each sing it in turn, with a slackening of the time to *Andante*, after which an explosive *coda* brings a rapid close to the movement.

5. *Allegro*, 2/4. The flutes have a characteristic phrase in three-part harmony, answered by sextolet figures in the strings. This is repeated and somewhat elaborated, other instruments (oboe, clarinet) taking a share. A brisk middle section (*più mosso*), in which flute and clarinet answer each other in lively triplet figures over *staccato* chords for strings, leads to a broad *maestoso*. Strings and woodwind then bring back the original theme, but this soon gives place to a climax built upon the middle section. A repetition of the first movement of the *Sinfonietta* (*Allegretto*) now clinches the work. The chief modifications in this repetition are the greater fullness of the scoring for brass and the prolonged trills for strings, and later for woodwind, in which form they take on an almost thematic significance and are conspicuous in the imposing peroration.

Appendix
Scores Annotated by František Neumann, Otto Klemperer and Henry Wood

Three notable copies of the *Sinfonietta* include annotations by conductors who performed the work during Janáček's lifetime, two of them in his presence. The first is annotated by František Neumann, conductor of the Brno premiere and of the last live performance Janáček heard. This copy is now part of the Universal Edition collection in the Wienbibliothek im Rathaus, Vienna; the other two are in the Royal Academy of Music (RAM) Library in London: the score used by Otto Klemperer for the Berlin performance attended by Janáček in 1927 and that used by Henry Wood for the British premiere in 1928. Neumann's and Klemperer's copies are of particular interest as both conductors performed the *Sinfonietta* in Janáček's presence, in Brno and Berlin, respectively. Henry Wood's copy was marked up by him for the first performance in London on 10 February 1928, about which Janáček corresponded with Rosa Newmarch.

All three copies are the first issue of the full score, published by Universal Edition (Vienna and New York) in January 1927, with a print run of one hundred copies (PN U.E. 8679, 72 pp.). Klemperer also owned a copy of the 1927 Wiener Philharmonischer Verlag miniature score (PN U.E. 8680, W.Ph.V. 224, 115 pp.), which is in the RAM Library. It has his ownership stamp on the front cover but contains no markings. The 1927 full score (72 pp.) is referred to below as UE 1927; the 1927 pocket score (115 pp.) is referred to as WPhV 1927.

Note: Page references are to the copies of UE 1927; bar numbers in square brackets are taken from the UE 2017 edition, which has written-out repeats.

František Neumann's conducting score

Wienbibliothek im Rathaus, Vienna, *UE Janáček 004*

František Neumann (1874–1929) was the conductor most closely associated with Janáček's music during the composer's lifetime: he conducted the world premieres of *Káťa Kabanová*, *The Cunning Little Vixen*, *The Makropulos Affair* and *Šárka*, as well as *Taras Bulba*, the *Ballad of Blaník* and the *Lachian Dances*. He also conducted the Brno premiere of the *Sinfonietta*. All these performances were given in the presence of the composer who was also involved in rehearsals. In other words, no other conductor was more intimately linked with Janáček and his music on such a regular basis. Following the composer's wishes, Neumann also conducted the final scene from *The Cunning Little Vixen* at Janáček's funeral in August 1928. Six months later, on 25 February 1929, Neumann himself died, at the early age of 54.

Given Neumann's importance as a Janáček conductor and their close working relationship, his corrected score of the *Sinfonietta* is a document of considerable interest. His markings are very neatly written in a mixture of pencil, red crayon and blue crayon and were probably made during preparations and rehearsals for the Brno premiere on 3 April 1927 and the second Brno performance on 27 May 1928 as part of the Brno Exhibition of Contemporary Culture. Both were attended by Janáček. In due course, this copy was sent to UE, and the corrections marked in it were taken into the 1937 reprint of the full score. Neumann almost certainly did not use this score to conduct from as there are none of the customary 'conductor's' markings. It is much more likely that he kept this clean copy of the score to note errors as he, or Janáček, found them. It should also be noted that the added *banda* trumpets in the last three bars are written into Neumann's score exactly as they subsequently appeared in the UE 1937 corrected reprint, not the more elaborate and interventionist solution proposed by Klemperer (discussed below). It is entirely possible – likely even – that Janáček authorised Neumann's addition here, as the other changes in this score reflects omissions and corrections that stemmed from consultation with the composer.

The following is a list of Neumann's corrections and annotations:

I.
p. 5, six bars after Fig. 4 [bars 100 and 106], tpt 1, second crotchet, corrected from E flat to F. Note that neither Neumann nor Klemperer (see below) made any correction four bars after Fig. 4 [bars 98 and 104] which contains the same error.

II.

p. 7, bars 2 and 3 [bars 14, 15, 18, 19], trbns 3 and 4: flat signs added to the Cs (second quavers) in each bar. These flat signs are present in WPhV 1927.

p. 7, one bar after Fig. 1 [bars 22 and 26]: trbns 1 and 2, first quaver corrected from A to B (almost certainly a copying error). Correct in WPhV 1927.

p. 7, four bars and two bars before Fig. 2 [bars 32, 34, 36 and 38], vn 1 and vn 2, slur added over last two (staccato) quavers of each bar, indicating the bowing.

p. 8, bars 8–11 [bars 48–51], ob 1, marked 'col Flöte' (the oboe line in 1927 FS and WPhV 1927 stops abruptly at the end of bar 47 but should double fl 1 until the end of bar 51).

p. 9, third system, bcl: clef at beginning of stave (two bars before Fig. 3) corrected from treble clef to bass clef. Correct in WPhV 1927.

p. 10, second bar of Fig. 3 [bar 62], bcl, first note corrected from written D to written F.

p. 11, bar 1 [bar 68], hn 1, first note corrected from written B flat to written D flat. Correct in WPhV 1927.

p. 15, three before Fig. 8 [bar 156], vn 2, G flat corrected to B flat at start of second beat. Correct in WPhV 1927.

p. 15, two before Fig. 8 [bar 157], vn 2 last semiquaver: G flat corrected to F flat.

III.

p. 26, third and fourth bars of Fig. 1 [bars 14–15], vn 1 and vc, long phrase marks from half bar in bar 3 to end of bar 4 deleted; new phrase marks added from F flat quavers in bar 4.

p. 29, *Con moto* four bars before Fig. 4 [bar 42], metronome mark corrected from minim = 100 to crotchet = 100 (see below for Klemperer's quite different correction here).

p. 29, *Con moto* [bar 42] vc, quaver on first beat, D flat corrected to E flat.

p. 34, upbeat to Fig. 10 [bar 139], trbn '1. Solo' corrected to '3. solo', i.e. 3 trbns.

p. 37, bars 13–18 after Fig. 11 [bars 165–170], bcl, corrected to an octave higher than written.

p. 38, three bars before Fig. 12 for three bars [bars 199–201], tuba, second notes of each bar corrected from G flats to A flats.

p. 39, *Più mosso* starting five bars after Fig. 12 [bars 206–8], 'rit – – –' marked over the three bars before *Meno*.

p. 39, last two bars [bars 213–4], va, quaver upbeats (Fs) missing in printed score added in pencil.

Plate 22. The end of the third movement in František Neumann's corrected score, with the added 'rit' marking over the three *Più mosso* bars, and the added upbeat Fs in the violas in the closing bars. Both corrections were incorporated into the 1937 Universal Edition reprint (Wienbibliothek im Rathaus).

IV.

p. 43, bars 1 and 2 [bars 92 and 93], hn 4, sharp signs added to written Fs.

p. 44, bar 1, bar 5 and Fig. 6 [bars 112, 116 and 120]: bcl, written low A (three ledger lines below stave) moved up a sixth to written Fs.

p. 45, bar 2 [bar 123], bcl, written low A (three ledger lines below stave) moved up a sixth to written F. Bcl does not play in this bar in UE 2017.

p. 46, Fig. 7, first two bars [bars 138–9], bcl, pitches corrected to written E flat, F, G, a third higher than printed.

V.

p. 49: printed tempo marking 'Allegro' corrected to 'Andante con moto'.

p. 49, third bar of Fig. 1 [bar 14]: bcl, second crotchet, written D flat corrected to written C flat.

p. 52, Fig. 3 [bar 64], db, crescendo hairpin added over two bars.

p. 52, third and fourth bars of Fig. 3 [bars 66–7], trbns, db, *p* and crescendo hairpin added over two bars.

p. 53, bar 3 (second time bar) [bar 76], vc, upper note of each of the four demisemiquavers group corrected from E to F sharp.

p. 53, start of second system [bar 79], trbns, db: *pp* added before crescendo hairpin.

p. 69, sixth bar of Fig. 13 [bar 261], tpt 1, second crotchet corrected from E flat to F. No correction to second crotchet of fourth bar of Fig. 13 [bar 259].

p. 70, bar 1 [bar 267], tpt 5 corrected from E flat to F (tpts 4, 5, 6: first chord should be A flat, F, E flat).

p. 71, last bar (third bar of Fig. 14) [bar 278], vn 1 and vn 2, slurs deleted.

p. 72, bars 1–6 [bars 279–84], vn 1, vn 2, all slurs deleted.

p. 72, last three bars [bars 283–5], on an added stave: 'alle Tromp. I–IX (Do)': four-part chord (D flat, F, A flat, D flat), marked *ffo* (i.e. *ff*) for two bars, then crotchet on the same pitches, for the final chord, marked *sfo* (i.e. *sf*).

Plate 23. František Neumann's corrected score, showing the *banda* trumpets playing in the last three bars, and the violin slurs deleted. These corrections were incorporated into the 1937 Universal Edition reprint. It is certainly possible that this version of the final bars was made with Janáček's approval (Wienbibliothek im Rathaus).

Erstaufführung U+g Klemperer September 1927 (Republikoper)
Berlin
Reprise: Februar 1933 (Lindenoper)

Věnováno paní R. Newmarchové   OTTO KLEMPERER

LEOŠ JANÁČEK
SINFONIETTA

pour Orchestre   für Orchester   for Orchestra

pro orchestr

(1926)

PARTITURA

Konzert-Revision: Dr. P. A. Pisk

Aufführungsrecht vorbehalten — Droits d'exécution réservés
UNIVERSAL-EDITION A. G.
WIEN ——————— NEW YORK
Copyright 1927 by Universal Edition Inc., New York
Pro Republiku Československou Hudebni Matice, Praha

Printed in Austria

Plate 24. Otto Klemperer's conducting score, signed and dated with his Berlin performances in September 1927 and February 1933 (Royal Academy of Music, London).

Otto Klemperer's conducting score
Royal Academy of Music, London

Otto Klemperer Collection: 25 JANACEK; accession no. 090573
Bound in contemporary black boards. Signed on the title page: 'Otto Klemperer / Erstaufführung Berlin, September 1927 (Republikoper) / Reprise: Februar 1933 (Lindenoper).' Ownership stamp on title page: 'Otto Klemperer'.

The orchestra list on the verso of the title page has annotations by Klemperer. Beside the tenor tubas, he has written '(ev. 2 Hr)' [or two horns], though he seems not to have followed this suggestion in performance. Next to the timpani, he has noted '(sehr hohe Pauken)' [very high timpani]. In general, Klemperer's markings in the score are quite sparing, neatly written in purple crayon or pencil.

The following is a summary of significant annotations. Page numbers refer to the 1927 UE full score; bar numbers refer to the UE 2017 edition.

I.
p. 5, third bar of Fig. 4 [bars 97 and 104], tpts 4–6, 'meno f'.
p. 5, six bars after Fig. 4 [bars 100], tpt 1, second crotchet, corrected from E flat to F.

II.
p. 6, metronome mark: quaver = 138 [printed mark is quaver = 112].
p. 6, over bar 5 [bar 5], *Allegretto*: quaver = crotchet (printed mark is crotchet = 138).
p. 7, bars 2 and 3 [bars 14, 15, 18, 19], trbns 3 and 4: flat signs added to the Cs (second quavers) in each bar. Correct in WPhV 1927.
p. 11, bar 1 [bar 68], hn 1, first note corrected from written B flat to written D flat. Correct in WPhV 1927.
p. 11, bar 2 [bar 69], *Più mosso*: hn 1, trbns 1–4, va, vc, db: 'leggiero'.
p. 11, five bars before Fig. 4 [bar 75], *Meno mosso*, va, vc, db: 'leggiero'.
p. 12, Fig. 4 [bar 80], vc and cb: '(ohne Bässen)' [i.e. without db].
p. 12, Fig. 5 [bar 104], vc and cb: '(mit Bässen)' [i.e. with db].
p. 13, three bars before Fig. 6 for three bars and repeat [bars 116–20]: vn 1, '8' [octave] marking deleted.
p. 14, five bars before Fig. 7 [bar 133]: vn 2, renotated in flats: D flat, D flat, E flat, C flat, D flat, F (printed score has C sharp, C sharp, D sharp, B, C sharp, E sharp).

p. 15, nine bars before Fig. 8 (and semiquaver upbeat) [bar 150], va, renotated in flats (and in treble clef).

p. 15, three bars before Fig. 8 [bar 156]: vn 2, second beat, G flat corrected to B flat.

p. 15, two bars before Fig. 8 [bar 157], vn 2 last semiquaver: G flat corrected to F flat.

p. 15, two bars before Fig. 8 [bars 157–8]: vn 1, accents added to the 3 crotchets before Fig. 8.

p. 16, bar 2, *Maestoso* [bar 163]: all woodwind and *banda* marked *p*; strings marked *mf*.

p. 16, bar 6 [bar 167]: all instruments marked *f*.

p. 17, three bars after Fig. 9 [bar 171], diminuendo marked in all parts (one bar before printed *dim.*).

p. 18, Fig. 10 [bar 187], hns marked *fp*, vn 1 and vn 2 marked *mf*.

p. 19, Tempo I [bar 194], crotchet = 138 (printed mark is minim = 69); harp marked *p* (printed dynamic is *mf*).

p. 22, one bar before Fig. 12 [bar 218], vn 1, vn 2: 'Spitze!', i.e. at tip of the bow, for four bars.

p. 23, bar 1 [bar 221], last six quavers, 'a tempo' (placed a half bar before printed 'Tempo I');

trbns: *mf* in place of printed *p*.

p. 23, starting five bars from end [bar 224–7], obs *f* (printed dynamic is *mf*).

p. 23, starting five bars from end [bars 224–8]: vn 2, va: '(die Hälfte)' [half the section], '*p.* subito' (printed dynamic is *mf*), presumably up to bar 228.

III.

p. 25, head of page: 'martern' [anguished].

p. 26, three bars after Fig. 1 [bar 14], vn 1, vn 2, *sf* added to first note.

p. 26, seven bars after Fig. 1 [bar 18], cor, tuba, va: *p* at start of bar.

p. 29, four bars before Fig. 4, *Con moto* [bar 42], metronome mark: crotchet = 168 (printed marking is minim = 100).

p. 29, four bars before Fig. 4 [bar 42], vc quaver on first beat, D flat corrected to E flat.

p. 32, five bars after Fig. 7 [bar 100], campanelli: 'in es' (i.e. in E flat).

p. 32, 2 bars before Fig. 8 [bar 110]: vn 1, vn 2, *pp* and *pizz* for next eight bars. The same marking appears to apply to va, particularly in light of Klemperer's *arco* marking at bar 116.

p. 33, bar 4 [bar 116] va: *arco*, presumably from last quaver.

p. 39, bar 3, *Più mosso* [bar 206], 'crotchet = 132'.

p. 39, last two bars [bars 213–4], va, quaver upbeats (Fs) missing in printed score added in pencil, with explanatory note at foot: 'Violen ein achtel hinzugefügt im vorletzten und ... letzten Takt' (violas: a quaver has been added in the penultimate and last bar).

The upbeat Fs are missing in UE 1927 FS, but they are present in the UE 1937 corrected score and in later editions such as Füssl 1980. However, in Zahrádka 2017, the upbeat Fs have been removed (and thus the violas are printed as in UE 1927). They are restored in Zahrádka's 2025 edition (SKV D/9).

IV.

p. 40 'Sordinen ab!' (a reminder).

p. 40, bars 8–10 [bars 8–10], vc, db: all crotchets marked as downbows.

p. 43, seven bars after Fig. 4 [bar 93], hn 3 and 4, *mf* and diminuendo for three bars.

p. 43, bar 5 [bar 96], hn 1 and 2, 'offen' (open).

p. 44, five bars before Fig. 6 [bar 115], campanelli marked 'Campane'.

V.

Tempo marking 'Allegro' replaced in pencil with 'Andante con moto', then erased.

p. 50, bar 2 [bar 23], halfway through bar: vn 1, vn 2, va: *cresc*.

p. 50, bar 4 [bar 25], vn 1, vn 2, va, *ff* with accent added to first note of vn 1.

p. 54, Fig. 4 [bar 87]: crotchet = 138.

p. 54, five bars after Fig. 4, *Più mosso* [bar 91], 'crotchet = quaver' and 'quaver = 138' (printed marking is crotchet = 69).

p. 54, twelfth bar of Fig. 4 [bar 98], vn 1: accent on first semiquaver; vn 1, vn 2 and va: *sfp* (printed marking is *sf*).

pp. 56–7, Fig. 6 [bars 122–3], handwritten stave for cl 1 and cl 2 in B flat added, *doubling E flat cl for two bars, marked 'ff espr.'*

p. 57, four bars after Fig. 6 [bar 125], fl and all strings marked *fp*.

p. 57, two bars before Fig. 7 [bar 126], vn 1, vn 2: *cresc* (up to Fig. 7). Large hairpin and *cresc* suggests this applies to all strings.

p. 57, Fig. 7, *Tempo I* [bar 128], 'crotchet = 92'.

p. 60, Fig. 8 [bar 150], 'crotchet = 92'.

p. 60, second bar of Fig. 8 [bar 151]: 'quaver = 92'.

p. 60, five bars after Fig. 8 [bar 154], all strings: *ff* (printed dynamic is *fp*).

p. 62, Fig. 9, *Allegretto* [bar 162], 'meno' [mosso]; vn 1 and vn 2, 'viel Bogen wechseln!' (many bow changes).

p. 69, six bars after Fig. 13 [bar 261], tpt I, second crotchet corrected from E flat to F.

p. 72, *Adagio* [bars 279–85], new handwritten stave added with *banda* parts for tpts 1–9 in C through to end; tpts 1–3 in F: doubling cl 1 and 2 an octave lower (without trills), later deleted; vn 1 and vn 2: slurs removed.

Klemperer's added parts for the *banda* were the subject of his letter to Janáček on 19 September 1927 asking, 'Would you allow the last bars to be played by all *12* trumpets?' If Janáček replied to this request, his letter does not survive. However, he was present at the Berlin premiere on 29 September 1927 (for which this score was used) and he attended the rehearsal earlier the same day. Had he objected, Klemperer would surely have deleted the extra trumpet parts. As it is, he did delete his rewriting of the orchestral trumpet parts. The likely conclusion is that Janáček was prepared to accept Klemperer's addition of the *banda* for the last six bars but not the rewriting of the orchestral trumpets. It has usually been stated, for instance in Füssl 1980 and Zahrádka 2017, that the *banda* played in the last three bars (bars 283–5) at Klemperer's suggestion. But Klemperer's score shows that his rewriting was more far-reaching, with parts for the *banda* throughout the concluding *Adagio* (bars 279–85). It is Neumann's score, not Klemperer's, that includes the version given in the 1937 UE reprint onwards. There is more compelling evidence for the possible authenticity (and composer's authority) of the version noted in Neumann's score.

Klemperer's score is an important and intriguing document in the early performance history of the *Sinfonietta*, used by a conductor Janáček is known to have admired. The question remains, how many – if any – of Klemperer's annotations stemmed from comments made by Janáček at the rehearsal he attended in Berlin on 29 September 1927? It is impossible to determine this with any certainty, but Klemperer was a conductor who was usually faithful to a composer's intentions, and a significant part of his repertoire at this stage in his career was of music by living composers, notably Stravinsky, Hindemith, Weill and Janáček. All we can do is speculate on the possible source of some of the adjustments to dynamics and metronome marks, comments on bowing and articulation, occasional changes in scoring and the correction of slips in the printed score. Some of the suggested annotations *may* have come from Janáček, but there is no firm evidence for that. The real value of Klemperer's score is that is gives us a much clearer picture of what his Berlin performance might have sounded like. After the rehearsal on the day of the concert, Janáček wrote that 'the performance under Klemperer is unmatched by anyone' (see Chapter 2). The inference from that surely has to be that Klemperer's adjustments were, at least, condoned by an enthusiastic composer. Unlike Neumann's annotated score discussed above, Klemperer's was the one he used for performances.

Plate 25. The last page of Otto Klemperer's conducting score, with additional parts for the *banda* and other retouchings written in his hand. Alterations to the orchestral trumpet parts have been crossed out. Klemperer – like Neumann – has deleted the superfluous slurs in the violin parts (Royal Academy of Music, London).

Henry Wood's conducting score
Royal Academy of Music, London

Henry Wood Collection: HW JANACEK, accession number 14143–2001
Unbound; as issued in the original printed wrappers (dated I.1927 on back wrapper), signed 'Henry J. Wood' in blue crayon on the front wrapper. A copy of UE's single-page typescript errata list ('Fehlerverzeichnis') is pasted on to verso of the title page (see below). This is not present in Neumann's or Klemperer's copies.

The score is quite heavily marked by Wood in blue crayon and occasionally ink, but Janáček did not hear Wood's performance, only Rosa Newmarch's enthusiastic report of it (see Chapter 2, p. 97). At the start of the Fanfares, Wood has adjusted the metronome mark, changing it from minim = 72 to crotchet = 92. This matches the printed metronome mark for the reprise of the fanfares in the last movement as given in both UE 1927 and WPhV 1927. This was an error (taken from Sedláček's authorised copy which served as the printer's model for both 1927 editions). It should have been minim = 72 in both the first movement and the reprise in the final movement, but Wood was not to know this. If he did follow a tempo around crotchet = 92, then the fanfares will have been unusually broad – and it's worth noting that Klemperer seems to have reached the same conclusion, on the evidence of his two surviving live recordings of the work, though there are no changes to the printed metronome mark at the start of the Fanfares in his score.

Annotations by Wood at the start of the third and fourth movements (p. 25 and p. 40, respectively) note that both movements require a 'glockenspiel', indicating that this was Wood's solution rather than tubular bells. At the relevant moment in the fourth movement where the campanelli enter (p. 44, five bars before Fig. 6), Wood has marked the entry as 'Glocken'. This on its own would be ambiguous, but the note on p. 40 seems to clarify Wood's intention to use a glockenspiel. On the last two pages of the score, it is evident that Wood played the concluding *Adagio* as printed in the first edition, without any contribution from the *banda* in the work's closing bars.

The UE errata list

An undated single-page typescript was inserted into copies of the score from mid-1927 onwards (including Henry Wood's copy). The corrections are only a small proportion of those noted in Neumann's score which formed the basis of the more thorough revised reprint issued in 1937. But this is an interesting document as its post-publication corrections were all sent to UE by Janáček himself. The following is a complete translation but with the information in the right order, rather than the more haphazard arrangement of the original (some corrections were evidently added as Janáček submitted them).

Errata List for Janáček's Sinfonietta
I. 6th bar after 4: trumpet 1, 2nd crotchet: F not E flat[1]
III. 4th bar before 4: *Con moto* (crotchet = 100) not (minim = 100)[2]
13th–18th bars after 11: bass clarinet an octave higher[3]
3rd bar before 12: tuba, 2nd quaver, A flat not G flat[4]
IV. 3rd bar before 5 until 7th bar after 5: bass clarinet an octave higher[5]
8th and 4th bars before 6; 1st and 4th bars after 6: bass clarinet: F not A (an octave higher)[6]
1st and 2nd bars after 7 bass clarinet: E flat–F–G not C–D–E flat[7]
V. 8th bar after 13 (second time), trumpet 5, F not E flat[8]

---

[1] Correction sent by Janáček to UE, 22 March 1927, BmJA B02063.
[2] Janáček to UE, 10 April 1927, BmJA A06018.
[3] Janáček to UE, 22 March 1927, BmJA B02063.
[4] Janáček to UE, 4 April 1927, BmJA B02064.
[5] Janáček to UE, 22 March 1927, BmJA B02063.
[6] Ibid.
[7] Ibid.
[8] Ibid.

Discography

This discography lists over eighty recorded performances. For the sake of clarity, in the case of performances reissued multiple times, one catalogue number is given for release in any given medium (i.e. one LP release and one CD release), but where it is helpful, later issues are listed.

The Brno State Philharmonic Orchestra (Státní filharmonie Brno) changed its name to Brno Philharmonic Orchestra (Filharmonie Brno) in 2006. Earlier recordings reissued after that date often use the orchestra's new name.

Entries in *italics* are unpublished broadcast performances of significant artistic interest preserved in sound archives or available online. YouTube links are live at time of writing but are liable to disappear without warning.

Abbreviations
78	78 r.p.m. records
BRSO	Bavarian Radio Symphony Orchestra
CD	compact disc
COA	Concertgebouw Orchestra, Amsterdam
ČF	Czech Philharmonic (Česká filharmonie)
DL	download
LP	long-playing record, 33 r.p.m.
LSO	London Symphony Orchestra
NYP	New York Philharmonic
unpubd	unpublished
VPO	Vienna Philharmonic Orchestra

Claudio Abbado, LSO
7 February 1968; Kingsway Hall, London
LP: Decca SXL 6398; CD: Decca 4485792

Claudio Abbado, Berlin Philharmonic Orchestra
19–21 November 1997; Jesus-Christus-Kirche, Berlin
CD: DG 4273232

KarelAnčerl, ČF
9–11 January 1961, Rudolfinum ('Dvořák Hall'), Prague
LP: Supraphon SUAST 50022; CD: Supraphon SU 1929–2, SU 3684-2

KarelAnčerl, Cologne Radio Symphony Orchestra (WDR)
28 February 1970 (live)
CD: En Larmes ELS 04-517

Břetislav Bakala, ČF
16–18 October 1950; Domovina Studio, Prague
78: Ultraphon H23508–11; LP: Supraphon LPM 21; CD: Supraphon SU 3613–2 001

Břetislav Bakala, Brno Radio Symphony Orchestra
9 September 1953[1]; Brno Radio recording
CD: Panton 8111052

Břetislav Bakala, Prague Radio Symphony Orchestra
25–27 January 1955, Prague Radio Recording
CD: Multisonic 3101842

Břetislav Bakala, Brno State Philharmonic Orchestra
October 1956; Warsaw[2]
LP: Polskie Nagrania Muza L 0167, Eterna 720077

Jiří Bělohlávek, Brno State Philharmonic Orchestra [Brno Philharmonic Orchestra on CD reissue]
22–23 December 1977; Stadion, Brno
LP: Panton 110728; CD: Supraphon SU 4250-2

Jiří Bělohlávek, ČF
3–6 June 1990; Smetana Hall, Prague
CD: Chandos CHAN 8897

Jiří Bělohlávek, ČF
22–24 February 2017; Rudolfinum, Prague
CD: Decca 4834080

---

[1] The CD booklet gives '1955', but fuller documentation for the download gives 9 September 1953.
[2] Bakala and the Brno State Philharmonic Orchestra performed at the Warsaw Autumn Festival in October 1956 (the *Sinfonietta* was in their second concert on 17 October). This recording was made during that visit. It was first released by Muza in c. 1957. The Eterna reissue dates from c. 1960.

Discography 215

Leon Botstein, American Symphony Orchestra
25 April 2015; Sosnoff Theater at the Fisher Center, Bard College
DL: ASO 062

Pierre Boulez, BBC Symphony Orchestra
15 August 2008; Royal Albert Hall, London
Unpubd broadcast
www.youtube.com/watch?v=Dshwl12juoM&list=RDDshwl12juoM

Semyon Bychkov, WDR Symphony Orchestra
March 2002; Cologne Philharmonie (live)
WDR Klassik YouTube channel
www.youtube.com/watch?v=E_sK4n61FOo

Sylvain Cambreling, Orchestra of La Monnaie, Brussels
22 March 1985; Théâtre de la Monnaie (live)
CD: Ricercar RIS 111082

Sylvain Cambreling, SWR Symphony Orchestra, Baden-Baden
20–21 June 2005; Hans-Rosbaud-Studio, Baden-Baden
CD: SWR Classic SWR 19135CD

Andrew Davis, Royal Stockholm Philharmonic Orchestra
November 1996; Stockholm Concert Hall, Stockholm
CD: Finlandia Records 3984-214492

Colin Davis, BRSO
October 1989; Gasteig, Munich (live)
Unpubd radio broadcast
www.youtube.com/watch?v=cgmjyK2IdPo

Christoph von Dohnányi, Cleveland Orchestra
24 September 1998; Severance Hall, Cleveland (live)
CD: Cleveland Orchestra MMA-01032

Charles Dutoit, Montreal Symphony Orchestra
October 1991; Eglise de St Eustache, Montreal
CD: Decca 4362112

Mark Elder, Hallé Orchestra
21 July 2011; Royal Albert Hall, London
Unpubd radio and TV broadcast
www.youtube.com/watch?v=9aFTv50AoEQ

Radomil Eliška, Sapporo Symphony Orchestra
16–17 April 2010; Sapporo Concert Hall (live)
CD: Pastier DCQ 561

Tibor Ferenc, Hungarian National Philharmonic Orchestra
1988; Budapest
CD: IMP Classics PCD 1016

Claus Peter Flor, Rotterdam Philharmonic Orchestra
3 October 1992; Concertgebouw, Amsterdam
CD: Rotterdam Philharmonic RPhO 9394/1–4

Edward Gardner, Bergen Philharmonic Orchestra
10–12 March 2014; Grieghallen, Bergen
CD: Chandos CHSA 5142

Jascha Horenstein, Orchestre National de RTF
11 February 1952; Paris
CD: Music & Arts CD 1146

Jascha Horenstein, Vienna Symphony Orchestra
September 1955; Vienna
LP: Vox PL 9710; CD: Vox 7805; Pristine PACO 173

Milan Horvat, ORF Symphony Orchestra
23 February 1971; Musikverein, Vienna
CD: ORF CD 3158

Jakub Hrůša, NHK Symphony Orchestra
14 April 2019; NHK Hall, Tokyo
Unpubd TV broadcast
www.youtube.com/watch?v=rRan287uEj8&t=7s

Jakub Hrůša, ČF
1 January 2020; Rudolfinum, Prague
Unpubd TV broadcast

Jos van Immerseel, Anima Eterna Brugge [period instruments]
March 2015; Concertgebouw, Brugge
CD: Alpha 206

Eliahu Inbal, Deutsches-Symphonie Orchester, Berlin
6, 9 May 1995; Philharmonie, Berlin
CD: Denon CO 18049

Neeme Järvi, Bamberg Symphony Orchestra
25–28 January 1989, Dominkanerbau, Bamberg
CD: BIS CD 436

František Jílek, Brno State Philharmonic Orchestra
3 [recte 13] October 1978[3]; Janáček Theatre, Brno (live)
CD: RadioServis CR 0269-2 031

František Jílek, Brno State Philharmonic Orchestra
14–16 April 1986; Stadion, Brno
CD: Supraphon SU 3888-2

Árpád Joo, LSO
1980 (year of issue)
LP: Sefel Records SEFD 5001

Herbert Kegel, Leipzig Radio Symphony Orchestra
29 September 1972; Leipzig, Kongresshalle
CD: Weitblick SSS 0024-2

Rudolf Kempe, BBC Symphony Orchestra
30 August 1974; Royal Albert Hall, London (live)
CD: BBC Legends BBCL 4087-2

Rudolf Kempe, BBC Symphony Orchestra
12 October 1975; Fairfield Hall, Croydon (live)
CD: BBC Legends BBCL 4215-2

Otto Klemperer, COA
11 January 1951; Concertgebouw, Amsterdam
CD: Archiphon ARC 101

---

[3] The disc gives the date as 3 October, but the programme book of the 1978 Brno International Festival and the listing in *Rozhlas* (2 October 1978, p. 9) both give the date as 13 October 1978 when the *Sinfonietta* was the final item in the closing concert of the festival. Another Czech Radio CD, RadioServis CR 0790-2, gives the date as 7 October 1979, but it is the same (1978) performance.

Otto Klemperer, Cologne Radio Symphony Orchestra
27 February 1956; Klaus-Bismarck-Saal, WDR, Cologne
CD: EMI 5754652

Zdeněk Košler, ČF
18–20 April 1977; Rudolfinum ['House of Artists'], Prague
LP: Supraphon 410 2167, Denon OX-7110-ND; CD: Praga PRD 250 377

Rafael Kubelík, ČF
4–5 October 1946; Slovanský Hall, Prague
78: HMV C3574–3575, C7671–7673; CD: Testament SBT 1181

Rafael Kubelík, VPO
26 July 1955, Musikverein, Vienna
LP: Decca LW 5213; CD: Decca Eloquence 4800955, 4841452

Rafael Kubelík, BRSO
27–29 May 1970; Herkulessaal, Munich
LP: DG 2530 075; CD: DG 4372542

Rafael Kubelík, LSO
16 October 1975; Royal Festival Hall, London
Unpubd radio broadcast
www.youtube.com/watch?v=5HrBT2pfxIU&t=18s

Rafael Kubelík, BRSO
16 October 1981; Herkulessaal, Munich (live)
CD: Orfeo C552011B

Rafael Kubelík, NYP
7 November 1981; Avery Fisher Hall, New York (live)
Unpubd radio broadcast

Ondrej Lenárd, Slovak Radio Symphony Orchestra (Bratislava)
4–6 February 1990; Concert Hall of Slovak Radio, Bratislava
CD: Naxos 8550411

Marko Letonja, Strasbourg Philharmonic Orchestra
23–28 August 2022; Palais de la musique et des Congrès, Strasbourg
CD : Warner Classics 019029 6280634

Zdeněk Mácal, Royal Philharmonic Orchestra

February 1978; Henry Wood Hall, London
LP: Aristocrate 7678; CD: PG Records PCD 7678

Charles Mackerras, Pro Arte Orchestra
19–24 July 1959; Walthamstow Assembly Hall
LP: CML 33007, GSGC 14004; CD: EMI CDM 7637792, Testament SBT 1325

Charles Mackerras, VPO
24–25 March 1980; Sofiensaal, Vienna
LP: Decca SXDL 7519; CD: Decca 4101382

Charles Mackerras, Brno State Philharmonic Orchestra
7 October 1990; Janáček Theatre, Brno (live)
Unpubd TV broadcast

Charles Mackerras, BBC Philharmonic
28 February 1998; Bridgewater Hall, Manchester
Unpubd radio broadcast

Charles Mackerras, ČF
17–18 October 2002; Rudolfinum, Prague (live)
CD: Supraphon SU 3739-2 032

Charles Mackerras, Berlin Philharmonic Orchestra
22 January 2004; Philharmonie, Berlin (live)
CD: Disclosure Classics DS 00552

Charles Mackerras, BBC Philharmonic
28 July 2007; Royal Albert Hall, London (live)
CD: BBC MM302

Charles Mackerras, Sydney Symphony Orchestra
11–13 October 2007; Concert Hall, Sydney Opera House (live)
CD: Sydney Symphony SSO 200705

Fuat Mansurov, Moscow Radio Large Symphony Orchestra
2004 (year of first issue)
DL: Music Square INDEDIGI 1209

Kurt Masur, NYP
5–9 October 1993; Avery Fisher Hall, New York (live)
CD: Teldec 4509-908472

Lovro von Matačić, NHK Symphony Orchestra
14 December 1973; NHK Hall, Tokyo (live)
CD: King Records KKC 2026–7

Lovro von Matačić, Zagreb Philharmonic Orchestra
19 December 1979;[4] Lisinski Concert Hall, Zagreb (live)
CD: Zagreb Philharmonic CD 37596; King Records 5632207

Daniel Nazareth, Slovak Philharmonic Orchestra
April 1987; Studio 1 of Radio Bratislava
CD: Opus 9350 2013

Tomáš Netopil, Prague Radio Symphony Orchestra
22–24 and 29 June 2012, 30 September 2012; Rudolfinum, Prague
CD: Supraphon SU 4131-2

Václav Neumann, Leipzig Radio Symphony Orchestra
1951
LP: Urania URLP 7030; CD: Forgotten Records FR 945

Václav Neumann, NHK Symphony Orchestra
7 December 1978; Tokyo
CD: King Records KKC 2051–2

Václav Neumann, ČF
4 August 1981; Grosses Festspielhaus, Salzburg
Unpubd radio broadcast

Václav Neumann, ČF
5–6 and 25 June 1982; Rudolfinum, Prague
CD: Supraphon 38C37-7056; Supraphon 110717-2

Václav Neumann, SWF Symphony Orchestra, Baden-Baden
21–22 June 1990; Südwestfunk, Baden-Baden
CD: Arte Nova Classics 74321 30481 2

Václav Neumann, ČF
23 and 24 April 1992; Smetana Hall (live)
Lupulus Clara 57008-2

---

[4] The King Records issue gives the date as 14 December 1979, but it is the same performance.

Jonathan Nott, Bamberg Symphony Orchestra
25–28 October 2004; Joseph-Keilberth-Saal, Bamberg
CD: Tudor 7135

Seiji Ozawa, Chicago Symphony Orchestra
June–July 1969; Medina Temple, Chicago
LP: HMV ASD 2652; CD: EMI CDC 547837

Libor Pešek, Philharmonia Orchestra
June 1990; Walthamstow Assembly Hall
CD: Virgin Classics VC 7915062

André Previn, Los Angeles Philharmonic Orchestra
3 May 1988; Royce Hall, UCLA, Los Angeles
CD: Telarc CD 80174

Simon Rattle, Philharmonia Orchestra
17–18 November 1982; Kingsway Hall, London
LP: HMV ASD 1435221; CD: EMI 566995-2

Simon Rattle, LSO
18–19 September 2018; Barbican Hall, London (live)
CD: LSO Live LSO 0850

Heinz Rögner, Berlin Radio Symphony Orchestra
1979; Berlin
LP: VEB Deutsche Schallplatten S27544; CD: Berlin Classics 0032422BC

Gennady Rozhdestvensky, USSR Radio Symphony Orchestra
1965; Moscow
LP: Melodiya/Angel SR 40075; CD: RCA 74321 29251-2

Gennady Rozhdestvensky, BBC Symphony Orchestra
28 October 1981; Royal Festival Hall, London (live)
CD: BBC Radio Classics 15656 91352

José Serebrier, Czech State Philharmonic Orchestra [Brno State Philharmonic Orchestra], Brno
2–5 April 1995; Stadion, Brno
CD: Reference Recordings RR 65CD; RR 2103

Georg Solti, VPO

7 June 1964; Theater an der Wien, Vienna (live)
DVD: VAI 4645

George Szell, Cleveland Orchestra
15 October 1965; Severance Hall, Cleveland
LP: Columbia MS 6815; CD: Sony Classical SBK 62404

Klaus Tennstedt, NDR Symphony Orchestra
9 March 1980
CD: St Laurent Studio YSL 0886 (Tennstedt Vol. 30)

Klaus Tennstedt, LPO
2 April 1991, Royal Festival Hall, London (live)
CD: BBC Legends BBCL 4139-2

Michael Tilson Thomas, LSO
2 October 1990; Watford Town Hall
CD: Sony Classical SK 47182

Otakar Trhlík, Ostrava Janáček Philharmonic Orchestra
1975; Ostrava Studios
CD: Panton 710457-2

Vladimír Válek, Czech Army Central Band;
arr. for band by Karel Bělohoubek
23–25 April 1997; Czech Radio, Prague, Studio No. 1
CD: Clarton CQ 0039-2 431

Vladimír Válek, ČF
13–15 May 1997; Rudolfinum, Prague
CD: Exton OVCL 00390

Antoni Wit, Warsaw Philharmonic Orchestra
29–30 September 2009; Warsaw Philharmonic Hall, Warsaw
CD: Naxos 8572639

David Zinman, Rotterdam Philharmonic Orchestra
1980 (year of issue)
LP: Philips 9500 874; CD: Philips 4426602

Select Bibliography

Archives

Beroun, Museum of the Bohemian Karst
Brno, Janáček Archives of the Moravian Museum (BmJA)
Brno, Nadace Leoše Janáčka [Leoš Janáček Foundation] (NLJ)
London, Royal Academy of Music Library (RAM)
Prague, Czech National Archives
Prague, Museum of Czech Literature
Vienna, Nationalbibliothek (ÖNB)
Vienna, Universal Edition archives (UE)
Vienna, Wienbibliothek im Rathaus
Private collections

Editions

(in chronological order of publication; for details see Supplement to Chapter 1)
'Sletové fanfáry Leoše Janáčka', *Lidové noviny*, vol. 34, no. 335, 4 July 1926, pp. 5–6 (fragment); complete facs of Fanfáry: Prague: SHV, 1963
Pocket score, first edn (variant 1), Vienna and New York: UE, 1927
Pocket score, first edn (variant 2), Wiener Philharmonischer Verlag, 1927
Full score, first edn, Vienna and New York: UE, 1927
Full score, rev. edn, Vienna: UE, 1937
Pocket score, rev. edn, Vienna: Philharmonia, 1951
Pocket score, ed. Miroslav Barvík and Reiner Zimmermann. Leipzig: Peters, 1980
Full score, ed. Karl Heinz Füssl. Vienna: UE, 1980
Pocket score, ed. Karl Heinz Füssl. Vienna: Philharmonia, 1980
Full score, critical-practical edn, ed. Jiří Zahrádka. Vienna: UE, 2017
Pocket score, critical-practical edn, ed. Jiří Zahrádka. Vienna: UE, 2017
Full score, critical edn, ed. Jiří Zahrádka. Prague: Bärenreiter, SKV D/9, 2025

Books and periodicals

Bartová, Jindřiška: *František Jílek: Osobnost dirigenta* (Brno: JAMU, 2014).
Brod, Max: *Leoš Janáček: Život a dílo* (Prague: Hudební matice, 1924).
Brod, Max: *Leoš Janáček: Leben und Werk* (Vienna: Wiener Philharmonischer Verlag, 1925).
Brod, Max ['M.B.']: 'Janáček Urauffūhrung', *Prager Tagblatt*, vol. 51, no. 152, 27 June 1926, p. 9.
Brown, A. Peter: *The Symphonic Repertoire. Vol. 4: The Second Golden Age of the Viennese Symphony* (Bloomington: Indiana University Press, 2003), pp. 513–25.
Černušák, Gracian: 'Janáčkovo jaro', *Lidové noviny*, vol. 34, no. 222, 1 May 1926, p. 9.
Černušák, Gracian, and Vladimír Helfert, ed.: *Pazdirkův hudební zlaník naučný. II: Část osobní. Svazek prvý A–K* (Brno: Pazdírek, 1937).
Československý hudební slovník osob a institucí, ed. Gracian Černušák, Bohumír Štědroň and Zdenko Nováček. vol. 1, A–L (Prague: Státní hudení vydavatelství, 1963); vol. 2, M–Z (Prague: Státní hudení vydavatelství, 1965).
Curtis, William D.: *Leoš Janáček. Discography series XVIII* (Utica, NY, J. F. Weber, 1978).
Downes, Olin: 'Music: Janacek's Sinfonietta Delights', *New York Times*, 5 March 1927, p. 9.
Duchoňová, Katarína: *Břetislav Bakala jako janáčkovský dirigent* (Brno: JAMU, 2016).
Fischmann, Zdenka, ed.: *Janáček–Newmarch Correspondence* (Rockville, MD: Kabel Publishers, 1986).
Heinsheimer, Hans: *UE: die ersten 37½ Jahre: eine Chronik des Verlags* (Vienna: Universal Edition, 2017).
Helfert, Vladimír: 'Janáčkovy nové skladby ... II. Symfonietta', *Hudební rozhledy*, vol. 3, no. 7 (April 1927), pp. 110–2.
Helfert, Vladimír: *František Neumann* (Prostějov, pubd for the Neumann family, 1936).
Helfert, Vladimír: *O Janáčkovi*, ed. Bohumír Štědroň (Prague: Hudební matice, 1949).
Heyworth, Peter: *Otto Klemperer: His Life and Times, vol. 1: 1885–1933* (Cambridge: Cambridge University Press, 1983).
Hilmar, Ernst, ed.: *Leoš Janáček: Briefe an die Universal Edition* (Tutzing: Schneider, 1988).
Hollander, Hans: *Leoš Janáček: His Life and Work*, trans. Paul Hamburger (London: John Calder, 1963).
Jacobs, Arthur: *Henry Wood: Maker of the Proms* (London: Methuen, 1994).
Janáček, Leoš: 'Meine Stadt', *Prager Presse*, 4 December 1927; 'Moje město', *Lidové noviny*, vol. 35, no. 648, 24 December 1927, p. 5. German version repr. in *Brünn: die Hauptstadt von Mähren* (Prague: Orbis, 1928), pp. 43–6.

Janáček, Leoš: *Literární dílo I*, ed. Theodora Straková and Eva Drlíková (Brno: Editio Janáček, 2003).
Janáček, Leoš: *Literární dílo II*, ed. Theodora Straková and Eva Drlíková (Brno: Editio Janáček, 2003).
Janáčková, Libuše: *Leoš Janáček a Břetislav Bakala: Edice vzájemné korespondence*, diss. (Brno: Masaryk University, 2007).
Janáčková, Libuše: *Leoš Janáček a Lidové noviny. Leoš Janáček and Lidové noviny* (Brno: Moravian Museum, 2014), text in Czech and English.
Korespondence Leoše Janáčka s Maxem Brodem, ed. Jan Racek and Artuš Rektorys (Prague: SNKLHU, 1953), Janáčkův archiv Vol. 9.
Kuna, Milan: *Václav Talich 1883–1961. Šťastný i hořký úděl dirigenta* (Prague: Academia, 2009).
Lambert, Patrick: 'Leoš Janáček and T. G. Masaryk', in Harry Hanak, ed.: *T. G. Masaryk (1850–1937), vol. 3: Statesman and Cultural Force* (London: Macmillan, 1989).
Lambert, Patrick: 'The Blare of Victorious Trumpets', unpubd typescript, n.d.
Lána, Oldřich: *Leoš Janáček a Umělecká beseda (1920–1928)*, diss. (Brno: Masaryk University, 2017).
Mackerras, Charles: 'My Life with Janáček's Music', interview with John Tyrrell, disc notes for Supraphon SU 3739-2 032.
Mikota, Jan: 'Leoš Janáček v Anglii', *Listy Hudební matice*, vol. 5 (1926), pp. 257–68.
Musikblätter des Anbruch 1919 bis 1937, CD-ROM (Universal Edition, UE 45014).
Newmarch, Rosa: *The Concert-goer's Library of Descriptive Notes*, vol. 5 (London: Oxford University Press, 1938), pp. 58–60 [note on the *Sinfonietta*].
Newmarch, Rosa: *The Music of Czechoslovakia* (London: Oxford University Press, 1942).
Novak, John K.: *The Symphonic Works of Leoš Janáček* (Munich: Peter Lang, 2016).
Pečman, Rudolf: 'Symfonické dílo Leoše Janáčka v pojetí Břetislava Bakaly', in *Leoš Janáček a soudobá hudba: mezinárodní hudebně vědecký kongres, Brno 1958* (Prague: Hudební rozhlédy, 1963).
Petrželka, Vilém ['–el']: 'Šestý a poslední symfonický koncert divadelní', *Moravské slovo*, 5 April 1927, p. 3.
Pospíšilová, Klára: *Historie Brněnských festival věnovaných odkazu Leoše Janáčka*, diss. (Brno: Masaryk University, 2016).
Přibáňová, Svatava, ed.: *Hádanka života (dopisy Leoše Janáčka Kamile Stösslové)* (Brno: Opus musicum, 1990).
Přibáňová, Svatava, ed.: *Thema con variazioni. Leoš Janáček korespondence s manželkou Zdeňkou a dcerou Olgou* (Prague: Bärenreiter, 2007).
Přibáňová, Svatava, and Jiří Zahrádka: *Leoš Janáček ve fotografiích. Leoš Janáček in Photographs* (Brno: Moravian Museum, 2008), text in Czech and English.

Procházková, Jarmila: 'Janáček and Military Music', *Sborník prací filozofické fakulty brněnské university, řada hudebněvědná (H)*, vol. 47, no. 33 (1998), pp. 43–53.
Pult und Taktstock, CD-ROM (Vienna: Universal Edition, UE 45015).
Šeda, Jaroslav: *Leoš Janáček* (Prague: SHV, 1961).
Simeone, Nigel: *The First Editions of Leoš Janáček: A Bibliographical Catalogue with Illustrations of the Title Pages* (Tutzing: Schneider, 1991).
Simeone, Nigel, John Tyrrell and Alena Němcová: *Janáček's Works: A Catalogue of the Music and Writings* (Oxford: Clarendon Press, 1997).
Simeone, Nigel, and John Tyrrell, ed.: *Charles Mackerras* (Woodbridge: Boydell Press, 2015).
Simeone, Nigel: *Břetislav Bakala Conducts Janáček*, booklet notes for CRQ Editions DVD10.
Simeone, Nigel: *The Janáček Compendium* (Woodbridge: Boydell Press, 2019).
Skoumal, Zdeněk: *The Music of Leoš Janáček: Motive, Rhythm, Structure* (Rochester, NY: University of Rochester Press, 2020).
Šourek, Otakar, ed.: *Václav Talich: život a práce* [Václav Talich: Life and work] (Prague: Hudební matice, 1943).
Štědroň, Bohumír: *Leos Janáček: Letters and Reminiscences*, trans. Geraldine Thomsen (Prague: Artia, 1955).
Štědroň, Bohumír: *Dílo Leoše Janáčka* (Prague: Hudební rozhledy, 1959).
Štědroň, Bohumír: *Leoš Janáček: Vzpomínky, dokumenty, korespondence a studie* (Prague: Editio Supraphon, 1986).
Štědroň, Miloš: 'Jak vlastně začíná Janáčkova Sinfonietta?!?', *Opus musicum*, vol. 20, no. 3 (1988), p. xxi.
Stevens, Lewis: *An Unforgettable Woman: The Life and Times of Rosa Newmarch* (Kibworth Beauchamp: Matador, 2011).
Stolařík, Ivo: *Jan Löwenbach a Leoš Janáček: vzájemná korespondence* (Opava: Slezský studijní ústav, 1958).
Susskind, Charles: *Janáček and Brod* (London: Yale University Press, 1985).
Telec, Vladimír: *Leoš Janáček 1854–1928: výběrová bibliografie* (Brno: Universitní knihovna, 1958).
Tyrrell, John, ed. and trans.: *Intimate Letters: Leoš Janáček to Kamila Stösslová* (London: Faber, 1993), edited translation of Přibáňová 1990.
Tyrrell, John, ed. and trans.: *My Life with Janáček: The Memoirs of Zdenka Janáčková* (London: Faber, 1998).
Tyrrell, John: *Janáček: Years of a Life. Vol. I (1854–1914): The Lonely Blackbird* (London: Faber, 2006).
Tyrrell, John: *Janáček: Years of a Life. Vol. II (1914–1928): Tsar of the Forests* (London: Faber, 2007).
Tyrrell, John: Disc notes for Janáček Orchestral Works Vol. 1, Chandos CHSA 5142, incl. *Sinfonietta*.
Vašek, Adolf: *Po stopách dra Leoše Janáčka. Kapitoly a dokumenty k jeho životu a dílu* (Brno: Brněnské knižní nakladatelství, 1930).

Vogel, Jaroslav: 'Hudba. Z pražské koncertní sine. Janáčkova "Vojenská symfonieta"', *Česká republika*, 29 June 1926, p. 29.
Vogel, Jaroslav: *Leoš Janáček: A Biography* [rev. edn by Karel Janovický] (London: Orbis Publishing, 1981).
Vomáčka, Boleslav ['B.V.']: 'O Janáčkově symfoniettě', *Lidové noviny*, vol. 34, no. 329, 1 July 1926, p. 7.
Wingfield, Paul: *Janáček: Glagolitic Mass* (Cambridge: Cambridge University Press, 1992).
Zahrádka, Jiří: 'Divadlo nesmí býti lidu komedií': *Leoš Janáček a Národní divadlo v Brně*. *'Theatre must not be comedy for the people': Leoš Janáček and the National Theatre in Brno* (Brno: Moravian Museum, 2012), text in Czech and English.
Zahrádka, Jiří: 'Od sokolských Fanfár přes Symfoniettu vojenskou, sletovou až po Sinfoniettu', *Opus musicum*, vol. 45, no. 5 (2013), pp. 6–34.

Online resources

ANNO: Austrian Newspapers Online: anno.onb.ac.at
Český hudební slovník osob a institucí, ed. Petr Macek, Petr Kalina, Karel Steinmetz and Šárka Zahrádková: ceskyhudebnislovnik.cz
Delpher: Dutch newspapers online: delpher.nl
Deutsche Zeitungsportal: deutsche-digitale-bibliothek.de/newspaper
Encyklopedie dějin města Brna: encyklopedie.brna.cz
Karel Ančerl, website: karel-ancerl.com
Korespondence Leoše Janáčka: korespondencejanacek.musicologica.cz
Leoš Janáček, website (in Czech and English): leosjanacek.eu
Lidové noviny online archive: lidovenoviny.cz/archiv.aspx
New York Philharmonic Digital Archives: archives.nyphil.org
New York Times, online: nytimes.com
Newspapers.com, online archives of UK, US and other English-language newspapers: newspapers.com
Österreichisches biographisches Lexikon, website: biographien.ac.at
Rozhlasový týdeník, online: kramerius.rozhlas.cz/periodical/uuid:4ddoofoc-423d-4cd9-b654-3413d3deda82. This website includes all issues of the Czech radio listings magazine from 1923 to 2022 under its various titles: *Radio-Journal* (1923–38), *Náš rozhlas* (1939–53) and later, *Rozhlas* and *Týdeník rozhlas*.
The Times Digital Archive via gale.com
Vienna Konzerthaus, online archive: konzerthaus.at/archive
Vienna Musikverein Konzertarchiv, online: musikverein.at/archiv/konzertarchiv

Index

Abbado, Claudio, 148, 150, 213
Abendroth, Hermann, 70, 107, 108
Adam, Franz, 70, 92, 93
Adler, Kurt, 114
Aleš, Mikoláš, 17
Alpenburg, Richard von, 116
Ančerl, Karel, 13, 125, 131–4, 139, 150, 151, 154, 155, 156, 157, 160, 161, 214
Anderson, W.R., 127
Ansermet, Ernest, 121
Axman, Emil, 16

Bach, David Josef, 99
Bach, Johann Sebastian, 86, 88, 90, 107
Bakala, Břetislav, 13, 35, 63, 111, 125, 128–31, 142, 143, 149, 154, 155, 156, 164–5, 172, 214
Balatka, Antonín, 142
Bartók, Béla, 104, 118, 175
Barvík, Miroslav, 55, 63, 150, 152
Beck, Walther, 70, 99
Beinum, Eduard van, 119
Bella, Jan Levoslav, 105, 106
Bělohlávek, Jiří, 144, 145, 150, 151, 152, 154, 155, 156, 160, 170, 214–15
Belza, Igor, 61
Berg, Alban, 82, 83, 85, 102, 103
Berlioz, Hector, 7, 93
Bie, Oskar, 117
Blanks, Fred, 137
Blom, Eric, 95
Blyth, Alan, 136
Boehe, Ernst, 116
Böhm, Karl, 70, 98
Bojanowski, Jerzy, 120

Botstein, Leon, 148–9, 215
Boulez, Pierre, 148, 158, 215
Boult, Adrian, 120, 158
Brno, as inspiration for the *Sinfonietta*, 36–8, 72–3, 84, 174
Braunfels, Walter, 102
Braus, Dorothea, 98
Brod, Max, 33, 35, 36, 38, 44, 71–3 (review of world premiere)
Brown, A. Peter, 180
Brown, Christopher, 139
Brown, Ismene, 139
Bruckner, Anton, 92, 101, 107, 109
Burghauser, Jarmil, 61, 62, 166, 175, 191
Busch, Fritz, 70, 103–5
Bychkov, Semyon, 146, 215

Calvocoressi, Michel-Dimitri, 96
Cambreling, Sylvain, 148, 150, 215
Capell, Richard, 119
Cardus, Neville, 120
Cassidy, Claudia, 127
Čech, Svatopluk, 15
Černušák, Gracian, 30 n. 37, 32 n. 46, 85, 89, 106
Chalabala, Zdeněk, 142, 165
Chlubna, Osvald, 2, 16
Colles, H.C., 96
Covell, Roger, 137
Curjel, Hans, 88, 90
Czech Composers' Club, 19

Davis, Andrew, 149, 215
Davis, Colin, 215
Dohnányi, Christoph von, 148, 215

Donath, Rudolf, 102
Downes, Olin, 81, 82, 123
Durdík, Josef, 15
Dutoit, Charles, 148, 215
Dvořák, Antonín, 1, 7, 18, 20, 109, 119, 126, 132, 137, 183

Editio Supraphon (music publisher), 61, 62, 65
Eichhorn, August, 77
Einstein, Alfred, 91
Elder, Mark, 149, 215
Elgar, Edward, 7
Eliška, Radomil, 144, 145, 150, 165, 216
Evans, Edwin, 120

Flor, Claus Peter, 216
Foerster, Josef Bohuslav, 19 n. 8, 105
Forsyth, Cecil, 7
Frey, Martin, 101
Fügner, Jindřich, 16
Füssl, Karl Heinz, 62, 150, 152, 160, 174, 208, 209

Gardner, Edward, 149, 150, 155, 216
Giannini, Dussolina, 107
Göhler, Georg, 70, 101–2
Gogol, Nikolai, 15
Graf, Max, 113
Gregor, Bohumil, 161, 164

Hába, Alois, 19 n. 8
Hanus, Tomáš, 13
Heger, Robert, 119–20
Heinrich, Arnošt, 37
Helfert, Vladimír, 83, 84, 85, 174, 175
Heller, Karel, 28, 29
Hertzka, Emil, 42, 43, 44, 45, 49, 50, 78; *see also* Universal Edition (UE)
Heyworth, Peter, 122
Holiš, Evžen, 157, 158, 165
Hollander, Hans, 174, 175, 180, 181, 183, 187, 188

Hollmann, Otakar, 6
Honegger, Arthur, 105
Horenstein, Jascha, 70, 99, 101, 111, 145, 153, 154, 155, 216
Horowitz, Vladimir, 116
Horvat, Milan, 146, 216
Hruby, Frank, 133
Hrůša, Jakub, 13, 145, 151, 152, 157–73, 216
Hudební matice, 34, 42–50, 51, 57, 58, 62, 75

Immerseel, Jos van, 149, 150, 152, 216
Inbal, Eliahu, 148, 217

Janáček, Leoš
  WORKS
  Ballad of Blaník (*Balada blanická*), 2, 10, 15, 83, 111, 200
  Beginning of a Romance, The (*Počátek románu*), 157
  Capriccio, 7, 15
  Concertino, 14, 15, 53, 71, 115
  Cunning Little Vixen, The (*Příhody lišky Bystroušky*), 2, 3, 4, 5, 9, 12, 13, 42, 43, 81, 83, 103, 130, 158, 164, 200
  Diary of One who Disappeared (*Zápisník zmizelého*), 89
  Excursions of Mr Brouček, The (*Výlety páně Broučkovy*), 2, 3, 9, 10, 12, 15, 30, 83 n. 27
  Fairy Tale (*Pohádka*), 15
  Fate (*Osud*), 2, 10, 11, 53, 113 n. 7, 169, 172
  Fiddler's Child, The (*Šumařovo dítě*), 2, 15, 151
  From the House of the Dead (*Z mrtvého domu*), 2, 3, 4, 9, 10, 11, 12, 88, 89, 110
  Glagolitic Mass, 2, 3, 4, 5, 6, 8, 9, 10, 13, 15, 39, 49, 94, 161
  Idyll, 1
  Jealousy (*Žárlivost*), 1, 7, 15, 83, 111

Jenůfa (*Její pastorkyňa*), 1, 2, 4, 7, 9, 10, 13, 71, 77, 78, 79, 81, 83, 89 n. 37, 94, 98, 104, 107, 108, 109, 113, 115, 117, 118, 122, 130, 145, 157, 165, 172
Káťa Kabanová, 2, 3, 4, 5, 7, 9, 10, 11, 12, 13, 15, 32, 33 n. 47, 53, 77, 83 n. 27, 107, 122, 130, 137, 169, 200
Lachian Dances (*Lašske tance*), 1, 42, 83, 94, 130, 200
Makropulos Affair, The (*Věc Makropulos*), 2, 3, 9, 10, 11, 15, 18, 53, 80, 83 n. 27, 169
Music for Club-Swinging (*Hudba ke kroužení kužely*), 17
Nursery Rhymes (*Říkadla*), 5, 11, 15
Rákoš Rákoczy, 1
Šárka, 83 n. 27, 130 n. 9, 200
String Quartet No. 1 (*Kreutzer Sonata*), 12
String Quartet No. 2 (*Intimate Letters*), 11, 12, 121
Suite for strings, 1
Taras Bulba, 2, 4, 5, 6, 7, 8, 9, 10, 12, 13, 15, 42, 49, 50, 74, 75, 83, 94, 109, 110, 120, 127, 137, 151, 157, 159, 172–3, 200
Youth (*Mládí*), 14, 71
Janáčková, Věra (niece), 39
Janáčková, Zdenka (wife), 17, 28, 33 n. 47, 34
Järvi, Neeme, 148, 150, 217
Jeremiáš, Otakar, 110
Jílek, František, 13, 65, 125, 142–3, 150, 154, 155, 156, 157–60, 161, 163, 164, 165, 217
Jirák, Karel Boleslav, 109–10
Jochum, Eugen, 117
Jungmann, Josef, 17

Kalmus, Alfred, 43 n. 74
Kanner, Hedwig, 113
Karajan, Herbert von, 158

Kde domov můj (Czech National Anthem), 18
Kdož jsú boží bojovníci ('You who are God's warriors'), 39
Kegel, Herbert, 148, 217
Keilberth, Josef, 65, 111, 114
Kempe, Rudolf, 147, 154, 155, 217
Kleiber, Erich, 33 n. 47, 80, 109, 114 n. 9
Klemperer, Otto, 34 n. 56, 44, 49, 50, 56, 70, 77–80 (German premiere), 80–2 (American premiere), 86–92 (Berlin premiere, in Janáček's presence), 98, 117, 122, 123, 125, 145, 149, 152, 153, 154, 155, 172, 193, 199, 200, 201, 206–9 (annotated score), 211, 217–18
Klíma, Alois, 111
Kmoch, František, 18
Kovařovic, Karel, 1, 13, 165
Košler, Zdeněk, 144, 218
Krauss, Clemens, 70, 93, 111
Krawc-Schneider, Bjarnat, 104–5
Krejčí, Antonín, 28, 29, 30, 31, 38
Krips, Josef, 70, 98, 102
Kroutil, Michael, 171, 172
Kubelík, Rafael, 13, 110–11, 125, 126–8, 132, 134, 144, 149, 150, 151, 154, 155, 156, 157, 160, 218
Kulhánek, Jaroslav, 6
Kvapil, Jaroslav, 142
Kylián, Jiří, 139

Laber, Heinrich, 116
Lambert, Patrick, 110 n. 3, 111 n. 4, 120
Latzko, Ernst, 114
Legge, Walter, 126
Leinsdorf, Erich, 123
Lenárd, Ondrej, 144, 218
Leonhardt, Carl, 116
Letonja, Marko, 151, 152, 218
Löwenbach, Jan, 43, 44, 75

Mácal, Zdeněk, 144, 218

Mackerras, Charles, 8, 13, 64, 123, 124, 125, 130, 134–42, 147, 149, 150, 151, 152, 153, 154, 155, 156, 157, 163–4, 168, 172, 219
Mahler, Gustav, 7, 88, 134, 137
Mánes, Josef, 17
Mansurov, Fuat, 219
Martinů, Bohuslav, 109
Masaryk, Tomáš Garrigue, 17, 18, 38
Masur, 150, 219
Matačić, Lovro von, 145–6, 220
Matějovský, František, 71
Medek, Rudolf, 71
Mikota, Jan, 33, 36 n. 60, 42, 50 n. 101
Mikota, Václav, 42, 43, 44, 45, 49
Monteux, Pierre, 117, 119
Morris, Don, 139
Mozart, Wolfgang Amadeus, 20, 80, 86, 89, 90, 91, 98, 103
Mucha, Alfons, 17, 113 n. 7
Muck, Karl, 115
Münch, Fritz, 121
Mussorgsky, Modest, 103, 115

Nazareth, Daniel, 220
Neruda, Jan, 17
Nesporý, Gustav, 141, 151, 170
Netopil, Tomáš, 144, 150, 220
Neumann, František, 1, 28, 50, 56, 61, 63, 64, 70, 82–5 (Brno premiere), 105–6, 111, 128, 130, 152–3, 165, 172, 193, 199–203 (annotated score), 209, 211, 212
Neumann, Václav, 143–4, 220
Newmarch, Rosa, 49–50 (dedicatee of *Sinfonietta*), 94, 97, 196–8 (programme note), 199, 211
Nick, Edmund, 121
Nott, Jonathan, 148, 221
Novak, John K., 175, 181, 187, 191
Novák, Vitězslav, 105, 106, 113, 126

Obrovský, Jakub, 17
Ostrčil, Otakar, 16, 105, 106

Ozawa, Seiji, 148, 221

Pacovský, Jaroslav, 20
Pečman, Rudolf, 130, 131
Peischer, Josef, 77
Pešek, Libor, 144, 150, 221
Petrželka, Vilém, 84, 85
Pijper, Willem, 118
Písek, as inspiration for the *Sinfonietta*, 11, 19–22, 75, 175
Pisk, Paul, 51, 57, 58, 61, 62
Ponsonby, Robert, 126
Porter, Andrew, 134, 135, 136
Previn, André, 148, 221

Rachlew, Anders, 121
Rachmaninoff, Sergei, 116
Rattle, Simon, 149, 150, 151, 152, 154, 155, 171, 221
Ravel, Maurice, 96, 98
Reiner, Fritz, 58 n. 119
Richter, Hans, 158
Řídký, Jaroslav, 16
Rimsky-Korsakov, Nikolai, 7, 13
Rodziński, Artur, 123
Rögner, Heinz, 148, 221
Rozhdestvensky, Gennady, 149, 153, 154, 156, 221

Sachs, Benno, 61
Sachs, Milan, 165
Sauer, Emil von, 92
Schalk, Franz, 109
Scheiner, Josef, 29
Scherchen, Hermann, 131
Schnabel, Artur, 86, 89, 90
Schoenberg, Arnold, 33 n. 47, 96, 118
Schönewolf, Karl, 103
Schreker, Franz, 33 n. 37
Schumann, Robert, 7
Seckerson, Edward, 138
Sedláček, Václav, 8, 26 n. 22, 28, 32, 35, 48, 51, 53, 56, 62, 63, 151, 152, 170, 211

Serebrier, José, 148, 221
Service, Tom, 140
Skoumal, Zdeněk, 175, 176, 177, 188
Skrýšovský, Josef Emanuel (pseud. for Josef Suk), 18
Smetana, Bedřich, 20, 81, 113, 115
  Libuše, 18, 37,
  Má vlast, 29, 31, 71
Sokol
  Seventh All-Sokol Rally, 1920, 18,
  Eighth All-Sokol Rally, 1926, 14, 18–19, 28–33, 35, 38–9, 71, 73, 74, 75, 77, 83, 174
  Tenth All-Sokol Rally, 1938, 109
  foundation and purpose, 16–18
  proposed dedication of Sinfonietta, 49–50
Solti, Georg, 147, 222
Stadlen, Peter, 132
Starý d'Albert, Karel, 82
Stefan, Paul, 114
Stein, Erwin, 52–3, 55, 61, 64, 65
Stein, Fritz, 116
Stejskalová, Marie, 17
Stiedry, Fritz, 123
Stolba, Heinz, 65
Stösslová, Kamila, 11, 19, 20, 28, 31, 33, 99, 130
Straková, Theodora, 2
Strauss, Richard, 7, 13, 77, 80, 92, 93, 147, 163, 171
Stravinsky, Igor, 3, 90, 102, 118, 121, 122, 209
Strobel, Heinrich, 90
Stupka, František, 35, 49, 50, 75, 109 n. 2
Suk, Josef, 18, 19, 30, 74, 82, 83, 85, 109, 120, 121, 132, 139, 171
Světlá, Karolina, 17
Szell, George, 120, 123, 147–8, 156, 222
Szendrei, Alfred, 114

Talich, Václav, 5, 13, 32, 33, 34–5 (recollections of Janáček at rehearsals), 42, 53, 56, 57, 63, 64, 70, 71–5 (world premiere), 77, 109, 131, 134, 135, 151, 164, 169, 171, 172, 193
Tchaikovsky, Pyotr Ilyich, 7, 107
Tennstedt, Klaus, 146–7, 150, 153, 156, 222
Tietjen, Heinz, 89
Tilson Thomas, Michael, 149, 222
Torkanowsky, Werner, 123
Trhlík, Otakar, 144, 222
Trkanová, Marie, 17 n. 4
Tyrrell, John, 2–3, 18, 103, 140
Tyrš, Miroslav, 16

Universal Edition (UE), 2, 28, 42–5, 48, 49, 50, 51, 52, 53, 55, 56–65, 78, 89, 97, 99, 116 n. 15, 122 n. 35, 130, 150, 152, 160, 163, 166, 168, 175, 181, 199, 200, 209, 211, 212
Uprka, Joža, 113–14

Vach, Ferdinand, 105
Válek, Vladimír, 144, 149, 152, 156, 222
Verdi, Giuseppe, 94, 96, 104, 107
Viklický, Emil, 150
Vlk, František, 164
Vogel, Jaroslav, 9, 14, 35 n. 58, 49, 63, 73–5 (review of world premiere), 84, 142, 151, 170, 171, 175, 176, 181, 183, 187
Vomáčka, Boleslav, 18, 19, 30, 42, 54, 73 (review of world premiere)
Von Rhein, John, 133
Vrchlický, Jaroslav, 15

Walton, Kenneth, 140
Warrack, John, 135
Weber, Carl Maria, 107, 109
Webern, Anton, 99
Weisbach, Hans, 114
Wendel, Ernst, 116, 117
Wiener Philharmonischer Verlag, 43 (esp. n. 74), 44, 50. 57, 58, 61, 199
Wingfield, Paul, 7–8

Wit, Antoni, 148, 222
Woess, Kurt, 123
Wolf, Hugo, 134
Wolf, N.H., 118–19
Wood, Henry, 56, 70, 93–7 (British premiere), 119, 196, 199, 211 (annotated score), 212

Zahrádka, Jiří, 2, 55, 63, 64, 144, 150, 151, 152, 165, 171, 172, 175, 208, 209
Ženíšek, František, 17
Zimmermann, Reiner, 55, 63, 150, 152
Zinman, David, 148, 222
Zweig, Fritz, 44, 79, 88
Zwissler, Karl Maria, 117

www.ingramcontent.com/pod-product-compliance
Lightning Source LLC
Chambersburg PA
CBHW070800230426
43665CB00017B/2430